TEIKYO WESTMAR

P9-BAW-926

PENGUIN BOOKS

THE MAGIC LANTERN

Ingmar Bergman is considered by many to be the world's greatest living film director and is also internationally well known as a theatre, television and opera director. He was born in 1918 in Uppsala, Sweden, and studied at Stockholm University. From 1943 to 1946 he was a producer and scriptwriter for Svensk Filmindustri and, later, Artistic Adviser. He has directed at theatres throughout Sweden as well as abroad and was Head of the Royal Dramatic Theatre in Stockholm from 1963 to 1966. His many films include *The Seventh Seal*, *Smiles of a Summer Night*, *Persona*, *The Virgin Spring*, *Through a Glass Darkly*, *Cries and Whispers*, *Scenes from a Marriage*, *Face to Face*, *Autumn Sonata*, *The Serpent's Egg*, *From the Life of the Marionettes* and *Fanny and Alexander*, winner of four Academy Awards. Ingmar Bergman has received many international awards and prizes for his films, including the Goethe Prize in 1976 and the Swedish Gold Medal in 1977.

GRAY LIBRARY

The Magic Lantern

An Autobiography by
Ingmar Bergman

Translated from Swedish by Joan Tate

PENGUIN BOOKS

PENGUIN BOOKS

Published by the Penguin Group
27 Wrights Lane, London w8 5TZ, England
Viking Penguin Inc., 40 West 23rd Street, New York, New York 10010, USA
Penguin Books Australia Ltd, Ringwood, Victoria, Australia
Penguin Books Canada Ltd, 2801 John Street, Markham, Ontario, Canada L3R 1B4
Penguin Books (NZ) Ltd, 182–190 Wairau Road, Auckland 10, New Zealand

Penguin Books Ltd, Registered Offices: Harmondsworth, Middlesex, England

First published, under the title *Laterna Magica*, by
Norstedts Förlag, Sweden, 1987
This English translation first published in Great Britain by Hamish Hamilton 1988
Published in Penguin Books 1988
3 5 7 9 10 8 6 4 2

Copyright © Ingmar Bergman, 1987
This translation copyright © Joan Tate, 1988
All rights reserved

Made and printed in Great Britain by Richard Clay Ltd, Bungay, Suffolk
Filmset in Sabon

Except in the United States of America,
this book is sold subject to the condition
that it shall not, by way of trade or otherwise,
be lent, re-sold, hired out, or otherwise circulated
without the publisher's prior consent in any form of
binding or cover other than that in which it is
published and without a similar condition
including this condition being imposed
on the subsequent purchaser

List of illustrations

The publishers would like to thank Ingmar Bergman for permission to reproduce photographs from his family albums, and are also extremely grateful to Peter Cowie for several photographs and for invaluable help with the picture research.

The Magic Lantern

Chronology
by
Peter Cowie

Index

1

When I was born in 1918, my mother had Spanish influenza. I was in a bad way and was baptized as a precaution at the hospital. One day the family was visited by the old house doctor, who looked at me and said: 'He's dying of under-nourishment.' My maternal grandmother took me with her to her summer house in Dalarna, and on the train journey, which in those days took a whole day, she fed me with sponge cake soaked in water. By the time we finally arrived, I was practically dead, but Grandmother managed to find a wet nurse – a kindly, fair-haired girl from a neighbouring village. I got better, but was always vomiting and had constant stomach-aches.

I suffered from several indefinable illnesses and could never really decide whether I wanted to live at all. Deep down in my consciousness, I can recall my actual condition, the stench of my body's secretions, the damp chafing clothes, the soft glow of the nightlight, the door into the next room just ajar, the nursemaid's deep breathing, pattering steps, whispering voices, reflections of the sun in the carafe of water. I can recall it all, but I do not remember any fear. That came later.

My family lived on the first floor in an apartment house on the corner of Skeppargatan and Storgatan in Stockholm. The dining room faced on to a dark back courtyard with a high brick wall, the outdoor privy, dustbins, fat rats and a carpet-beating stand. I am sitting on someone's knee being fed with gruel. The plate is on grey oilcloth with a red border, the enamel white, with blue flowers on it, and reflecting the sparse light from the window. By bending my head sideways and forwards, I try out various viewpoints. As I move my head, the reflections in the gruel plate change and form new patterns. Suddenly, I vomit over everything.

That is probably my very first memory.

In the autumn of 1920, we moved to Villagatan 22 in the Östermalm district of Stockholm. It smelt of new paint and polished parquet flooring. The nursery had sun-yellow linoleum on the floor and light-coloured blinds with castles and meadow flowers on them. Mother's hands were soft and she made time to tell me stories. Father stepped on the chamber pot one morning when he got out of bed and swore loudly. Two country girls from Dalarna inhabited the kitchen, and they sang often and spontaneously. A playmate of my own age lived on the other side of the landing. She was called Tippan and was imaginative and enterprising. We compared our bodies and found interesting differences. Someone caught us at it but said nothing.

When I was four, my sister was born and the situation changed radically. A fat monstrous creature had suddenly acquired the main rôle. I was banished from my mother's bed and my father beamed over this bawling bundle. The demon of jealousy fastened its claws into my heart. I raged, wept, crapped on the floor and messed myself. My elder brother and I, usually mortal enemies, made peace and planned various ways of killing this repulsive wretch. For some reason, my brother considered I should do the deed. I was flattered and we looked for a suitable moment.

I thought I was alone in the apartment one quiet sunny afternoon and crept into my parents' bedroom, where the creature was asleep in her pink basket. I pulled up a chair, climbed on to it and stood looking at the swollen face and dribbling mouth. My brother had given me perfectly clear instructions, but I had misunderstood. Instead of squeezing my sister's throat, I tried to press her chest in. She woke at once with a penetrating scream. I pressed my hand against her mouth and her watery blue eyes squinted and stared. I took a step forward to get a better grip, lost my footing and fell to the floor.

I recall that the deed itself was associated with acute pleasure that rapidly turned into terror.

＊　　＊　　＊

Today, as I lean over photographs of my childhood to study my mother's face through a magnifying glass, I try to penetrate long vanished emotions. Yes, I loved her and she is very attractive in the photograph, with her thick centre-parted hair above a broad forehead, her soft oval face, gentle sensual mouth, her warm unaffected gaze below dark shapely eyebrows, her small strong hands.

My four year-old heart was consumed with doglike devotion.

Nevertheless, our relationship was not uncomplicated. My devotion disturbed and irritated her. My expressions of tenderness and my violent outbursts worried her. She often sent me away with cool ironic words and I wept with rage and disappointment. Her relationship with my brother was simpler, for she was always defending him against Father, who brought him up with rigorous sternness in which brutal flogging was a recurrent argument.

I slowly realized that my adoration, alternately gentle and furious, had little effect, so I soon started to test out behaviour that would please her and arouse her interest. Illness immediately attracted her sympathy. As I was a sickly child with endless ailments, this did indeed become a painful but successful route to her tenderness. On the other hand, as Mother was a trained nurse, shamming was swiftly seen through and punished in public.

Another way to gain her attention proved more harmful. I learnt that Mother could not bear indifference and preoccupation. She used them as *her* weapons. I also learnt to subdue my passions, and started on a peculiar game, the primary ingredients of which were arrogance and a cool friendliness. I can remember nothing about what I did, but love makes one enterprising and I quickly succeeded in creating interest in my combination of sensitivity and self-esteem.

My greatest problem was simply that I was never given the opportunity to reveal my game, throw off the mask and allow myself to be enveloped in a love that was reciprocated.

Many years later, when Mother was in hospital with a tube in her nose after her second heart attack, we talked about our lives. I told her about my sufferings in childhood and she admitted she had been distressed by them, but not in the way I had thought. She had taken her troubles to a famous paediatrician and he had warned her in solemn terms to reject firmly what he called my 'sickly approaches'. Every indulgence would damage me for life.

I have a clear memory of a visit to this child specialist. I had refused to go to school, although I was already more than six. Day after day I was dragged or carried, screaming with anguish, into the classroom. I vomited over everything I saw, fainted and lost my sense of balance. In the end, I won the day and school was postponed, but the visit to this famous paediatrician was unavoidable.

He had a large beard, a high collar and smelt of cigars. He pulled down my trousers, seized my insignificant organ in one hand and with the forefinger of his other hand drew a triangle round my crotch, then said to my mother, sitting behind me in her fur-edged coat and dark green velvet hat with a veil, 'The boy still looks like a child *here*.'

When we got back from doctor's, I was dressed in my faded yellow smock with its red border and a cat embroidered on the pocket. I was given hot chocolate and cheese sandwiches. Then I went into the nursery, now recaptured from the baby.

My brother had scarlet fever and was elsewhere. (Naturally I hoped he would die. The disease was dangerous in those days.) Out of the toy cupboard I took a wooden cart with red wheels and yellow spokes and harnessed a wooden horse to the shafts. The threat of school had faded into a pleasing memory of a success.

*   *   *

One windy day in early 1965, Mother phoned me at the theatre to tell me Father had been taken to hospital and was to be operated on for a malignant tumour in his gullet. She wanted me to go to see him. I told her that I had neither time nor desire to do so, that my father and I had nothing to say to each other, that he was a person to whom I was indifferent and I would probably only frighten and embarrass him by going to see him on what could be his deathbed. Mother was angry. She persisted. I was upset and refused to be emotionally blackmailed. This eternal blackmail. *Can't you do it for my sake?* Mother was furious and started crying. I pointed out that tears had never made any impression on me, and I slammed down the receiver.

That same evening I was on duty at the theatre. I went backstage and talked to the actors. I hustled in members of the audience who had arrived late because of a raging snowstorm. I sat in my room working on the scenery for Peter Weiss' *Die Ermittlung* [*The Investigation*]

The telephone rang and the girl on the switchboard reported that Mrs Bergman was there asking to speak to the theatre manager. As there were several Mrs Bergmans to choose from, I snappily asked which damned Mrs Bergman. The switchboard girl replied with some trepidation that it was the theatre director's mother and she wished to speak to her son – *immediately*.

I went to fetch my mother, who had made her way to the theatre through the snowstorm and was still breathing heavily from the effort, her bad heart and her anger. I asked her to sit down and whether she would like a cup of tea. She replied that she was certainly not going to sit down and neither had she any desire for tea. The purpose of her visit was to hear me repeat the heartless and brutal abuse I had expressed over the telephone that same morning. She wanted to see what I looked like when I rejected and insulted my parents.

The snow melted round the little fur-clad person, making dark patches on the carpet. She was very pale, her eyes black with anger and her nose red.

I tried to embrace her and kiss her, but she pushed me away and slapped my face. (Mother's slapping technique was unsurpassed. The blow was dealt like lightning and with her left hand on which two heavy wedding rings added painful emphasis to the punishment.) I laughed and Mother burst into tears. She sank, with considerable skill, on to a chair at the table and hid her face in her right hand while fumbling for a handkerchief in her bag with the other.

I sat down beside her and assured her that of course I would go to see my father, that I regretted what I had said and that with all my heart I asked her forgiveness.

She flung her arms round me and said she would not disturb me for a minute longer.

After which we had tea and talked calmly until two o'clock in the morning.

All that happened on a Tuesday. On the following Sunday, an acquaintance of the family, who was staying with Mother while Father was in hospital, telephoned to ask me to come at once as Mother had been taken ill. Her doctor, Professor Nanna Svartz, was on her way and for the moment the attack had abated. I hurried over to Storgatan 7. The professor opened the door and at once told me that Mother had died a few minutes earlier.

To my surprise, I began to weep loudly and uncontrollably. That soon passed and the old doctor stood in silence holding my hand. When I had calmed down, she told me it had all happened quite quickly, in two waves of twenty minutes each.

Not long afterwards, I was alone with Mother in the silent apartment.

She was lying in her bed, wearing a flannel nightgown and a knitted blue bed-jacket. Her head was turned slightly sideways and her lips were parted. She was pale, with shadows round her eyes. Her still dark hair was neatly combed – no, her hair was no longer dark, but iron-grey, and in recent years had been cut short, but the image of her in my memory tells me her hair was dark, possibly streaked with grey. Her hands were resting on her breast. On her left forefinger was a small band aid.

The room was suddenly filled with bright early spring light, the little alarm clock ticking away busily on the bedside table.

I thought that Mother was breathing, that her breast was heaving and that I could hear a quiet indrawn breath. I thought her eyelids twitched. I thought she was asleep and just about to wake, my habitual illusory game with reality.

I sat there for several hours. The church bells of Hedvig Eleonora rang for morning service, the light shifted and I could hear piano music somewhere. I don't think I was grieving, or that I was thinking, or even that I was observing myself or playing a rôle – that professional disease which has followed me mercilessly throughout my life and so often robbed or diminished my most profound experiences.

I don't recall much of those hours in Mother's room. What I remember most is the band aid on her left forefinger.

That same afternoon I went to see Father in hospital and told him about Mother's death. He had survived the operation, as well as the consequent pneumonia, and was now sitting in the ward's blue armchair in his old dressing gown, shaved and tidy, his long gnarled hand on the handle of his stick. He looked steadily at me, his eyes clear, calm and wide open. When I had told him what I knew, he just nodded and asked me to leave him alone.

*   *   *

Most of our upbringing was based on such concepts as sin, confession, punishment, forgiveness and grace, concrete factors in relationships between children and parents and

God. There was an innate logic in all this which we accepted and thought we understood. This fact may well have contributed to our astonishing acceptance of Nazism. We had never heard of freedom and knew even less what it tasted like. In a hierarchical system, all doors are closed.

So punishments were something self-evident, never questioned. They could be swift and simple, a slap over the face or a smack on the bottom, but they could also be extremely sophisticated, refined through generations.

If I wet myself, which often happened, and all too easily, I was made to wear a red knee-length skirt for the rest of the day. This was regarded as harmless and funny. Major crimes reaped exemplary punishment, starting from when the crime was discovered. In minor instances the criminal confessed, say to maids, or to Mother or one of the innumerable female relations living at our parsonage on various occasions.

The immediate consequence of confessing was to be frozen out. No one spoke or replied to you. As far as I can make out, this was to make the criminal long for punishment and forgiveness. After dinner and coffee, the parties were summoned to Father's room, where interrogation and confessions were renewed. After that, the carpet beater was fetched and you yourself had to state how many strokes you considered you deserved. When the punishment quota had been established, a hard green cushion was fetched, trousers and underpants taken down, you prostrated yourself over the cushion, someone held firmly on to your neck and the strokes were administered.

I can't maintain that it hurt all that much. The ritual and the humiliation were what was so painful. My brother got the worst of it. Mother often used to sit by his bed, bathing his back where the carpet beater had loosened the skin and streaked his back with bloody weals. As I hated my brother and was frightened of his sudden flaring rages, I found great satisfaction in seeing him punished so severely.

After the strokes had been administered, you had to kiss Father's hand, at which forgiveness was declared and the burden of sin fell away, deliverance and grace ensued. Though of course you had to go to bed without supper and evening reading, the relief was nevertheless considerable.

There was also a spontaneous kind of punishment which could be very unpleasant for a child tormented by fear of the dark: being shut inside a special cupboard. Alma in the kitchen had told us that in that particular cupboard lived a little creature which ate the toes of naughty children. I quite clearly heard something moving in there in the dark and my terror was total. I don't remember what I did, probably climbed on to shelves or hung from hooks to avoid having my toes devoured.

This form of punishment lost its terror when I found a solution. I hid a torch with a red and green light in a corner of the cupboard. When I was shut in, I hunted out my torch, directed the beam of light at the wall and pretended I was at the cinema. Once when the door was opened, I lay on the floor with my eyes closed, pretending to be unconscious. Everyone was horrified except Mother, who suspected shamming, but no evidence could be found and further punishment was not forthcoming.

Other punishments were no excursions to the cinema, no food, being sent to bed or sent to your room, extra homework, caning on your hand, hair-pulling, working in the kitchen (which could be rather pleasant), no one speaking to you for a specific time and so on.

Nowadays, I understand my parents' desperation. A pastor's family lives as if on a tray, unprotected from other eyes. The parsonage must always be open to criticism and comments from the congregation. Both Father and Mother were perfectionists who sagged beneath this unreasonable pressure. Their working day was open-ended, their marriage difficult, their self-discipline iron-hard. Their two sons reflected characteristics they unremittingly punished in themselves. My brother was rebellious and unable to protect himself. Father used all his willpower to break him, and almost succeeded. My sister was loved very much and possessively, by both parents. She responded with self-effacement and gentle timidity.

I think I came off best by turning myself into a liar. I created an external person who had very little to do with the real me. As I didn't know how to keep my creation and my person apart, the damage had consequences for my life and creativity far into adulthood. Sometimes I have to console myself with the fact that he who has lived a lie loves the truth.

My first conscious lie stands out clearly in my memory. Father had become a hospital chaplain. We had moved to a yellow house on the edge of the great park that borders Lill-Jansskogen in Stockholm. It was a cold winter's day and my brother and I and his friends had been throwing snowballs at the greenhouse on the edge of the park, breaking a great many panes. The gardener at once suspected us and reported the matter to Father. Interrogations followed. My brother confessed and so did his companions. I was in the kitchen drinking a glass of milk, Alma baking at the kitchen table, when Siri, the housemaid, came into the kitchen and relayed the progress of the awful punishments. She asked me if I had had any part in this vandalism, something I had already denied at a preliminary interrogation (I had been temporarily released owing to lack of evidence). When Siri jokingly asked me as if in passing whether I had succeeded in breaking any panes, I realized she was trying to trap me, so I replied in a calm voice that I had just watched for a while and thrown a few loose snowballs that had hit my brother, but then I'd left because my feet were so cold. I clearly remember thinking: This is just what you do when you lie.

It was a decisive discovery. In roughly the same rational way as Molière's Don Juan, I decided to be A Hypocrite. I cannot say I was always successful: owing to lack of experience, I was sometimes seen through, and occasionally outsiders intervened.

The family had an immensely rich benefactor called Aunt Anna. She invited us to children's parties with conjurors and other delights. She always gave us expensive and much coveted Christmas presents and took us every year to the

Schumann Circus première in Djurgården. This event drove me
into a state of feverish excitement: the car journey with Aunt
Anna's uniformed chauffeur, going into the huge brightly lit
wooden building, the secret smells, Aunt Anna's voluminous
hat, the blaring orchestra, the magic of the preparations and the
roaring of lions and tigers behind the red draperies of the circus
entrance. Someone whispered that a lion had appeared in a
dark opening under the cupola and that the clowns were
frightening and aggressive. I fell asleep from sheer emotion and
awoke to wonderful music – a young woman dressed in white
was riding around on a huge black stallion.

I was overcome with love for this young woman. She was
included in my fantasy games and I called her Esmeralda
(perhaps that was her name). My fiction finally took an all-too-
hazardous step out into reality. Under an oath of secrecy, I
confided in the boy called Nisse who sat next to me at school. I
told him that my parents had sold me to Schumann's Circus and
I was soon to be taken away from home and school to be trained
as an acrobat, together with Esmeralda, who was considered
the most beautiful woman in the world. The next day my
fantasy was revealed and desecrated.

My class teacher considered the matter so serious that she
wrote an agitated letter to my mother. There was a dreadful
court scene. I was put up against the wall, humiliated and
disgraced, at home as well as at school.

Fifty years later, I asked Mother if she remembered my sale to
the circus; she did, very well. I asked why no one had laughed or
at least been affectionately amused when faced with so much
imagination and daring. Did no one question the deeper
reasons why a seven year-old wished to leave home and be sold
to a circus? Mother replied that they had already been troubled
on several occasions by my lies and fantasies. In her anguish,
she had consulted the paediatrician. He had emphasized how
important it was for a child to learn at an early stage to
differentiate between fantasy and reality. As they were now
faced with an insolent and flagrant lie, it had to be punished
accordingly.

I had my revenge on my former friend by taking my brother's sheath-knife and chasing him around the school playground. When a teacher threw herself between us, I tried to kill her.

I was removed from school and severely beaten. Then my false friend caught polio and died, which pleased me. The whole class was sent home for three weeks as was the custom, and everything was forgotten.

But I still fantasized about Esmeralda, our adventures becoming more and more dangerous and our love more and more passionate. Meanwhile, I became engaged to a girl in my class called Gladys, thus betraying Tippan, my faithful playmate.

The park of Sophiahemmet, the royal hospital, is large, the front facing on to the Valhallavägen, the Stadium on one side and the College of Technology on the other. It penetrates deep into Lill-Jansskogen. The buildings, not many in those days, were scattered over the rolling landscape.

I roamed around freely and experienced all kinds of things. The chapel, a small brick building deep in the park, aroused my special interest. Through my friendship with the hospital caretaker, who was in charge of transport between hospital and chapel, I heard a great many good stories and was allowed to see a lot of corpses in various stages of decay. Another building, entrance to which really was forbidden, was the boiler room with its four huge roaring furnaces. Coal was brought on trolleys and tipped into the furnaces by black figures. Carts, harnessed to heavy Ardennes horses, arrived several days each week and the sacks were humped to the open steel furnace doors by men in sacking hoods. Now and again, secret loads of bloody organs and amputated limbs were cremated in the furnaces.

Every other Sunday, Father conducted communion service in the hospital chapel, which filled with nurses in black Sunday uniforms and starched white aprons, the Sophiahemmet cap on their well-groomed heads. Opposite the parsonage was Solhemmet, where lived very old nurses who had devoted their lives to the hospital. They were like an order of nuns with strict convent regulations.

The inhabitants of Solhemmet could look right into the parsonage. And they did.

To be honest, I think back on my early years with delight and curiosity. My imagination and senses were given nourishment, and I remember nothing dull, in fact the days and hours kept exploding with wonders, unexpected sights and magical moments. I can still roam through the landscape of my childhood and again experience lights, smells, people, rooms, moments, gestures, tones of voice and objects. These memories seldom have any particular meaning, but are like short or longer films with no point, shot at random.

The prerogative of childhood is to move unhindered between magic and oatmeal porridge, between boundless terror and explosive joy. There were no boundaries except prohibitions and regulations, which were shadowy, mostly incomprehensible. For instance, I know I did not grasp the concept of time. *You really must learn to be punctual. You've been given a watch and you know how to tell the time.* But time ceased to exist, something told me I was probably hungry, there was a row.

It was difficult to differentiate between what was fantasy and what was considered real. If I made an effort, I was perhaps able to make reality stay real. But, for instance, there were ghosts and spectres. What should I do with them? And the sagas, were they real? God and the Angels? Jesus Christ? Adam and Eve? The Flood? What was it truly like to be with Abraham and Isaac? Was he *really* going to cut Isaac's throat? I stared in dismay at Doré's engraving, identifying myself with Isaac. That was real. Father was going to slit Ingmar's throat. What would happen if the Angel came too late? Then they would *have* to weep. Blood running and Ingmar smiling bleakly. Reality.

Then came the cinematograph.

The weeks before Christmas. The immensely rich Aunt Anna's uniformed Mr Jansson had already delivered a quantity of presents. As usual, they were placed in the Christmas present basket in the cupboard under the stairs. One parcel in particular aroused my excited curiosity. It was brown and angular with 'Forsners' on the wrapping paper. Forsners was a photographic store in Hamngatan which sold not only cameras but real cinematographs.

More than anything else, I longed for a cinematograph. The year before, I had been to the cinema for the first time and seen a film about a horse. I think it was called *Black Beauty* and was based on a famous book. The film was on at the Sture cinema and we sat in the front row of the circle. To me, it was the beginning. I was overcome with a fever that has never left me. The silent shadows turned their pale faces towards me and spoke in inaudible voices to my most secret feelings. Sixty years have gone by and nothing has changed; the fever is the same.

Later that autumn, I went to see a school friend who had a cinematograph and a few films, and he put on a dutiful performance for Tippan and me. I was allowed to wind the machine while our host necked with Tippan.

Christmas was an explosion of amusements. Mother directed it all with a firm hand, and there must have been considerable organization behind this orgy of hospitality, meals, visiting relatives, Christmas presents and church arrangements.

At home, Christmas Eve was a fairly quiet affair which began with Christmas prayers in church at five o'clock, then a happy but restrained meal, the lighting of the candles on the tree, the reading of the Christmas story and early bed. (We had to be up for early mass the next day, in those days really early.) No presents were handed out, but the evening was joyful, an exciting prelude to the festivities of Christmas Day. After early Church service with lighted candles and trumpets came Christmas breakfast. By then Father had carried out his professional duties and had exchanged his cassock for his smoking jacket. He was in his most merry mood and made an improvised speech in verse to our guests, sang a song composed for the occasion, toasted everyone in schnapps, gave imitations of his colleagues and made everyone laugh. I sometimes think about his cheerful light-heartedness, his kindness, friendliness and extravagance, everything that had been concealed behind darkness, severity, brutality and remoteness. I think that in my memory I have often done my father an injustice.

After breakfast, everyone went to bed for a few hours. The internal domestic routine must have gone on working, for at two o'clock, just as dusk was falling, afternoon coffee was served. We had open house for anyone who cared to come and wish the parsonage a happy Christmas. Several friends were practising musicians and part of the afternoon festivities was usually an improvised concert. Then the sumptuous culmina-tion of Christmas Day approached: the evening meal. This was held in our spacious kitchen, where the social hierarchy was temporarily set aside. All the food was laid out on a serving table and covered working surfaces, and the distribu-tion of Christmas gifts took place at the dining-room table. The baskets were carried in, Father officiated with a cigar and glass of sweet liqueur, the presents were handed out, verses were read aloud, applauded and commented on; no presents without verses.

That was when the cinematograph affair occurred. My brother was the one who got it.

At once I began to howl. I was ticked off and disappeared under the table, where I raged on and was told to be quiet immediately. I rushed off to the nursery, swearing and cursing, considered running away, then finally fell asleep exhausted by grief.

The party went on.

Later in the evening I woke up. Gertrud was singing a folk song downstairs and the nightlight was glowing. A transparency of the Nativity scene and the shepherds at prayer was glimmering faintly on the tall chest-of-drawers. Among my brother's other Christmas presents on the white gate-legged table was the cinematograph, with its crooked chimney, its beautifully shaped brass lens and its rack for the film loops.

I made a swift decision. I woke my brother and proposed a deal. I offered him my hundred tin soldiers in exchange for the cinematograph. As Dag possessed a huge army and was always involved in war games with his friends, an agreement was made to the satisfaction of both parties.

The cinematograph was mine.

It was not a complicated machine. The source of light was a paraffin lamp and the crank was attached with a cogwheel and a Maltese cross. At the back of the metal box was a simple reflecting mirror, behind the lens a slot for coloured lantern slides. The apparatus also included a square purple box which contained some glass slides and a sepia-coloured film strip (35mm). This was about three metres long and glued into a loop. Information on the lid stated that the film was called *Mrs Holle*. Who this Mrs Holle was no one knew, but later it turned out that she was a popular equivalent of the Goddess of Love in Mediterranean countries.

The next morning I retreated into the spacious wardrobe in the nursery, placed the cinematograph on a sugar crate, lit the paraffin lamp and directed the beam of light on to the whitewashed wall. Then I loaded the film.

A picture of a meadow appeared on the wall. Asleep in the meadow was a young woman apparently wearing national costume. *Then I turned the handle*! It is impossible to describe this. I can't find words to express my excitement. But at any time I can recall the smell of the hot metal, the scent of mothballs and dust in the wardrobe, the feel of the crank against my hand. I can see the trembling rectangle on the wall.

I turned the handle and the girl woke up, sat up, slowly got up, stretched her arms out, swung round and disappeared to the right. If I went on turning, she would again lie there, then make exactly the same movements all over again.

She was moving.

2

Childhood in the grace and favour parsonage of Sophiahemmet, the everyday rhythm, birthdays, church festivals, Sundays. Duties, games, freedom, conformity and security. The long dark way to school in winter, the games of marbles and bicycle rides in spring, and reading aloud by the fire on autumn Sunday evenings.

We didn't know Mother had gone through a passionate love affair or that Father suffered from severe depression. Mother was preparing to break out of her marriage, Father threatening to take his own life. They were reconciled and decided to continue together 'for the sake of the children', as was said at the time. We noticed nothing, or very little.

One autumn evening, I was busy with my film apparatus in the nursery. My sister was asleep in Mother's room and my brother was out practising shooting. I suddenly heard a violent argument going on downstairs, Mother crying and Father talking angrily, frightening sounds I had never heard before. I crept out on to the stairs and saw Mother and Father in violent altercation in the hall, Mother trying to pull her coat towards her, but Father holding firmly on to it. Then, she let go of the coat and rushed towards the porch. Father got there before her and, pushing her aside, stood in front of the door. Mother went for him and they struggled. She struck him in the face; he threw her against the wall and she lost her balance and fell. My sister woke in the tumult, came out onto the landing and began to cry. Mother and Father stopped.

I can't remember clearly what happened next. Mother was sitting on the sofa in her room, her nose bleeding. She was trying to calm my sister. I was in the nursery looking at my cinematograph. I fell pathetically to my knees and promised God he could have my films and all my apparatus as long as Mother and Father became friends again.

My prayers were heard. The Pastor of Hedvig Eleonora parish (Father's superior) intervened, my parents were reconciled, and the immensely rich Aunt Anna took them off on a long holiday trip through Italy. Grandmother stepped in, and order and the illusion of security were restored.

Grandmother lived mostly in Upsala, but she owned a country house up in Dalarna. When widowed at scarcely thirty, she divided the handsome apartment in Trädgårdsgatan in half and moved into five rooms, a kitchen and a maid's room. When I was very young, she lived there alone with Miss Ellen Nilsson, a timeless monument to the character of the Småland region, who cooked good food, was sternly religious and spoilt us children. When Grandmother died, she came to Mother, and was both loved and feared. At the age of seventy-five, she was afflicted with cancer of the throat, tidied her room, wrote her Will, changed the second-class ticket Mother had purchased for her to third-class and went to her sister's in Paraholm, where she died a few months later. Called 'Lalla' by us children, Ellen Nilsson had lived with Grandmother's and Mother's families for over fifty years.

Grandmother and Lalla existed in moody mutual dependence, which entailed a great deal of stepping over the mark and then making up, but none of this was ever questioned. To me, the large (perhaps not that large) apartment in the quiet of Trädgårdsgatan, was the epitome of security and magic: the numerous clocks measuring the time, the sunlight wandering across the infinite green of the carpets, the fires fragrant in the tiled stoves, the chimney pipe roaring and the little stove-doors tinkling. Down in the street, a sleigh with its jingling bells sometimes passed, the cathedral bells rang for divine service or a funeral and, morning and evening, the delicate and distant Gunilla bell could be heard.

Old furniture, heavy curtains, dim pictures. At the end of the long dark hall was an interesting room with four holes bored in the door near the floor, red wallpaper, a mahogany-and-plush thronelike chair with brass fittings and ornamentations. Two steps covered with soft carpeting led up to the throne and, when you opened the heavy lid of the chair, you stared down into a chasm of darkness and odours. Courage was required to sit on Grandmother's throne.

A tall iron stove in the hall gave off its own special smell of burning coal and hot metal. When Lalla prepared dinner in the kitchen, a nourishing cabbage soup, the fragrance spread warmly throughout the apartment and merged into a higher union with the vague scents from the secret room.

For someone small with his nose close to the ground, the rugs smelt fresh and strong of the moth-proofing they absorbed as they lay rolled up throughout the summer months. Every Friday, Lalla polished the old parquet floor with beeswax and turpentine, an overpowering aroma. The knotted and splintery wooden floors smelt of soft-soap, and the linoleum was polished with an evil-smelling mixture of sour skimmed milk and water. People went around like symphonies of smells – powder, perfume, tar-soap, urine, sex, sweat, pomade, snuff and cooking. Some smelt of human beings in general, some smelt safe, others menacing. Father's fat Aunt Emma wore a wig which she stuck on to her bald pate with a special kind of glue. All of Aunt Emma smelt of glue. Grandmother smelt of 'glycerine and rose-water', a lotion bought artlessly at the chemist's. Mother smelt sweet like vanilla, and when she was cross her downy moustache turned moist and gave off a scarcely perceptible odour of metal. My favourite smell was of a plump red-haired young nursemaid called Marit, who was lame. The best thing in the world was to lie on her arm in her bed with my nose pressed against her coarse nightgown.

A sunken world of lights, odours and sounds. Today, if I am calm and just about to fall asleep, I can go from room to room and see every detail, know and feel it. In the quietness of Grandmother's home, my senses opened and decided to keep all this for ever and ever. Where has everything gone? Have any of my children inherited the impressions of my senses? Can one inherit impressions of senses, experiences, insights?

The days, weeks and months spent with my maternal grandmother gratified my constant and importunate need for silence, regularity and order. I played my solitary games with no desire for company, while Grandmother sat at her desk in the dining room, clad in black, a large blue and white striped apron on top. She read a book, or did accounts or wrote letters, her steel nib scratching faintly. Lalla would be in the kitchen, humming quietly to herself. I leant over my toy theatre, letting the curtain rise voluptuously on Red Riding Hood's dark forest or Cinderella's bright ballroom, my games making me ruler of the stage, my imagination populating it.

One Sunday I go down with a sore throat, so am excused morning service and left alone in the apartment. It is early spring and the sunlight keeps coming and going with swift soundless movements over the curtains and pictures. The huge dining-room table towers above me as I sit with my back against one of its bulging legs. The chairs round the table and the walls are covered with yellow leather, darkened with age and smelling old. The sideboard rises fortresslike behind me, the carafes and cut-glass bowls glimmering in the changing light. Along the long wall on my left hangs a large picture of white, yellow and red houses growing out of blue water, and oblong boats floating on the water.

The dining-room clock, which rises to the ornamental ceiling, is talking to itself in a morose and introverted way. From where I am sitting, I can see the shimmering green of the drawing room, green walls, rugs, furniture, curtains, ferns in green pots. I can see the naked white lady with her arms chopped off. She is leaning slightly forward, looking at me with a small smile. A gilt clock under a glass dome stands on the bulging bureau with its gold fittings and feet; a young man leans against the clockface, playing a flute; close to him is a little lady in a big hat and a short wide skirt. Both of them are gilded. When the clock strikes twelve, the young man plays his flute and the girl dances.

The sunlight turns fiery, lighting up the prisms in the chandelier, sweeping over the picture of houses growing out of the water and caressing the whiteness of the statue. Then the clocks strike, the golden girl dances, the boy plays, the naked lady turns her head and nods at me and Death drags his scythe across the linoleum in the dark porch. I can just see him, his smiling yellow skull and dark gangling figure against the panes of glass in the front door.

* * *

I want to see Grandmother's face, so I hunt out a photograph, a picture of my grandfather the Transport Manager, with Grandmother and her three stepsons. Grandfather is looking at his young bride with pride. His dark beard is well-tended, his pince-nez gold-framed, his collar high and his morning suit impeccable. His sons have drawn themselves up, young men with wavering eyes and weak features. I fetch a magnifying glass and study Grandmother's features. Her eyes are pale but sharp, her face plumply round, her chin stubborn and mouth determined, despite the polite studio smile. Her hair is thick and dark, carefully arranged. I couldn't say she was beautiful, but she radiates strength of will, intelligence and humour.

The newly weds give the impression of well-to-do self-assurance: we have accepted our rôles and we intend to act them out. But the sons seem disorientated, oppressed, perhaps even rebellious.

Grandfather had built a summer house at Dufnäs, one of the most beautiful places in Dalarna, with its wide view over the river, the heathlands, out-barns and hills, blue beyond the hills. He loved trains and the railway line ran through his land, along a slope a hundred metres below the house. He could sit on his veranda and time the eight trains, four in each direction, two of them goods trains. He could also see the railway bridge across the river, a masterpiece of engineering, his pride and joy. It is said that I sat on his knee, but I have no memory of him. I have inherited my angled little fingers from him, and possibly my enthusiasm for steam engines.

So Grandmother was widowed early. She wore black and her hair turned white. The children married, left home and she was left alone with Lalla. Mother once told me that Grandmother never loved anyone, except her youngest son, Ernst. Mother tried to gain her love by resembling her in every possible way but, being a softer kind of person, she failed.

Father described Grandmother as a domineering bitch, and he was certainly not alone in that judgement.

Despite this, the best times of my childhood were with Grandmother. She treated me with a harsh tenderness and intuitive understanding. Among other things, we had perfected a ritual, at which she never failed me. Before dinner, we sat down on her green sofa, where we 'discussed' things for about an hour. Grandmother told me about the World, about Life, but also about Death (which was occupying my thoughts a good deal at the time). She wanted to know what I thought. She listened carefully, saw through my fibs or brushed them aside with friendly irony. She allowed me to have my say as a real person in my own right without camouflage.

Our 'discussions' were always enveloped in twilight, intimacy and winter afternoons.

Grandmother had another delightful quality. She loved going to the 'movies', and if children were allowed to see the film she took me along. There was only one disturbing element in our joy. Grandmother possessed a terrible pair of galoshes and she didn't like love scenes, which I adored. When the hero and heroine, endlessly and excessively languishing, gave expression to their emotions, Grandmother's galoshes started to squeak. The ghastly sound filled the whole cinema.

We read aloud to each other, we invented stories, especially ghost stories or other horrors, and we also drew 'people', a kind of serial. One of us started by drawing a picture, then the other continued with the next picture and thus the action developed. We drew 'actions' for several days. They could amount to forty or fifty pictures, and in between the pictures we wrote explanatory texts.

Domestic routine at Trädgårdsgatan was of time-honoured orderliness. When the fires were lit in the tiled stoves, we got up. Then it was seven o'clock. A rubdown in a tin bath in icy cold water, breakfast of porridge and hard crispbread open sandwiches, morning prayers, homework or lessons super-vised by Grandmother. At one o'clock we had afternoon tea and sandwiches. Then out in all weathers. A walk to see what the cinemas might be showing. Dinner at five o'clock. Take out the old toys, preserved since Uncle Ernst's childhood. Reading aloud. Evening prayers. The Gunilla bell ringing. At nine o'clock it was night.

Lying on the little couch listening to the silence, seeing the beam from the streetlamp throwing light and shade on the ceiling. When snowstorms swept across the Upsala plain, the lamp swung, the shadows intertwined and there was a squeaking and revelling in the tiled stove.

On Sundays, we had dinner at four o'clock and that was when Aunt Lotten came. She lived in a home for old missionaries and had been to the same high school as Grandmother, from which they were among the first women in the country to graduate. Aunt Lotten went to China, lost her looks, her teeth and one eye.

Grandmother knew I thought Aunt Lotten was disgusting, but she believed I ought to be hardened, so I was placed beside Aunt Lotten at Sunday dinner. I could see straight up into her hairy nose, and inside her nostril there was always a greenish-yellow blob of snot. She also smelt of dried pee. Her false teeth clattered when she spoke and she held her plate close to her face and slurped when she ate, a subdued growling sometimes rising from her stomach.

This revolting person owned a treasure. After dinner and coffee, she unpacked a Chinese shadow theatre from a yellow wooden box. A sheet was stretched across the doorway between the drawing room and the dining room, the light was turned out and Aunt Lotten performed her shadow play. She must have been very skilful, for she manipulated several figures simultaneously and acted all the parts. First the screen would turn red or blue, suddenly a demon would hurtle through the red, a thin moon would appear against the blue, then all at once everything was green and amazing fish were moving in the depths of the sea.

The uncles sometimes came on a visit, with their terrifying wives. The men were fat, had beards and spoke in loud voices. The women had big hats and stank of sweaty officiousness. I held my breath as much as I could. I was lifted up, hugged, kissed. I was pinched and nipped. I was also the butt of intimate questions. Has the boy wet himself this week? Rather a lot of that last week, was there not? Open your mouth and let me see if you've got a loose tooth. Here we are, naughty thing, shall we pull it out? You'll get ten öre. I think the boy's developing a squint. Look at my little finger, yes, one eye isn't following. You'll have to wear a patch like a pirate. Shut your mouth, Putte, you gape too much. Adenoids, I assume. People look stupid with their mouths open. Your grandmother will have to arrange for an operation. It's bad for you to go around with your mouth open.

They moved jerkily and glanced around awkwardly. The wives smoked and in Grandmother's presence they perspired with anxiety, their voices sharp and quick, their faces painted. They didn't look like Mother, although they were mothers.

Uncle Carl, however, was different.

3

Uncle Carl was sitting on Grandmother's green sofa, the recipient of her reproaches. He was a big fat man with a high forehead, which at this particular moment was creased with worry. His head was bald with brown spots and a few thin curls at the nape of his neck. His hairy ears were red. His round stomach bulged over his thighs and his glasses kept misting over with moisture, hiding his mild violet-blue eyes. He was holding his soft fat hands pressed together between his knees.

Grandmother sat small and straight in the armchair by the drawing-room table, a thimble on her right forefinger, occasionally emphasizing a word by striking the thimble on the shiny tabletop. As usual, she was in black, with a white collar and a cameo brooch. Her everyday apron was blue and white striped, and her thick white hair was shining in a ray of sunlight. It was a cold winter's day, the fire roaring in the stove and the windows starred with frosty flowers. The clock under its glass dome struck twelve sharp notes and the shepherdess danced for her shepherd. A sleigh passed through the entrance porchway, bells jingling, its runners scraping against the cobblestones, the heavy hooves echoing.

I was sitting on the floor in an adjoining room. Uncle Carl and I had just laid out the railway lines for the train I had had for Christmas from the immensely rich Aunt Anna. Grandmother had suddenly appeared in the doorway and summoned Uncle Carl in a curt and chilly voice. He had got up, sighing, put on his jacket and straightened his waistcoat across his stomach. They had gone to sit in the drawing room. Grandmother had closed the door, but it had slid open. I could follow everything, as if they were on a stage.

Grandmother was speaking and Uncle Carl was pouting his bluish-red lips, his great head sinking lower and lower between his shoulders. Uncle Carl was really only a half-uncle, as he was Grandmother's eldest stepson – not all that much younger than she.

Grandmother was his guardian. He was soft in the head, incapable of looking after himself, and sometimes he went into an asylum, but he mostly lived as a paying guest with two middle aged ladies, known as Aunt Beda and Aunt Ester, who cared for him in every way. He was as devoted and gentle as a large dog, but now he had gone too far. One morning he had come rushing out of his room without either long underpants or trousers, and had violently embraced Aunt Beda with a shower of kisses and improper words. Aunt Beda had not panicked but had calmly nipped Uncle Carl in the right place, just as the doctor had recommended. Then she had telephoned Grandmother.

Uncle Carl was all anguish and tears. He was a man of peace. He went to the Mission Church every Sunday with Aunt Ester and Aunt Beda and, in his neat dark suit, with his gentle looks and his melodious baritone voice, he might almost have been one of the preachers. He helped with all the appropriate activities, a kind of unpaid verger, and was looked on with approval at coffee parties and sewing bees, at which he read aloud while the ladies devoted themselves to their handiwork.

Uncle Carl was really an inventor. He besieged the Royal Patent Office with drawings and descriptions, but with little success. Out of a hundred or so applications, only two were approved, a machine that made all potatoes the same size, and an automatic lavatory brush.

Uncle Carl was extremely suspicious. He was horribly anxious that someone might steal his latest ideas, so he carried them about in an oilcloth wrapper between his trousers and long underpants. The oilcloth was necessary, for Uncle Carl suffered from urinomania. Sometimes, especially at large gatherings, he simply couldn't resist his secret passion. He would wind his right foot round the leg of a chair, half rise to his feet and allow his trousers and underpants to be soaked through with a gentle self-induced flood.

Grandmother, Aunt Ester and Aunt Beda knew of his weakness and were able to curb his need with a short sharp 'Carl', but to her horror Miss Agda had once heard a sizzling from the hot stove. Caught out, Uncle Carl cried: 'Whoops, here I am making pancakes.'

I respected him and willingly believed Aunt Signe, who maintained that Carl had been the most gifted of the three brothers, but that out of jealousy Albert had struck his older brother on the head with a hammer, thus causing a lifelong feeble-mindedness in the poor boy.

I admired him because he invented things for my magic lantern and my cinematograph. He rebuilt the slideholder and lens, mounted a concave mirror inside, and then worked away on three more movable pieces of glass, which he himself painted. In this way, he created mobile backgrounds for the figures. Their noses grew, they floated, ghosts appeared from moonlit graves, ships sank and a drowning mother held her child above her head until both were swallowed up by the waves.

Uncle Carl bought strips of film at five öre a metre, then put them in hot soda-water to remove the emulsion. When the strip had dried, he drew moving pictures directly on to the film with Indian ink. Sometimes he drew non-figurative patterns that could be transformed, exploding, swelling and shrinking.

He sat, leaning laboriously over his worktable in the overfurnished room, the film lying on a matt sheet of glass illuminated from below, his glasses pushed up on his forehead and a magnifying glass wedged into his right eye. He smoked a short crooked pipe and kept a whole row of similar pipes, ready cleaned and filled, in front of him on the table. I stared intently at the small figures emerging swiftly and without hesitation from the frames. While Uncle Carl worked, he chattered away, puffing on his pipe, talking and groaning and puffing:

'Here's Teddy the circus poodle doing a forward somersault. It goes fine. He knows how to do it. Now the cruel ringmaster is making the poor dog do a backward somersault — Teddy can't do it. He hits his head on the ring and sees suns and stars. We'll have another colour for the stars. They're red. Now he's got a great bump on his head. That's red, too. I don't think Aunt Ester and Aunt Beda are at home. Go into the dining room, open the little drawer on the left of the buffet, and inside there's a bag of chocolate creams they've hidden because Ma says I mustn't eat sweet things. Take four chocolate creams, but mind they don't catch you.'

I carried out the assignment and was given one of the chocolate creams. He stuffed the others through his thick lips, slavering shinily at the corners of his mouth, then leant back in his chair and peered out at the grey winter dusk. 'I'll show you something,' he said suddenly. 'But you mustn't tell Ma.' He got up, went over to the table under the central lamp and switched it on. The light shone yellow on the oriental pattern of the tablecloth. He sat down and invited me to sit opposite him. Then he wound a piece of the cloth round his left wrist, starting cautiously, then twisting and turning more and more roughly. Finally his hand and wrist loosened at the level of the starched cuff and a few drops of a cloudy fluid floated out on to the tablecloth. Or so it seemed.

'I've got two suits. Every Friday I'm told to go to your grandmother's to change my underclothes and suit. That's gone on for twenty-nine years. I have to stick to it as if I were a child. It's not fair. God will punish her. God punishes power people. Look at that, there's a fire in the house opposite.'

The winter sun had opened a crack in the iron-grey clouds and was shining directly on to the windowpanes of the building opposite in Gamla Ågatan, the reflections throwing dark yellow squares across the pattern of the wallpaper and half of Uncle Carl's face in the glowing light. The 'detached' hand lay between us on the table. Or so it seemed.

When Grandmother died, Mother became Carl's guardian. He was moved to Stockholm, where he rented two small rooms from an elderly Free Church lady who lived in Ringvägen, quite near Göyhsysn.

The routine went on. Every Friday, he came to the parsonage, was given clean underclothes, changed into a spotless freshly pressed suit and had dinner with the family. His appearance was unchanged, his body just as heavy and round, his face just as rosy, the violet-blue eyes just as mild behind the thick glasses. He went on indefatigably besieging the Patent Office with his inventions and, on Sundays, he sang hymns at the Mission Church. Mother managed his finances and he was given pocket-money. He called Mother 'Sister Karin' and was occasionally ironic about her attempts to imitate Grandmother. 'You're trying to be Stepmother. Do stop it. You're much too good-natured. Mammchen was hard right through.'

One Friday, Uncle Carl's landlady appeared and she and Mother carried on a long conversation together. The landlady wept so loudly, it was audible through several walls. After an hour or two, she said goodbye, her face swollen and red from crying. Mother went into the kitchen to Lalla, sank down on a chair and started laughing.

'Uncle Carl,' she said, 'has got engaged to someone thirty years younger than he is.'

A few weeks later, the newly engaged couple came on a visit. They wanted to talk about the marriage ceremony, which indeed was to be simple, but High Church. Uncle Carl was dressed casually in sports shirt and no tie, a check blazer and well-pressed flannel trousers without a spot on them. He had exchanged his old-fashioned spectacles for modern horn-rimmed ones and his button-boots for loafers. He was taciturn, collected and grave, not a word of confusion or boisterous flights of fancy escaping from him.

He had got the post of verger at Sofia Church. He had given up inventing. 'It was an illusion, you see, Schwesterchen.'

His fiancée was just over thirty, thin and small, with angular shoulders and long thin legs. She had big white teeth, piled-up honey-coloured hair, a long shapely nose, a narrow mouth and round chin. Her eyes were dark but very bright. She regarded her fiancé with all the tenderness of possession, and, as if in distraction, her strong hand rested on his knee. She was a gym teacher.

The lifelong guardianship was to cease. 'My stepmother's view of my mental state was one of her illusions. She was a power person. She had to have someone to dominate. Schwesterchen can never be like Stepmother, however much she tries. It's an illusion.'

His fiancée looked at the family with her bright eyes and said nothing.

A few months later the engagement was broken off. Uncle Carl moved back to his rooms in Ringvägen and stopped being verger at Sofia Church. He confided in Mother that his fiancée had tried to stop him inventing. It had all ended in screams and scuffles. Carl had scratches on his cheek. 'I thought I could stop inventing. It was an illusion.'

Mother again became his guardian. Every Friday, Uncle Carl came to the parsonage, changed his suit and underclothes and had dinner with the family. His desire to pee on himself increased.

He had another rather more dangerous habit. On his way to the Royal Library or the City Library, where he liked to spend his days, he took a short cut through the railway tunnel beneath southern Stockholm. After all, he was the son of a transport engineer who had built the railway between Krylbo and Insjön, and he loved trains. As they thundered past him in the tunnel, he pressed himself against the rocky wall; the sound fascinated him, the ancient rock shuddered, and the dust and smoke intoxicated him.

They found him one spring day, lying between the tracks with multiple injuries. Inside his trousers was the oilcloth folder containing a design to facilitate the changing of light bulbs in streetlamps.

4

When I was twelve, I was allowed to accompany a musician who was playing the celeste backstage in Strindberg's *A Dream Play*. It was a searing experience. Night after night, hidden in the proscenium tower, I witnessed the marriage scene between the Advocate and the Daughter. It was the first time I had experienced the magic of acting. The Advocate held a hairpin between his thumb and forefinger, he twisted it, straightened it out and broke it. *There was no hairpin, but I saw it.* The Officer was backstage waiting for his entrance, leaning forward looking at his shoes, his hands behind his back. He cleared his throat soundlessly, a perfectly ordinary person. Then he opened the door and stepped into the limelight. He was changed, transformed: he *was* the Officer.

* * *

As I harbour a constant tumult within me and have to keep watch over it, I also suffer agony when faced with the unforeseen, the unpredictable. The exercise of my profession thus becomes a pedantic administration of the unspeakable. I act as an intermediary, organizing, ritualizing. There are producers who make their own chaos and at best create a performance from this chaos. I loathe that kind of amateurism. I never partake in the drama, but translate and make concrete. Most important of all, I have no room for my own complications except as keys to the secrets of the text or as controlled impulses for the creativity of the actor. I hate tumult, aggression or emotional outbursts. My rehearsals are operations in premises equipped for the purpose, where self-discipline, cleanliness, light and quiet prevail. A rehearsal is proper work, not private therapy for producer and actor.

I despise Walter, who appears slightly drunk at half-past ten in the morning and spews out his private complications. I am disgusted by Teresa, who rushes up and embraces me in a cloud of sweat and perfume. I would like to hit Paul, the maddening gay who turns up in high-heeled shoes when he knows he has to run up and down stage stairs all day. I detest Vanja, who tumbles in exactly a minute late with her hair on end, puffing and blowing and untidy, laden with bags and carriers. I am irritated by Sara, who has forgotten her copy of the play and always has two important telephone calls to make. I want calm, order and friendliness. Only in that way can we approach a limitless world. Only in that way can we solve the mysteries and learn the mechanisms of repetition. Repetition, living throbbing repetition. The same performance every night, the same performance and yet reborn. For that matter, how do we grasp the lightning-swift rubato so necessary for a performance not to become deadly routine or insufferable wilfulness? All good actors know the secret, the mediocre have to learn it, and the bad never learn.

So my work is to administer texts and working hours. I am responsible for days not seeming entirely pointless. I am never my private self. I observe, register, establish and control. I am the actor's surrogate eye and ear. I suggest, entice, encourage or refuse. I am not spontaneous, impulsive or a fellow actor. It only looks as if I am. If I were to raise the mask for one moment and say what I really feel, my friends would turn on me and throw me out of the window.

Despite the mask, I am nevertheless not in disguise. My intuition speaks swiftly and clearly. I am totally present. The mask is a filter but nothing irrelevantly private is allowed to penetrate through. My own tumult must be kept in place.

I lived for a considerable time with an older, extremely talented actress. She scorned my cleanliness theory and maintained that theatre is shit, lust, rage and wickedness. 'The only boring thing about you, Ingmar Bergman,' she said, 'is your passion for the wholesome. You should abandon that passion. It's false and suspect. It sets limits you daren't exceed. Like Thomas Mann's Doctor Faustus, you should seek out your syphilitic whore.'

Perhaps she was right, perhaps it was all romantic drivel in the wash of pop art and shady drug scenes. I don't know. All I know is that this beautiful and brilliant actress lost her memory and her teeth and died at fifty in a mental hospital. That's what she got for expressing her feelings.

For that matter, artists who are clever with words are a hazard. Suddenly their speculations happen to become fashionable and that can be disastrous. Igor Stravinsky loved expressing himself. He wrote a good deal on interpretation. As he bore a volcano within him, he urged restraint. Mediocrities read him and nodded in agreement, so people without even the slightest vestige of a volcano within them raised their batons and observed restraint, while Stravinsky himself, who never practised what he preached, conducted his own *Apollon Musagète* as if it were Tchaikovsky. We who had read him listened and were astonished.

*   *   *

In 1986, I was to direct Strindberg's *A Dream Play* for the fourth time, a decision that seemed good. *Miss Julie* and *A Dream Play* within the same production year. My room at the Royal Dramatic Theatre, always known as Dramaten, had been repaired. I moved in and felt at home.

Our preparatory work started off with complications. I engaged a stage designer from Gothenburg and then his partner of ten years left him for a young actor. The stage designer acquired a stomach ulcer and arrived in a wretched state at my home on Fårö (Sheep Island) just after midsummer.

In the hope that work would contain his depression, we started our daily meetings. The designer's lips trembled and he looked at me with his slightly protruding eyes. 'I want her to come back,' he whispered. I did not embark on a cure of souls, and persisted, but a few weeks later, he broke down and said that he couldn't cope, after which he packed his bags and returned to Gothenburg, where he hoisted sail and went to sea with a new lover.

In my need, I turned to my old friend and colleague, Marik Vos. She was friendly and enthusiastic and installed herself in our guest house. We were already well behind schedule, but started off in a good mood. Many years before Marik had done *Dream Play*, produced by Olof Molander, the founder of the Strindberg tradition.

I had been dissatisfied with my previous three productions of this seminal play. The Swedish TV version had come to grief owing to technical disasters (video tapes couldn't even be edited in those days); the performance on the Small Stage turned out poor despite excellent actors; and the German adventure had been ruined by overwhelming sets.

This time I wanted to play the text with no changes or deletions, just as the writer had written it. My intention was also to translate the very complicated stage directions into technically possible and beautiful solutions. I wanted the audience to experience the stench of the backyard of the Advocate's office, the cold beauty of Fagervik's summer countryside in snow, the sulphurous mist and glint of hell in Skamsund and the magnificent flowers round the Rising Castle, the old theatre behind the theatre corridor.

The Small Stage at Dramaten was impractical, cramped and shabby, in reality a converted cinema which had not had any major repairs since it was opened in the early 1940s. To achieve space and intimacy, we decided to remove four rows of seats and extend the stage by five metres.

In that way, we obtained an outer room and an inner room. The outer room, nearest to the audience, was to be the Writer's domain with his desk by a multi-coloured art-nouveau window, the palm with its coloured lights, the bookcase with its secret door. To the right of the stage was a heap of rubbish dominated by a large but damaged crucifix and the mysterious pantry door. In the corner, as if buried in the dusty junk, 'Ugly Edit' sat at her piano. The actress was a skilled pianist, accompanying the events with both action and music.

The front room, achieved by extending the stage, opened on to a magical back room. As a child, I had often stood in the dark dining room at home, peeping into the salon through the half-open sliding doors. The sun lit up furniture and objects, glittered in the chandelier and cast moving shadows on to the carpet. Everything was green, as in an aquarium. Inside, people moved, disappeared, reappeared, stood quite still and spoke in low voices. The flowers in the window glowed, the clocks ticked and struck, a magical room. We were now to recreate such a room on the inner stage. Ten strong projectors were acquired to play on to five specially constructed screens. We didn't know what images they were to show, but we considered we had plenty of time to think about that. The stage floor was covered with a soft greyish-blue carpet, and a ceiling of the same colour was fixed above the outer room. Thus the usually unpredictable acoustics on the Small Stage became stable and extremely sensitive. The actors could speak quickly and lightly; the chamber music principle was established.

In May 1901, Strindberg marries a young, rather exotic beauty at the Royal Dramatic Theatre. She is thirty years younger than he is and already successful. Strindberg rents a five-room apartment in a new building on Karlaplan, and chooses the furniture, wallpapers, pictures and bric-à-brac. His young bride enters a décor entirely created by her ageing husband. The contracting partners lovingly, loyally and cleverly take pains from the start to reproduce the rôles expected of them. However the masks soon begin to crack and an unforeseen drama breaks through the carefully planned pastoral. The wife flees the home in rage and goes to stay with relatives out in the islands. The writer is left alone with his handsome décor. It is high summer and the city is deserted. He is afflicted with a pain hitherto unknown to him.

In *To Damascus*, when the Lady reproaches him for playing with Death, the Stranger replies: 'Just as I play with life. I was a writer. Notwithstanding my innate melancholy, I have never been able to take anything really seriously, not even my own great sorrows, and there are moments when I doubt that life has any more reality than my writing.'

The wound is now deep and bleeding profusely. The hurt cannot be turned on or off as in other disasters in life. The pain bores its way towards the unknown room and opens the floodgates. Strindberg writes in his diary that he wept, but the tears cleansed his eyes and he could look on himself and his fellow men with conciliatory indulgence. He was certainly speaking a new language.

There is a great deal of discussion on how large a part of *Dream Play* had been conceived before Harriet Bosse returned to an acceptance of her pregnancy and a conciliatory idyll. The first half is an incomparable flow, nothing difficult to interpret, all is pleasure and torment, alive, original, unexpected. The drama sets its own stage, the inspiration culminating in the Advocate's home. The start, the disillusion and the disintegration of a marriage are demonstrated in exactly twelve minutes.

Then things became more difficult for the producer of *A Dream Play*. Skamsund was followed by Fagervik, the inspiration stumbled and tripped rather as if, in the insoluble fugue in Beethoven's Hammerklavier sonata, the precision were to be replaced by too many notes. If you eliminated too much, the scenes died; if you acted it all, the audience tired.

It meant keeping a cool head and introducing a rhythm that had been lost. That was possible and paid dividends, as the text was still strong, harsh, amusing and poetically tenable. The unexpected intrusion of the school scene, for instance, is splendid. On the other hand, the unhappy coal-heavers are a taxing affair. *A Dream Play* is no longer a dream play, but a topical review with one number of doubtful quality.

However, the most complex problems remained. First Fingal's Cave. We know peace reigns in the house. The pregnant young wife is devoting herself to sculpture and reading good books and the Writer has stopped smoking to show his goodwill. They go to the theatre and opera, give dinner parties and arrange musical soirées. The dream play flourishes. Strindberg now discovers the drama is shaping into a panorama of human life supervised by a preoccupied God. He suddenly feels himself called to put into words the Divide of Being he has previously demonstrated in the text in such an unforced way. Indra's Daughter takes the Writer by the hand and, unfortunately for him, leads him to the Fingal's Cave farthest out to sea, where they declaim beautiful and worthless verses about each other, the vilest and the most lovely side by side.

A producer who doesn't give up but lets Strindberg stew in his own juice is faced with almost insuperable problems. How to create Fingal's Cave so that it doesn't sabotage itself? How shall I manoeuvre the Writer's great lament directed at Indra? It consists largely of complaints. How shall I create the storm, the shipwreck and, most difficult of all, Christ walking on the water? (A quiet, gripping moment in a turgid piece of ham theatre.)

I tried to make a small theatre performance within the performance. The Writer arranges an acting space with a screen, a chair and a horn gramophone. He wraps Indra's Daughter in an oriental shawl. He crowns himself in front of the mirror with the crown of thorns from the crucifix. He gives some manuscript pages to his fellow player. They slide from playing games into seriousness, from parody into irony, seriousness again, the joy of the amateur, great theatre and pure and simple harmony. The sublime stays sublime and what is governed by time is given a touch of tender-hearted irony.

We were pleased with our solution; at last we had found a practicable way.

The following scene in the theatre corridor is dull and says nothing, but cannot be excluded. The game with The Righteous, the Secret behind the door and the Advocate's murder of the Daughter's soul runs perfectly smoothly, hastily sketched and never deeply gone into. The only way to overcome this is lightness, swiftness and menace. The Righteous must unconditionally become dangerous when they are seized with anxiety when faced with the emptiness behind the open door.

Despite everything, the final scene at the altar is superb and the Daughter's departure simply gripping. It is preceded by a strange excrescence: Indra's Daughter betrays the Solution of the Mystery of Life. According to his diary, Strindberg was reading about Indian mythology and philosophy at the time of the final production of the drama. He threw the fruits of his reading into the pot and stirred it. They refused to sink to the bottom or give the dish any taste, remaining a piece of Indian saga with no place in the rest of the text.

In the final scene, and in the brisk opening scene, there is an insoluble but well-concealed problem. At the beginning a child is apparently speaking to his father: 'The Castle is still growing out of the earth. Do you see how much it has grown since last year?' At the very end, an ageing writer is speaking: 'Oh, now I feel the whole pain of existence. So this is what it is to be a human being.' At first a child and at the end an old man, a human life in between. I shared Indra's Daughter between three actresses. That paid dividends. The beginning glowed, the end was adequate, and even the Mystery of Life became a moving saga in the life experience and sincerity of a great actress. The adult Daughter was to be strong, inquisitive, vital, cheerful, capricious and tragic as she walked through life.

I had never before found the solution to a production with so much labour or so aggravatingly slowly. It had meant wiping out memories of earlier results. At the same time, it was important not to throw the baby out with the bathwater.

Good solutions which fitted neatly into the new conception had to be saved. But elimination was also necessary, following Faulkner's harsh advice: 'Kill your darlings.' While the production of *Miss Julie* had been an enjoyable game, the conquest of *A Dream Play* turned out to be a troublesome crusade.

For the first time, increasing age seemed to be undermining me. Images appeared reluctantly, decision-making became long drawn-out and I felt unusually selfconscious. What was impossible remained impossible and was suffocating me. Several times, I felt like giving up, a very rare impulse indeed in me.

Rehearsals began on Tuesday 4 February with a meeting at which we discussed practical details, planning and technicalities. We had already agreed that the text should be learnt as soon as possible. All that old drifting around with nose in book and one arm immobilized, originally launched by Lars Hanson who hated learning lines, was now a thing of the past. Lazy actors appropriated his gospel with the vague idea that they would absorb the text organically during the course of rehearsals. This always resulted in chaos, some knowing their lines, others not, glances and gestures, the whole interplay becoming a patchwork.

The most important task of an actor is of course to focus on and respond to his fellow player. With no *you*, no *I*, as a wise person once put it.

I look through my diary notes from work on *A Dream Play*, not very encouraging reading. I was in bad shape, uneasy, dejected, tired, my right hip hurting and aching continually, and mornings were troublesome. My stomach was sabotaging me with cramps and attacks of diarrhoea. Tedium hung like a damp dishcloth round my soul.

But I showed nothing. It is dereliction of duty to let private afflictions obtrude at work. Your mood must be even and forceful but, on the other hand, indefinable creative desires must not be encouraged. You have to rely on careful preparation and hope for better things.

A month or so before rehearsals started, Lena Olin asked to speak to me. She was to play Indra's Daughter. She had been infected by the prevailing fertility rife in the theatre. At the première, she would 'presumably' be at the beginning of the fifth month and was to give birth in August. So an autumn season was out of the question and the personally demanding *Dream Play* could not be put on the following spring. We would have forty performances at the most.

The situation was rather amusing. My television play, *After the Rehearsal*, was about a meeting between a young actress (played by Lena Olin) and an old director who was producing *A Dream Play* for the fourth time. She says she is with child. The old director, who started it all so as to work with the young actress, is devastated. Eventually the actress reveals that she has already had an abortion.

Lena Olin had no intention of having an abortion. She was a strong, beautiful and lively person, extremely emotional, sometimes chaotic, but stable and full of commonsense. She was pleased to be pregnant. She could see difficulties, but said that if she was going to have a child it had to be now, although she was just beginning to be known.

For the director, at least, the situation had its comic side. But a young mother-to-be is never comic. Lena was lovely and decent, and had also given up her career to have her child.

Emotions are for the most part ungovernable. I thought she had left me in the lurch. So-called reality had revised both dream and planning. My bitterness faded almost at once. What sort of whining was this? In the long run, our theatrical exertions are a matter of some indifference, but the birth of a child brought with it a touch of meaning. Lena Olin was happy. I was happy for her happiness.

The dullness of the rehearsals had nothing, or almost nothing, to do with this. The weeks went by. The results of our labours were and remained stodgily respectable. Also, Marik Vos, my stage designer, had a blackout or had perhaps been overworking. Dramaten's male costume department had for many years been 'manned' by incompetent nitwits. Marik struggled silently and stubbornly with stupidity, laziness and self-importance; nothing looked as it should and nothing was finished, with the result that she forgot our projections. She had delegated the picture research to a young lady who had been shifted elsewhere owing to her general incompetence, but had been extremely industrious and ordered photographs costing tens of thousands of kronor without anyone noticing. When I thought there was a suspicious silence, I started poking my nose in. It turned out that we had excellent projectors (costing nearly half a million kronor) but no projections. Disaster was imminent, but we were in luck. A young photographer who both wanted and was able to do them appeared and devoted day and night to the problems. The last photographs were ready in time for the dress rehearsal.

On Friday 14 March we had the first run-through, letting it all go through without interruptions or re-runs. In my diary I wrote: 'Frustrating run-through. Sitting there glaring. Totally outside. Totally unmoved. Well, time enough.' (The première had been planned for 17 April, seventy-nine years to the day after the world première.)

On the Sunday, Erland Josephson and I were in my room at the theatre talking about Bach, who had returned from a journey to find that his wife and two of their children had died during his absence. He wrote in his diary: 'Dear Lord, may my joy not leave me.'

All through my conscious life, I had lived with what Bach calls his joy. It had carried me through crises and misery and functioned as faithfully as my heart, sometimes overwhelming and difficult to handle, but never antagonistic or destructive. Bach called this state his joy, a joy in God. Dear Lord, may my joy not leave me.

Suddenly I heard myself saying to Erland: 'I'm about to lose my joy. I can feel it physically. It's running out. I'm just drying up, inside.'

I started crying and that frightened me, because I never wept. I had been an enthusiastic weeper as a child. My mother saw through my tears and punished me. I stopped crying. Occasionally I sense an insane wail deep down in the pit, the echo alone reaching me, striking without warning, a child weeping uninhibitedly, imprisoned for ever.

On that darkening afternoon in my room at the theatre, the attack came quite unexpectedly, my grief dark and bitter.

A few years ago, I visited a friend who was dying of cancer; he was eroding away, transformed into a shrivelled gnome with huge eyes and large yellow teeth. He was lying on his side, connected to a number of machines, holding his left hand close to his face and moving his fingers. He smiled a terrible smile and said: 'Look, I can still move my fingers. That's always a distraction.'

I thought: It means adapting oneself, pulling back the front lines, the battle already lost, nothing more to expect although I lived under the cheerful delusion that Bergman would remain intact for ever. 'Aren't there special regulations for hypocrites?' the actor Skat says in *The Seventh Seal*, clutching at the top of the Tree of Life. 'There are no special regulations for actors,' says Death, putting his saw to the trunk.

On the Monday night, I had a high temperature and was shaking and sweating, every nerve rebelling. This was an unfamiliar experience. I am practically never ill. I sometimes felt ill, but was never so ill that I couldn't direct rehearsals or filming.

I had a high temperature for ten days, unable even to read, but simply lay there mostly dozing. When I got up, I almost immediately lost my balance. I was so ill it was almost interesting. Dozing, falling asleep, waking, coughing, sniffling, influenza blossoming untiringly, my temperature leaping about. I had my opportunity. If I was going to leave *A Dream Play*, this was the moment.

We had recorded the unhappy run-through on video. I played it over and over again, noting the weaknesses and analysing the failings. The chance of getting out of it had given me the courage to go on. The meaninglessness was still just as meaningless and the listlessness just as listless, but I had been overcome by a rage demanding adrenalin. *I am not yet dead.*

I decided I would rehearse again on 1 April regardless of my condition. The night before, I had a relapse with a temperature and stomach cramps. However, we worked normally. I tore up long sections and started again from the beginning. The actors responded with friendly enthusiasm. My nights were sleepless, filled with anxiety and physical discomfort, the influenza leaving me with a depression I did not recognize, living its own poisonous life within my body.

On Wednesday 9 April we completed our last day in the rehearsal room. I wrote: 'Apprehensions verified and reinforced. Must drive on harder. Sad, but by no means crushed.'

Then we moved down to the crush and discomforts of the Small Stage. Distance and the bright working light mercilessly showed up the unevennesses in the play. We corrected and changed things, lighting, costumes, masks. My laboriously constructed house of cards collapsed, everything chafing, creaking and refractory.

The whole world is quaking and collapsing. Am I really to have this beard! If I'm to have one pair of trousers on top of the other, I won't have time to change. A Velcro-strip is needed here. Your make-up is too white. Palme's killer is still at liberty. The snow machine is out of order, the snow's coming in lumps, there's something wrong with the suspension, why is the left projector giving a warmer light than the others? There's something wrong with the mirror, a manufacturing fault, there are no mirrors in Sweden, we'll have to order one from Austria. Riots in South Africa, fourteen people killed, many injured. Why are the fans making that noise? The ventilation is hopeless, there's a cold spot in the middle of the salon, why haven't you got your shoes? The shoemaker's ill, the order has been put out in town, the shoes may come on Friday. Can I take it a little easy today? I've got a sore throat, no, no temperature, I'm not taking part in *The Government Inspector*, but I have a reading on the radio.

Stay there, take two steps to your right, that's good, can you feel that spot?

Patience and humour, laugh instead of quarrelling. It goes more quickly that way, but it's painful. Now we've got to that place, no, no change, still speechless. I can see him shaking as though with cramp, have I done wrong? Would other scenery have helped? No, nothing helps. He wants so badly to get it right, battering at the prison walls, there must be some way.

The world is quaking and collapsing, we buzz officiously and rather excitedly inside the thick walls of the House. A little world of troubled disorder, industry, love and skill. This is all we know.

The morning after the assassination of Olof Palme, we assembled in the waiting room of the rehearsal hall. It was impossible to start the day's work. We spoke uncertainly and fumblingly, trying to get through to each other. Someone was crying. Our profession becomes so peculiar when reality smashes its way in and massacres our illusory games. When Germany occupied Norway and Denmark, my amateur theatre was to have put on *Macbeth* in the hall of Sveaplan school. We had constructed an imitation stage and had been working for a year. The school became a garrison and most of us were called up, but for some unfathomable reason we were given permission to go ahead with our performance. Anti-aircraft guns were installed in the school playground, the floors in the corridors and classrooms were covered with straw and the place was secthing with more or less uniformed soldiers. Blackout.

I was playing Duncan and had been given far too small a wig. I painted my hair white with greasepaint and stuck a beard on my chin. No Duncan has ever looked so like a goat. Lady Macbeth had never rehearsed without her glasses and tripped over her gown. Macbeth fenced more wildly than ever (we had been given our swords at the very last minute) and hit Macduff on the head so that blood spattered in all directions. He was taken to hospital after the performance.

But now Olof Palme had been murdered. How should we behave in our confusion? Should we cancel the rehearsal? Should we cancel the evening performance? Let's abandon *A Dream Play* for ever. One can't put on a play about someone going round preaching that 'it isn't easy to be a human being'. An unendurably out-of-date artistic product, beautiful but distant, perhaps dead.

'Maybe I'm wrong,' said one of the younger actresses, 'but I think we should rehearse. I think we should go on. Whoever killed Palme wanted chaos. If we abandon it, we just add to the chaos. We let our emotions take over. This is something more than incidental private feelings. Chaos mustn't decide.'

Slowly and hesitantly, *A Dream Play* became a performance. We rehearsed to an audience. Sometimes they were attentive and enthusiastic, sometimes silent and withdrawn. A cautious optimism began to colour our cheeks. Colleagues were complimentary, we received letters and encouragement.

For the producer, the last week of rehearsals is always hard to endure. The venture has lost its edge, the weariness is suffocating, faults dazzle you and a cold damp indifference sits like a never-lifting mist on your brain and mind.

I sleep badly: calamities, tones of voice and gestures march past. Wrongly placed lights stand like sturdy scioptican slides before my eyes. My nights become long and miserable. Lack of sleep doesn't worry me. It's emotions that tire me. Where is the innermost failing? Is it in the text itself, the breach between brilliant inspiration and preachy attitudes, harsh beauty and saccharine twaddle? Is the playful parody in Fingal's Cave blasphemous? May one not laugh at a giant even when laughing affectionately? I mustn't forget to spread spotlight thirty six over the bed in the Advocate's room, otherwise the lighting's good there, few lights and lots of atmosphere. Sven Nykvist ought to be pleased with me.

Almost asleep, I see the cows on the meagre patch below the forge staring at me, clouds of flies round their muzzles and eyes; the little multi-coloured one has short pointed horns and is said to be fierce.

There's Helga with her blouse damp across her bulging bosom, laughing with her big white teeth, a gap in the middle where Brynolf has struck her. Helga went down to the river bank and sank Brynolf's boat, then opened a tin of anchovies and hid behind the door. When Brynolf came back for dinner, she pressed the tin into her spouse's face, pushed it in and twisted it. Brynolf brooded. When he had got his sight back, he took his little round hat and set off on foot to Borlänge with blood pouring down his forehead and cheeks and anchovies hanging in his beard. He went straight to Hultgren the photographer and asked to be photographed in his round hat and bespattered overalls, his nose bloody and anchovies on his chin and cheeks. That's what happened. Helga was given the photograph as a birthday present. I'll go to sleep, now, now the alarm clock's ringing.

I lie motionless, wide awake and anxious. I could murder anyone who says anything unfavourable about my actors. Now there's the dress rehearsal and we are to part. They will read the papers the day after tomorrow even if they say they don't, and they will be carved up, patted, congratulated, encouraged, snubbed or met with silence. That same evening, they have to go on stage. They know the audience knows.

Many years ago I saw a friend standing in a corner, dressed and made-up. He had chewed his lower lip so that blood was running down his chin and he had froth in the corners of his mouth. He was shaking his head, I'm not going on, I'm not going on. Then he went on.

The dress rehearsal was in the evening on 24 April. In the daytime, we had a *Hamlet* meeting, a whole crowd sitting round a table planning a production, the première planned for 19 December. I told them what I thought, empty stage, possibly two chairs, but not necessarily. Immobile lights, no coloured filters, no special atmospherics. A circle of five metre radius welded into the floor near the audience. This is where the action would take place. Fortinbras and his men break down the door in the back wall of the stage, the snowstorm blows in, the bodies are hurled down into Ophelia's grave, Hamlet is honoured in scornful formal phrases. Horatio is assassinated.

At some point I was furious and wanted to abandon the project. Many months earlier, I had asked to have Ingvar Kjellson as the gravedigger and he had accepted. Then, behind my back, Kjellson had moved or been moved into a major part in another production. A young actor scarcely dry behind the ears said he was thinking of requesting paternity leave. A third actor had been taken out of my cast on an ultimatum from a visiting producer. A spineless but talented youth did not want to play Guildenstern. Young men on their way up do not like standing beside a Hamlet of their own age or even younger. They have fits and imaginary problems; they even remember their new-born sons. Nor was it any longer so important to keep in with Bergman. He'd stopped making films.

At the same time I understood, of course I understood, I found it easy to understand. An actor is closest to himself, he squirms and changes course, speculates and weighs things up. I understood, but was furious all the same. I remembered when Alf Sjöberg was going to beat me up because I had taken Margaretha Byström out of his *Alcestis*. The present situation was similar. At Sjöberg's funeral, one of the members of the theatre board turned to one of the actors representing the theatre and said: 'Congratulations. Now you've one producer problem fewer at Dramaten.' I remembered how I had dismissed Olof Molander. Must have the sense to give up and leave in time. When does 'in time' come? Has 'in time' already come?

On Thursday 24 April at seven in the evening (the fact that no one was allowed in after the start of the performance had been announced in all the papers), at last the dress rehearsal started. The actors sensed a slight whiff of success and were cheerfully light-hearted. I took pains to share their happy expectations. Somewhere deep down in my consciousness I had already registered our failure, not that I was dissatisfied with our performance, on the contrary. After all our afflictions, a first-class, well thought through and under the circumstances well-acted performance was at last on stage. There was no reason for self-reproach.

Nevertheless, I already knew our venture would not make it.

The performance began. The C-major chord was struck and I left the Small Stage together with the theatre manager. As we came out on to the street through a rear door, we were assailed by photographers pushing and letting off their flashes. A sun-tanned Someone grasped me by the shoulder and said I must let him in, he was ten minutes late and couldn't get to the performance on any other occasion. He had tried to persuade the doormen who, obeying orders, had refused. I said irritably that I neither could nor wished to help him, that he only had himself to blame. Then I recognized the editor of the *Svenska Dagbladet*'s arts page, who was also its theatre critic. With an attempt at friendliness, I added that he must understand and respect the rules. At the same time I had an irresistible desire to hit him. He was supposed to be there in his professional capacity and had arrived late. He had also been tactless enough to assail the director with demands to be let in. He went away. Sensing lasting persecution by the arts page of *Svenska Dagbladet*, I ran after the infuriated man and found him a seat.

An unimportant episode had finally confirmed my feeling of utter dejection. My first stage designer's stomach ulcer and defection. Lena Olin's pregnancy, reluctant solutions, the flat acting in the middle of rehearsal time, my influenza and attached depression, our technical calamities, the casting of *Hamlet*, the offended arts editor. And on top of that, the assassination of Olof Palme, temporarily or for ever changing the light around our efforts. All those together, minor as well as major, had created insight. I knew how it would go.

After the dress rehearsal, we assembled in one of the new rehearsal rooms above the Small Stage for sandwiches and champagne. The atmosphere was happy, but also melancholy. It is always hard to part company after a long and close association. I felt a helpless love for these people. The umbilical cord had been cut, but my whole body hurt. We talked about Andrzej Wajda's *The Conductor* in which he shows that you can't make music without love. In the emotional high tension of the moment, we agreed that you certainly can make theatre without love, but it neither lived nor breathed. Without love, it doesn't work. With no *you*, no *I*. We had indeed experienced brilliant theatre, growing out of orgiastic hatred, but the hatred is also contact and the love just as acute as the hatred. We pondered on it and found examples.

The candles on the tables burnt down and flickered, candlegrease dribbling. It was time to part. We embraced and kissed each other as if we were never to meet again. We would meet the next morning, for Christ's sake, we said and laughed. The première was the next day.

For the first time in my professional life, I grieved over a failure for more than forty-eight hours. Usually one could console oneself with full houses. The attendance at the Small Stage's forty performances was not bad but insufficient. *So* much effort, pain, anxiety, tedium, hope, all to no avail.

5

The summer house in Dalarna was called 'Våroms', a dialect word meaning 'Ours'. I went there the first month of my life and still dwell there in my memory. It is always summer, the huge double birches rustling, the heat shimmering above the hills, people in light clothes on the terrace, the windows open, someone playing the piano, croquet balls rolling, goods trains shunting and signalling far down there in Dufnäs station, the river flowing black and secretive even on brightest days, the felled timber floating indolently or circling swiftly. There is the fragrance of lily-of-the-valley, ant heaps and roast veal. The children all have grazed knees and elbows. We bathe in the river or in the lake, Svartsjön; we learn to swim young, for both places have treacherously soggy clay beds and sudden ledges.

Mother had employed a young girl from the district whose name was Linnéa. She was quiet, kindly and used to younger brothers and sisters. I was six years old and adored her cheerful smile, her white skin and mass of reddish-fair hair. I obeyed her slightest whim and picked chains of wild strawberries to please her. She taught me to swim. She herself was a good swimmer and when we went swimming alone together, she omitted to put on her clumsy black bathing costume, a habit I appreciated. She was tall and thin, with broad freckled shoulders and hard small breasts. Her pubic hair was a flaming red. I have never swum as much as I did that summer. My teeth chattered, my lips turned blue, and she made a tent out of a big bath towel under which we warmed ourselves.

One evening in September, just before we were to return to Stockholm, I went out into the kitchen, where Linnéa was sitting at the table, a coffee cup in front of her. She had not even bothered to light the paraffin lamp. She was resting her head on one hand and was weeping profusely, but silently. I was terrified and flung my arms round her, but she pushed me away, something she had never done before, so I started crying too, for everything seemed miserable. I wanted her to stop crying at once and to console me, but she ignored me.

When we left Våroms a few days later, she did not accompany us to Stockholm. I asked Mother why and was given evasive answers.

Forty years later, I asked Mother what had happened to Linnéa. She told me that the girl had been pregnant and the man had denied paternity. As a pastor's family could hardly house a pregnant servant girl, Father was forced to dismiss her, despite Mother's violent protests. Grandmother wanted to intervene to help the girl, but she had already disappeared. A few months later, she was found near the railway station, wedged under a sunken log with a contusion on her forehead. The police assumed she had thrown herself off the bridge.

Dufnäs railway station consisted of a red station building with white corners and gables, a privy labelled 'Men' and 'Women', two signals, two shunting tracks, a goods warehouse, a stone-laid platform and an underground cellar with wild strawberries growing on its turf roof. The main track curved away towards the heel of Djurmo, past Våroms, which was visible from the station. A few hundred metres to the south, the river changed direction in a mighty curve called Grådan, a dangerous place of deep whirlpools and jagged protruding rocks. High above the curve of the river rose the railway bridge with its narrow footpath on the right. It was forbidden to cross the bridge, but no one took any notice of this because it was the quickest route to the wealth of fish in Svartsjön.

The stationmaster's name was Ericsson. With his wife, who suffered from goitre, he had lived in the station-house for twenty years and was regarded as a newcomer to the village, to be treated with suspicion. A great many silences surrounded Uncle Ericsson.

I had Grandmother's permission to be on the station. Uncle Ericsson was never consulted, but he treated me with absent-minded friendliness. His office smelt of pipe smoke, sleepy flies buzzed on the windows, and now and again the telegraph tapped and a narrow ribbon full of dots and dashes emerged. Uncle Ericsson sat over his desk writing in black books and sorting freight forms. Occasionally someone banged on the hatch through to the waiting room and bought a ticket to Repbäcken, Insjön or Borlänge. The silence was that of eternity and as dignified. I did not disturb it with unnecessary talk.

But suddenly the telephone would ring, a brief message, the train from Krylbo had left Lännheden, and Uncle Ericsson muttered something in reply, put on his uniform cap, picked up his red flag, went out and wound up the south signal. There was no one in sight. The hot strong sunlight was reflected off the goods-store wall and the rails, and there was a smell of tar and iron. Over by the bridge, the river murmured, the heat trembled above the oil-flecked sleepers and the stones sparkled. Silence and expectation. Uncle Ericsson's cat had settled on the station trolley.

Then the locomotive whistled over the curve before Långsjön and far away the train appeared like a black blot in the heavy greenery, at first almost soundlessly, then with a rising thunder; then it was out over the river, the thunder deepening;

the points crashed, the ground shook and the locomotive raced past the platform, rhythmical clouds of smoke puffing out of its stack, the pistons steaming. The wagons rushed by, the speed of their passing leaving a wind blowing in their wake, the wheels striking the rails, the ground shaking. Uncle Ericsson saluted the train driver, who replied likewise. Within a few moments the sound faded and the train curved round below Våroms and vanished below the mountain, whistling now at the sawmill. Then all was silent again.

Uncle Ericsson wound the telephone handle and said, 'Departed Dufnäs two thirty-three.' The silence was complete, the flies not even bothering to buzz against the windowpanes. Uncle Ericsson retreated up to the first floor for his dinner and a nap before the southbound goods train arrived sometime between four and five. That train was never punctual because it switched wagons at almost every station.

On the road up to the station was a blacksmith's forge whose occupier looked like a Mongol chieftain. He was married to a still beautiful but exhausted woman called Helga. They had a great many children and lived in two small rooms above the smithy, where everything was disordered but friendly. My brother and I liked playing with the blacksmith's children. Helga was still breast-feeding her youngest and, when the baby boy had had his fill, she would call over to my playmate, who was the same age as me, saying 'Come on, Jonte, come and get yours.' I would look on with envy while my friend stood between his mother's knees. She held out her heavy breast and he leant forward and sucked greedily at it. I asked if I might have a taste, but Helga laughed and said I would probably have to ask Mrs Åkerblom for permission first. Mrs Åkerblom was my grandmother, and I realized with shame that I had stumbled over one of those incomprehensible rules that kept piling up in my path.

A momentary image! I am lying in my bed with its high ends, it is evening. The nightlight is on. I'm pleasurably occupied squeezing a sausage between my hands. It is soft and malleable and smells intimate. Suddenly I throw it out on to the floor and excitedly call out for Linnéa, the nursemaid. The door opens and Father comes in. He stands there, large and dark against the light from the hall, points at the sausage and asks what on earth it is. I look up and with trembling heart reply that I don't think it's anything at all. Next scene: my bottom has been well and truly spanked and I am sitting yelling loudly on the pot in the middle of the floor. The ceiling light is on and Linnéa is angrily changing the sheets on my bed.

Secrets. Sudden silences. Vague physical disquiet. Are *those* qualms of conscience, as Indra's Daughter says in *A Dream Play*? What have I done? I ask in terror. You know that best yourself, answers Authority. Of course I've sinned. There's always some undiscovered misdemeanour gnawing at me. We've sat squeezed in by the privy tubs spying on backsides. We've stolen raisins from the spice cupboard. We've been swimming in deep whirlpools down by the railway station. We've stolen small change from Father's overcoat. We've blasphemed against God by exchanging His name with Satan's in the Blessing: Satan bless us and keep us, Satan turn his face upon us and give us a fuck. 'We' were my brother and I, occasionally united in common actions, but more often kept apart by a corroding hatred. Dag considered I lied and got away with it, and also that I was spoilt because I happened to be Father's favourite. I thought my brother, four years older than I was, had unfair advantages. He was allowed up late in the evenings and could go to films banned to children. He used to beat me up whenever it suited him. I did not understand until much later that he was constantly exposed to my father's jealous dislike.

Fraternal hatred almost led to fratricide. Dag had maltreated me badly and I was determined on revenge, whatever the cost.

I seized a heavy glass carafe, climbed up on a chair behind the door into our shared room at Våroms. When my brother opened the door, I crashed the carafe down on his head. The carafe shattered, my brother fell with blood pouring out of a gaping wound. A month or so later, he attacked me without warning and knocked out two of my front teeth. I responded by setting light to his bed when he was asleep. The fire went out by itself and hostilities temporarily ceased.

*   *   *

In the summer of 1984, my brother and his Greek wife came on a visit to my home on the island of Fårö. He was then sixty-nine and a retired consul general. He had dutifully stayed in his post despite severe paralysis. By now he could move only his head, his breathing was jerky and his speech difficult to understand. We spent our days talking about our childhood.

He remembered much more than I did. He spoke of his hatred of Father and his strong ties to Mother. To him, they were still parents, mysterious creatures, capricious, incomprehensible and larger than life. We made our way along overgrown paths and stared at each other in astonishment, two elderly gentlemen, now at an insuperable distance from each other. Our mutual antipathy had gone, but had left space for emptiness; there was no contact, no affinity. My brother wanted to die, but was at the same time frightened of dying; a raging will to live keeping his lungs and heart going. He also pointed out that he had no chance of committing suicide because he could not move his hands.

This strong, arrogant, clever man had constantly taken risks. He'd sought out danger, enjoyed life as fisherman, forest roamer. He was ruthless, selfish, humorous, always ingratiating with Father despite his hatred, always tied to Mother despite his exhausting conflicts and his attempts to free himself.

To me, my brother's illness is understandable, paralyzed as he was by rage, paralyzed by two overwhelming twilight figures, suffocating and incomprehensible, Father and Mother. Perhaps it should also be mentioned that his contempt for art, psychoanalysis, religion and spiritual reality was total. He was a rational human being through and through, spoke seven languages and had a preference for reading history and political biographies. He also dictated his autobiography on to tape. I had the material typed out; it came to eight hundred pages, written in a dry, jocular, academic style. He speaks in straightforward terms about his wife, and there are also a few pages about Mother; otherwise it is all surface, sarcasm and jovial indifference, life as an adventure story without excitement. In all those eight hundred pages, there is not one line about his illness. He never complained, but he despised his fate. He faced pain and humiliation with angry impatience, and made quite sure he was so unpleasant that no one could ever feel pity for him.

He celebrated his seventieth birthday with a party at the Embassy in Athens. He was very weak and his wife thought the party should be cancelled, but he refused and made a brilliant speech in honour of his guests. A few days later, he was taken to hospital, was given the wrong treatment and died during a long drawn-out attack of asphyxiation. He was conscious all the time, but unable to speak as they had made a hole in his windpipe. As he could not communicate, he died raging and struck dumb.

*   *   *

My young sister Margareta and I got on quite well together. She was four years younger than I, but we liked playing games together with her dolls and we invented complicated series of events in her ingeniously fitted-out doll's house. In a photograph in the family album, I see a small round little person with ash-blonde hair and terrified wide-open eyes. All is sensitivity, from her soft mouth to the uncertainty of her hands. She was greatly loved by both parents and attempted to meet them halfway, trying to be the gentle child to compensate for two difficult, unruly boys.

My childhood memories of Margareta are obscure and

keep eluding me. We made a toy theatre. She sewed the costumes and I painted the sets. Mother was a patient and interested spectator and gave us a lovely embroidered velvet curtain. We played quietly with good humour. I don't think we ever quarrelled.

When I was eleven and my sister seven, we spent a summer at Långängen, just outside Stockholm. Mother had had a major operation and was in Sophiahemmet for several months. Father wanted us nearby, and a gentle housekeeper, who was really a primary school teacher, was engaged. My sister and I were left very much to ourselves. There was an old bathhouse facing over the water, inside it a changing room and an outer room with no ceiling but with a bathing pool. We spent hours there playing our diffuse guilt-ridden games, but then, without any explanation or questions asked, we were suddenly forbidden to be alone in the bathhouse.

Margareta became more and more absorbed in her relationships with the parents and she and I lost contact. When I was nineteen, I ran away from home and since then we have hardly ever met. Margareta maintains she once showed me an attempt at writing, which in my youthful ignorance I critically tore to shreds; I myself have no memory of this. Nowadays she writes a book from time to time. If I have understood rightly what I have read, her life must have been sheer hell.

We occasionally talk to each other on the telephone and we once met unexpectedly at a concert. Her tormented face and peculiar toneless voice frightened me and made me feel ill at ease.

I have occasionally thought about my sister with brief qualms of conscience. She started writing in secret and no one was allowed to see what she had achieved. She finally plucked up her courage and let me read it. I was in a quandary. I was being favourably received as a promising young producer but condemned as a writer. I wrote badly, affectedly and was much influenced by Hjalmar Bergman and Strindberg. Then I found the same strained, laboured style in my sister's writing and murdered her attempt without recognizing that this was her only means of expression. According to her own words, she then gave up writing, whether to punish me or herself, or from discouragement, I do not know.

6

My decision to give up the movie camera was undramatic and grew out of my work on *Fanny and Alexander*. Whether it was my body ruling over my soul, or my soul influencing my body, I don't know, but physical distress became more and more difficult to overcome.

In the summer of 1985, I had what I thought was a captivating idea for a film. I would approach the world of silent film, working in long sections with no dialogue or acoustic effects; at last I saw a chance to break with the talkies.

I at once started writing the script. To put it melodramatically, I had once again been touched by Grace. The desire was there and my days were filled with a kind of secret contentment, sure evidence of sturdy vision.

After three weeks of good work, I suddenly fell violently ill. My body reacted with cramps and disorders of balance. I seemed to have been poisoned and was rent with anguish and contempt in the presence of my misery. I realized I would never again make a film. My body was refusing to cooperate and the continuous tension that is part of film-making was now a thing of the past. I put aside the manuscript, in which I made Finn Komfusenfej, a character from a nursery rhyme, into an anonymous old maker of silent movies, whose decaying films were found in countless metal cassettes underneath a country house about to be restored. A dimly perceived connection ran between these images, a deaf-and-dumb expert trying to read the actors' lips in order to interpret their lines. All kinds of montage were tried resulting in various action sequences. The project involved more and more people, grew and thrived, costing more and more money. It became more and more difficult to handle. One day, it all caught fire, the nitrate original as well as the acetate copies, and the whole lot went up in smoke. The relief was universal.

I have always suffered from what is called a nervous stomach, a calamity as foolish as it is humiliating. With a never-ebbing and often sophisticated wealth of invention, my bowels have sabotaged my efforts. Thus school was an unremitting misery, as I could never calculate when the attacks were going to hit me. Suddenly shitting in your trousers is a traumatic experience. It does not have to happen often for it to become a constant worry. The attack comes like lightning and without warning and the pain is hard to endure.

Over the years I have patiently taught myself to master my troubles sufficiently to be able to carry on working without all too obvious disturbances. It is like housing an evil demon in the most sensitive core of your body. With strict rituals, I can keep my demon under control. His power lessened considerably when *I* was the one to decide on my actions, not *him*.

No medicaments help, as they either cause apathy or arrive too late. A wise doctor once told me to accept my handicap and adapt. That is what I have done. In all the theatres I have worked in for any length of time, I have been given my own lavatory. These conveniences are probably my most lasting contribution to the history of the theatre.

For more than twenty years, I have suffered from chronic insomnia. That is nothing harmful as such, for you can manage with considerably less sleep than you imagine, five hours being quite sufficient for me. The wear and tear comes with the vulnerability of night, the altered proportions, the harping on stupid or humiliating situations, regrets over thoughtless or deliberate malice. Flocks of black birds often come and keep me company: anxiety, rage, shame, regret and boredom. Even for insomnia, there are rituals: changing beds, switching on the light, reading a book, listening to music, eating biscuits or chocolate, drinking mineral water. A well-timed Valium can be extremely effective, but may also be devastating, resulting in petulance and reinforced anxiety.

The third reason for my decision was ageing, a process I neither regret nor delight in. Solving problems became more sluggish, staging caused greater worries, decisions took longer and I became paralyzed by unforeseen practical difficulties.

With exhaustion, I also became more pedantic; the wearier, the grumpier. My senses were sharpened to a fine point and I saw faults everywhere.

I scrutinized my more recent films and productions and here and there found a perfectionist restriction which had driven out life and spirit. The danger was not so great in the theatre, where I could keep an eye on my weakness, and at worst the actors could put me right. In film, everything is irretrievable. Three minutes of completed film each day, all of which must live, breathe, be a creation.

Sometimes I perceived clearly, almost physically, a primaeval monster, half-beast, half-man, moving inside me to which I was about to give birth. One morning I was chewing on a rough evil-smelling beard. I had an inkling of a twilight which had nothing to do with death, but with extinction. Sometimes I dreamt I was losing my teeth and was spitting out worn yellow stumps.

I decided to retreat before my actors or collaborators caught sight of this monster and were seized with disgust or pity. I had seen far too many of my colleagues falling in the ring like tired clowns, bored by their own dullness, booed off or killed by polite silence and dragged out of the lights by kindly or contemptuous circus hands.

I shall take my hat while I can still reach the hatrack, and walk off by myself, although my hip hurts. The creativity in ageing is certainly not obvious, but periodic and conditional, pretty much like quietly diminishing sexuality.

*   *   *

I have chosen a day's filming in 1982. According to my notes, it was cold — twenty degrees Celsius below zero. I woke up as usual at five o'clock, which means I was woken, drawn as if in a spiral by some evil spirit out of my deepest sleep, and I was wide awake. To combat hysteria and the sabotage of my bowels, I got out of bed immediately and for a few moments stood quite still on the floor with my eyes closed. I went over my actual situation. How was my body, how was my soul and, most of all, what had got to be done today? I established that my nose was blocked (the dry air), my left testicle hurt (probably cancer), my hip ached (the same old pain), and there was a ringing in my bad ear (unpleasant but not worth bothering about). I also registered that my hysteria was under control, my fear of stomach cramp not too intensive. The day's work consisted of the scene between Ismael and Alexander, in *Fanny and Alexander*, and I was worried because the scene in question might be beyond the capacity of my brave young actor in the title rôle, Bertil Guve. But the coming collaboration with Stina Ekblad as Ismael gave me a jolt of happy expectation. The first inspection of the day was thus completed and had produced a small but nevertheless positive profit: if Stina is as good as I think, I can manage Bertil-Alexander. I had already thought out two strategies: one with equally good actors, the other with a principal actor and a secondary actor.

Now it was a question of taking things calmly, of being calm.

At seven o'clock, my wife Ingrid and I had breakfast together in friendly silence. My stomach was acquiescent and had forty-five minutes in which to create hell. While I was waiting for it to decide on its attitude, I read the morning papers. At a quarter to eight, I was fetched and driven to the studio, which at that particular time was in Sundbyberg and was owned by Europafilm Ltd.

Those once so reputable studios were decaying. They produced mainly videos and any staff left from the days of film, were disorientated and downhearted. The actual film studio was dirty, not sound-proof, and badly maintained. The editing room, at first sight comically luxurious, turned out to be useless. The projectors were wretched, incapable of keeping either definition or stills. The sound was bad, the ventilation did not function and the carpet was filthy.

At exactly nine o'clock, the day's filming started. It was important that our collective start was punctual. Discussions and uncertainties had to take place *outside* this innermost circle of concentration. From this moment on, we were a complicated but uniformly functioning machine, the aim of which was to produce living pictures.

The work quickly settled into a calm rhythm, and intimacy was uncomplicated. The only thing to disturb this day was the lack of sound-proofing and the lack of respect for the red lamps outside in the corridor and elsewhere. Otherwise it was a day of modest delight. From the very first moment, we all felt Stina Ekblad's remarkable empathy with the ill-fated Ismael and, best of all, Bertil-Alexander had at once accepted the situation. In that strange way children have, he gave expression to a complicated mixture of curiosity and fear with touching genuineness.

The rehearsals moved on smoothly and a quiet cheerfulness reigned, our creativity dancing along. Anna Asp had created a stimulating set for us. Sven Nykvist had done the lighting with that intuition which is difficult to describe, but which is his hallmark and makes him one of the leading lighting camera men in the world, perhaps the best. If you asked him how he did it, he would point out some simple ground rules (which have been of great use to me in my work in the theatre). He could not – or had no wish to – describe the actual secret. If for some reason he was disturbed, pressurized or ill at ease, everything went wrong and he would have to start all over again from the beginning. Confidence and total security prevailed in our collaboration. Occasionally I grieve over the fact that we shall never work together again. I grieve when I think back to a day such as the one I have depicted. There's a sensual satisfaction in working in close union with strong, independent and creative people: actors, assistants, electricians, production staff, props people, make-up staff, costume designers, all those personalities who populate the day and make it possible to get through.

Sometimes I really feel the loss of everything and everyone concerned. I understand what Fellini means when he says filming to him is a way of life and I also understand his little story about Anita Ekberg. Her last scene in *La Dolce Vita* took place in a car erected in the studio. When the scene had been taken and filming was over as far as she was concerned, she started crying and refused to leave the car, gripping firmly onto the wheel. She had to be carried out of the studio with gentle force.

Sometimes there is a special happiness in being a film director. An unrehearsed expression is born just like that, and the camera registers that expression. That was exactly what happened that day. Unprepared and unrehearsed, Alexander turned very pale, a look of sheer agony appearing on his face. The camera registered the moment. The agony, the intangible, was there for a few seconds and never returned. Neither was it there earlier, but the strip of film caught the moment. That is when I think days and months of predictable routine have paid off. It is possible I live for those brief moments.

Like a pearl fisher.

*　　*　　*

I was director of Helsingborg Theatre, and the year was 1944. I was twenty-six. For a long time I had been employed as a scriptwriter by Svensk Filmindustri, and I had had one script filmed (*Frenzy*, directed by Alf Sjöberg). I was considered talented but difficult. I had a kind of rights contract with SF, of no financial advantage to me but it prevented me from working for other film companies. That danger was not very great. Despite a certain success with *Frenzy*, no one got in touch with me, except Lorens Marmstedt who phoned now and again, asking in amiably mocking tones how long I considered it worth while hanging on with SF, adding that they would be sure to finish me off, but that he, Lorens, would probably be able to make a good film director out of me. I was in two minds and still authority-bound, so I always decided to stay with Carl Anders Dymling, who treated me both paternally and with some condescension.

One day a play landed on my desk. It was called *Moderdyret (The Mother)* and was written by a Danish hack. Dymling suggested I should write a script from the play and, if the script was approved, I would get my first film to direct. I read the play and found it appalling. But, if anyone had asked me to, I would certainly have filmed the telephone directory. So I wrote the script in fourteen nights and had it approved. The film was to be made in the summer of 1945. So far so good. I was crazy with delight and naturally did not see the realities, with the result that I fell headlong into every single pit I and others had helped to dig.

The film-town of Råsunda was a factory producing between twenty and thirty films a year during the 1940s. It contained a wealth of professional and skilled trade traditions, routine and bohemian. During my years as script slave, I had spent a great deal of time in the studios, in the film archives, the laboratory, the editing room, the sound department and the canteen, so I knew the premises and the people fairly well. I was also convinced I would show myself to be the world's greatest film director.

What I didn't know was that they were aiming to produce a cheap B-film in which they could largely use the company's contract actors. After considerable argument, I was given permission to make a test film with Inga Landgré and Stig Olin. Gunnar Fischer was the cameraman. We were contemporaries, enthusiastic, and we got on well together. It became a long test film. After I had seen it, my enthusiasm knew no bounds. I telephoned my wife, who had stayed in Helsingborg, and shouted excitedly down the phone that Sjöberg, Molander and Dreyer could now go into retirement. Ingmar Bergman was on his way.

While I was frothing away with self-confidence, they took the opportunity to exchange Gunnar Fischer with Gösta Roosling, a battle-scarred Samurai, who had won praise with a number of short films showing broad skies with beautifully illuminated clouds. He was a typical documentarist and had hardly ever worked in a studio; when it came to lighting, he was relatively inexperienced. He also despised feature films and disliked being indoors. From the very first moment, we detested each other and, as we were both unsure of ourselves, we concealed our uncertainty behind sarcasm and rudeness.

The first days of filming on *Crisis* were nightmarish. I realized at once that I had landed myself in an apparatus I had by no means mastered, and I also realized that Dagny Lind, whom I had argued my way into having in the title rôle, was not a film actress and lacked experience. I saw with icy clarity that they all realized I was incompetent. I confronted their distrust with an offensive outburst of rage.

The results were deplorable. There was something wrong with the camera, some of the scenes were blurred, the sound was bad and one could make out only with difficulty what the actors were saying.

Intense activity was going on behind my back. The studio management considered the film should either be dropped or the director and main actor replaced. After we had toiled away for three weeks, I received a letter from Carl Anders Dymling, who was on holiday. He wrote to say he had seen the material and he didn't think it particularly good, but it was promising. He suggested we should start again from the beginning. I gratefully accepted, without noticing the trapdoor that had been supporting my thin body.

As if by chance, Victor Sjöström, the great silent film-maker, turned up. He grasped me firmly by the nape of the neck and walked me like that back and forth across the asphalt outside the studio, mostly in silence, but suddenly he was saying things that were simple and comprehensible. You make your scenes too complicated. Neither you nor Roosling can cope with those complications. Work more simply. Film the actors from the front. They like that and it's best that way. Don't keep having rows with everyone. They simply get angry and do a less good job. Don't turn everything into primary issues. The audience just groans. A minor detail should be treated like a minor detail without necessarily having to look like one. We walked round and round, back and forth across the asphalt, he holding on to the back of my neck and being down-to-earth, factual, not angry with me, although I was being so unpleasant.

It was a hot summer. The days in the studio under the covered glass roof were miserably oppressive. I was living in lodgings in Old City. Every evening, I fell into bed and lay paralyzed with anxiety and shame, and, at dusk, I went to a milk bar and had a meal. Then I went to the cinema, always the cinema. I watched American films and thought – I ought to learn that. That camera movement is simple. Roosling could manage that. That was a nice cut. I'll remember that.

On Saturdays I got drunk, sought out bad company and got mixed up in brawls. Sometimes my wife came to see me. She was pregnant. We quarrelled and she left. I also read plays and prepared for the coming season at Helsingborg Theatre.

We were to film in Hedemora of all places. I don't know why. Perhaps I had an obscure need to show off to my parents, who were staying at Våroms that summer, some miles further north. We set off. In those days this meant a safari of cars, generator units, sound trucks and the crew. We stayed at Hedemora Municipal Hotel.

Two things happened.

The weather changed and the rain came down unremittingly. Roosling, at last allowed out of doors, saw no interesting clouds, only an even grey sky, so he stayed in his hotel room, got drunk and refused to shoot.

Secondly I very soon realized that I had indeed been a

wretched team manager in the studio, but here, in rainy Hedemora, I was even worse.

Most of the crew stayed in the hotel playing cards and drinking; the others grew depressed. All agreed that the director was to blame for the vile weather. Some directors were lucky with the weather, others unlucky. I was the latter kind.

We rushed out several times, erected our camera stand, rigged up our clumsy lights, brought up the generators and sound equipment, set up the heavy Debrie camera, rehearsed with the actors, the clapper clacked – and down came the rain again. We stood about in entrances, sat in cars or crouched in some café as the rain poured down and the light faded. Then it was time to drive back to the hotel for dinner. When we occasionally did succeed in taking a scene during a few seconds of sunlight, I was so confused and excited that – according to sober witnesses – I behaved like a lunatic, screaming, swearing and raging, insulting bystanders and cursing Hedemora.

In the evenings there was often noisy brawling around the hotel and the police had to be called in. The hotel manager threatened to throw us out. Marianne Löfgren danced the cancan on a restaurant table (very skilfully and amusingly) but fell to the floor and cracked the parquet. After three weeks, the elders of the town wearied of us, contacted Svensk Filmindistri and besought the management to take these insane people away, for God's sake.

The next day we received orders to disperse immediately. In twenty days of filming, we had shot four scenes out of twenty.

I was called in to Dymling and given a terrible dressing-down. He openly threatened to take the film away from me. It is possible that Victor Sjöström intervened, but I don't know.

That was hard enough, but what was to come was much worse. There was a beauty salon in the film, situated, according to the script, next door to a music hall. Music and laughter were to be heard from the theatre in the evening. I insisted on a set of a street being built, as I could not find a suitable place in Stockholm. It would be an expensive business, I realized that, despite my insane state of mind. But I had a vision of Jack's bloody head under the newspaper, the winking lights of the theatre signs, the beauty salon's illuminated window with the rigid wax faces beneath elaborate wigs, the rain-washed asphalt, the brick walls in the background. I was going to have my little stretch of street.

To my surprise, the project went through without discussion. The great building enterprise was launched immediately on a cleared area about a hundred metres from the big studio. I often went to the site and was quite proud of my success in driving this expensive enterprise through. I assumed the management believed in my film, despite all the rows and difficulties. What I hadn't grasped was that my street was to turn out to be an excellent weapon in the hands of a power-mad studio management, aimed at me and Dymling who had hitherto protected me. There were always strong tensions between head office, which reigned supreme, and the studio, which made the films. The costly and utterly pointless street set was to be debited to my film, thus making it impossible to recoup its budget.

The shooting itself took an ugly turn. The first scene was filmed one autumn evening after nightfall. It was a single shot, the camera on a nine-foot stand. The theatre lights winked. Jack had shot himself and Marianne was lying prone over his body, screaming to make one's blood run cold. The ambulance drove up, the asphalt glistened and the beauty-salon dummies stared. I was clinging to the stand, sick and dizzy, but intoxicated with a sense of power: all this was my creation, my reality, anticipated, planned and carried out.

The truth struck swiftly and cruelly. An assistant was poised on the edge of the stand with another assistant, ready to lift down the camera. It suddenly came free and the man hurtled headlong to the ground with the heavy camera on top of him. I don't remember all that well what happened, but an ambulance was there on the spot and was able to take the injured man straight to Karolinska Hospital. The crew insisted on breaking off filming, as they were convinced their colleague was dead or dying.

I was panic-stricken and refused, shouting that the man had been drunk, that they were all drunk filming at night (which was partly true) and that I was surrounded by rabble and riffraff, that the shooting would continue until the hospital informed us that the injured man was dead. I accused my fellow workers of being careless, lazy and sloppy. No one responded and a sullen Swedish silence surrounded me. The filming went on, the programme was completed, but everything I had imagined in the way of approaches to faces, objects and gestures had been wiped out. I couldn't do it. I went away into the darkness and wept with rage and disappointment.

The matter was later glossed over. The injured man was not that badly hurt and neither had he been sober.

The days dragged on. Roosling was openly hostile and mocked my suggestions for camera set-ups. The laboratory made our pictures either too light or too dark. My first cameraman, a contemporary who had already made one film, laughed a lot and thumped me on the back. I repeatedly quarrelled with the electricians' foreman over breaks and hours. The last remnant of discipline vanished and people came and went as they pleased. I was frozen out.

But I did have one friend who refused to run with the pack. That was the film's editor, Oscar Rosander. He actually looked like a pair of scissors, everything about him sharp and clearly defined. He spoke with a dignified guttural southern accent and was rather supercilious in the English way, pouring kindly contempt on directors, the studio management and the bigwigs at head office alike. The great moment of his life had been working with Prince Wilhelm, who now and again made a short film with SF. Everyone was afraid of Oscar and no one knew when he was going to be amiable or murderous. He treated women with old-fashioned chivalrous courtesy, but from a distance. He was a widely read man and possessed an estimable collection of pornography. It was said that he had frequented the same whore for twenty-three years, twice a week, in all seasons.

When I went to him after shooting was completed, disappointed and furious, he received me with abrupt and friendly objectivity, and mercilessly pointed out what was bad or unacceptable in my film. He also initiated me into the secrets of editing, among other things a fundamental truth – that editing occurs during filming itself, the rhythm created in the script. I know that many directors hold the opposite view. For me, Oscar Rosander's teaching has been fundamental.

The rhythm in my films is conceived in the script, at the desk, and is then given birth in front of the camera. All forms of improvisation are alien to me. If I am ever forced into hasty decisions, I grow sweaty and rigid with terror. Filming for me is an illusion planned in detail, the reflection of a reality which the longer I live seems to me more and more illusory.

When film is not a document, it is dream. That is why Tarkovsky is the greatest of them all. He moves with such naturalness in the room of dreams. He doesn't explain. What should he explain anyhow? He is a spectator, capable of staging his visions in the most unwieldy but, in a way, the most willing of media. All my life I have hammered on the doors of the rooms in which he moves so naturally. Only a few times have I managed to creep inside. Most of my conscious efforts have ended in embarrassing failure – *The Serpent's Egg, The Touch, Face to Face* and so on.

Fellini, Kurosawa and Buñuel move in the same fields as Tarkovsky. Antonioni was on his way, but expired, suffocated by his own tediousness. Méliès was always there without having to think about it. He was a magician by profession.

Film as dream, film as music. No form of art goes beyond ordinary consciousness as film does, straight to our emotions, deep into the twilight room of the soul. A little twitch in our optic nerve, a shock effect: twenty-four illuminated frames a second, darkness in between, the optic nerve incapable of registering darkness. At the editing table, when I run the strip of film through, frame by frame, I still feel that dizzy sense of magic of my childhood: in the darkness of the wardrobe, I slowly wind on one frame after another, see the almost imperceptible changes, wind faster – a movement.

The mute or speaking shadows turn without evasion towards my most secret room. The smell of hot metal, the wavering flickering picture, the rattle of the Maltese cross, the handle against my hand.

7

Before the primaeval darkness of puberty lowered itself round me and confused both body and soul, I had a happy love affair during the summer I was living alone with Grandmother at Våroms.

I cannot remember the reason for this arrangement, but I do remember my contentment and feeling of wellbeing and security. Guests came occasionally, stayed a few days and left again, enhancing my delight. Although I was still childish, looked childish and my voice had not yet broken, Grandmother and Lalla regarded me as a Young Man and treated me accordingly. Apart from the obligatory participation in domestic duties (chopping wood, collecting pinecones, drying dishes and carrying water), I was left to roam quite freely. I was mostly alone and enjoyed my solitude. Grandmother left me in peace with my dreams. Our confidential conversations and evening reading aloud still went on but there was no compulsion. I was allowed to decide things for myself as never before. Nor was punctuality considered all that important. If I was late for meals, there was always a sandwich and a glass of milk in the larder.

The only unwavering rule was early mornings, reveille at

seven o'clock, on Sundays as well as weekdays, and cold rubdowns supervised by Grandmother personally. Clean nails and washed ears were encroachments on my freedom which I bore with equanimity, but with no understanding. I think Grandmother imagined external cleanliness would maintain and strengthen all things spiritual.

In my case, the problem was as yet nonexistent. My sexual fantasies were diffuse, perhaps vaguely guilt-ridden. The Terrible Sin of Youth had still not afflicted me. I was innocent in all respects. The mantle of lies that had burdened me at the parsonage had fallen away and I lived trouble-free from day to day without anxiety or guilty conscience. The world was understandable and I was in control of my dreams as well as my reality. God kept quiet and Jesus did not torment me with his blood and murky invitations.

I am not entirely certain where Märta came into all this. A family from Falun with several children had for many summers rented the upper floor of the Good Templars' hall used jointly by Dufnäs and Djurmo for educational classes and cinema shows in the winter. The railway ran a few metres from the building, there was a pool of water in the grounds, and at the bottom of the slope was a small sawmill driven by water power from the Gimå just before it flowed into the river. There was also a very deep mere full of leeches which were caught and sold to the local chemist. The good smell of sun-warmed newly-sawn timber in stacks round the decaying engine house hung over everything.

My brother had long ago found friends of his own age among Märta's brothers. They were bold, aggressive and loved trouble. They joined up with the mission-hall children who lived at the south end of the village and together they challenged the village's own hooligans to fights on a steep bracken-covered slope. They dived in from each side, hunted each other out and fought with sticks and stones. I kept away from their ritual fights, for I had quite enough to do defending myself against my brother, who hit me whenever he got the chance.

One hot high-summer day, Lalla sent me to an outlying barn on the other side of the river, beyond the heath, where lived an old woman called Liss-Kulla, known as Aunt. She was a mysterious person, much respected for her medical skills and cheese-making. She had been mentally ill for a few years and instead of sending her to the lunatic asylum in Säter, regarded as a disgrace by the family, she was shut in a shed on the farm and her bellows could sometimes be heard all over the village. One early morning, she was found standing outside Våroms holding a handkerchief between her hands like a tray, and she asked Grandmother for four kronor to be placed on the handkerchief. If she wasn't given the money, she threatened, she would put heaps of brushwood across the road so that adders would assemble and bite the children's bare feet. Grandmother invited Liss-Kulla in and gave her some food and some money, then Liss-Kulla called down God's blessing, stuck out her tongue at my brother and loped off.

One cold winter's day she tried to drown herself in the Gråda at Bäsna. Some men on the ferry saw her and fished her out. She later became calm and sensible, but spoke little. She retreated to the outfield barn, where she wove cloths and brewed herbal medicines considered to be much superior to the local doctor's concoctions.

It was, as I say, a hot day. I swam in the black waters of Svartsjön where the water lilies rose out of the depths on insidious stalks. The water was always icy and the lake was considered bottomless, with an unexplored underground canal leading to the river. A boy who had gone down in it was found months later on the boom at Solbacken, his stomach full of eels and eels coming out of his mouth and backside.

I took the route across the marsh, which was forbidden, but I knew the path. It smelt astringent, the brown water bubbled up between my toes and a little cloud of flies and horseflies followed me.

The outfield barn lay on the edge of the forest below the ridge, the grazing grounds sloping away in waves to the south. The cattleshed, barns and dwelling house were in good condition and painted red, their tiled roofs newly laid, the flowerbeds well kept. Liss-Kulla's family were well-off farmers and, now that Aunt had come to her senses, nothing was too good for her.

The old woman was tall with grey-streaked hair parted in the middle, her eyes dark blue. She had a forceful face, a wide mouth, large nose, broad forehead and protruding ears. She was standing bare-armed and bare-legged out in the yard sawing wood. Märta was holding the other end of the saw.

It turned out that Märta had moved up to the outfield barn to help Liss-Kulla, for a modest payment, with the animals and other duties.

I was given blackcurrant juice and sandwiches and seated at the gate-legged table under the window. Liss-Kulla and Märta stood by the stove slurping coffee out of saucers. The cramped hot room smelt of sour milk, and flies crawled and buzzed all over the place, the sticky flypapers black with a gently moving mass.

Liss-Kulla enquired after Miss Nilsson's and Mrs Åkerblom's health. I replied that they were well. The huge cheese was packed into my knapsack, I shook hands, bowed, and thanked them for the pleasure, then said goodbye. For some reason, Märta came with me for a bit of the way.

Although we were the same age, Märta was half a head taller than me. She was broad and angular, her straight hair cut short and almost white from the sun and swimming. Her lips were thin, her mouth broad and when she laughed it seemed to me that her mouth went out to her ears, revealing strong white teeth. Her eyes were pale blue and her gaze seemed surprised, her eyebrows as fair as her hair, her nose long and straight, with a little blob on the very end. She had powerful shoulders and no hips, her arms and legs long and sunburnt, and covered with golden down. She smelt of the cowshed, as astringent as the marsh. Her dress had originally been blue but was faded and torn, with dark patches of sweat under her arms and between her shoulder blades.

Love was immediate – as between Romeo and Juliet, the

difference being that we never even thought of touching each other, not to mention kissing.

On the pretext of time-consuming duties, I disappeared from Våroms early in the mornings and returned after dusk. This went on for several days until Grandmother finally asked me straight out and I confessed. In her wisdom, she granted me unlimited leave from nine o'clock in the morning until nine at night. She also told me that Märta was always welcome to come to Våroms, a kindness we seldom made use of, as Märta's younger brothers had swiftly taken note of our passion. One afternoon, when we dared go down to the Gimå to fish and were sitting close together without touching each other, a horde of little boys appeared out of a bush and sang: 'Screwer and Fucker wanna be fine but Pricker and Cunter at once start t'whine'. I leapt on the mob and hit some of them, but got quite badly beaten. Märta did not come to my rescue. Presumably she wanted to see how I would cope.

She didn't talk. We never touched each other, but we sat, lay or stood close together, licking the scabs of our sores and scratching our mosquito bites, swimming in all weathers, but shyly, ignoring each other's nakedness. I also helped as best I could with the chores at the outfield barn, but I was rather frightened of the cows. The elkhound watched me jealously and kept nipping at my legs. Sometimes Märta was scolded. Aunt was very thorough about the duties assigned to her and once Märta had her ears boxed and she wept with rage. I was quite unable to console her.

She was quiet and I did the talking. I told her that my father was not my real father, but I was the son of a famous actor called Anders de Wahl. Pastor Bergman hated and persecuted me, which was quite understandable. My mother still loved Anders de Wahl and went to all his premières. I had been allowed to meet him once outside the theatre. He had looked at me with tears in his eyes and kissed me on the forehead. Then he had said 'God bless you, my child' in his melodious voice. 'Märta, you can hear him when he reads the *New Year Bells* on the radio! Anders de Wahl is my father and as soon as

I leave school, I'm going to be an actor at the Royal Dramatic Theatre.'

I had lugged Grandmother's old bicycle across the railway bridge and we were wobbling along the paths and winding roads down below the forest, Märta pedalling and I on the carrier at the back, holding on to the springs of the saddle with stiffening fingers. We were going to a revivalist meeting in Lännheden. Märta was a true believer and sang the ever-hopeful hymns in a loud voice, while I was unable to conceal my aversion. I hated God and Jesus, especially Jesus, with his revolting tone of voice, his slushy communion and his blood. God didn't exist. No one could prove he existed. If he existed, then he was evidently a horrid god, petty-minded, unforgiving and biased, they could keep him! Just read the Old Testament and there he is in all his glory. And that's supposed to be the God of Love who loves everyone. The world's a shithole, just as Strindberg says!

The full moon was white above the hills, the mist above the mere absolutely motionless. The silence would have been complete if I hadn't talked so much. I simply had to tell Märta I was afraid of Death. An old pastor in the congregation had suddenly died. On the day of his funeral he was lying in an open coffin while the guests were drinking wine and munching cakes in the next room. It was hot, flies buzzing round the corpse. His face was covered with a white cloth because his illness had eaten away his lower jaw and upper lip. A sweetish stench came through the heavy aroma of the flowers. Suddenly, the damned pastor rose to a sitting position, tore off the stained cloth, revealing a rotting face, then fell to one side, the coffin tipping over and the whole lot landing on the floor. Then you could see the pastor's wife had threaded a gold ring round the pastor's willie and jammed a thimble up his arse. 'It's true, Märta. I was there myself and if you don't believe me, ask my brother who was there too, but he fainted, of course. No, Death's horrid. You don't know what comes afterwards. All that stuff Jesus says about in my father's house are many mansions, I don't believe it. Not for me, thanks. If I've at last escaped my own father's mansions, I'd prefer not to move in with someone who's probably worse. Death's an insoluble horror, not because it hurts, but because it's full of beastly dreams you can't wake up from.'

One day it was raining, drizzling and dripping, and Aunt was visiting a neighbour with severe stomach pains. We were alone in the cramped hot room. It was a mild day, the rain streaking the small windows and rustling above the loft. 'You'll see,' said Märta. 'Autumn'll be here after this rain.' I suddenly realized our days were now numbered, that eternity did have an end and separation was approaching. Märta was leaning over the table, her breath smelling of milk. 'A goods train from Borlänge leaves at quarter past seven,' she said. 'I can hear when it leaves. I'll think about you then. You hear and see it when it passes Våroms. Then you must think about me.'

She stretched out her broad sunburnt hand with its dirty bitten nails. I put my hand on hers and she closed hers round it. At last I stopped talking, for an overwhelming grief had silenced me.

Autumn came and we were forced to wear shoes and socks. We helped with the turnips, the apples ripened, the frost came and everything turned to glass in space and on the ground. The pond outside the Good Templars' hall had a thin layer of ice on it and Märta's mother started packing. The sun was hot in the middle of the day, but it turned bitterly cold towards evening. The fields were ploughed and the threshing machines thundered away in the barns. We helped occasionally, but liked to go off on our own. One day we borrowed Berglund's boat and went fishing for pike. We caught a huge one which bit my finger. When Lalla cut open the pike, she found a wedding ring in its stomach. With a magnifying glass, Grandmother could see the name Karin engraved inside the ring. Some years earlier, Father had lost his ring up by the Gimå. It did not necessarily follow that it was the same ring.

One raw cold morning, Grandmother told us to go to the

village store half way between Dufnäs and Djurmo. We got a lift with Berglund's son, who was going the same way to sell an old horse. We sat on the back flap of the wagon. The journey was slow and difficult along the road full of potholes made by the rain. We counted cars passing or coming towards us, and they added up to three in two hours. At the store, we packed our knapsacks and started off home on foot. When we came to the old ferry place, we sat down on a black log that had been washed ashore and drank apple juice and ate sandwiches. I talked to Märta about the Nature of Love, explaining that I didn't believe in eternal love, human love was egoism, and Strindberg had said that in *The Pelican*. I maintained that love between man and woman was mostly lechery. I told her about a beautiful but fat lady who made love to my father in the vestry after communion service every Thursday evening.

The apple juice all gone, Märta threw the bottle into the river. I went on about tragic loving couples in literature and paraded my knowledge a little. Suddenly I felt depressed, almost dizzy, and asked in embarrassment whether Märta thought I talked too much. 'No, not at all,' she said, shaking her head gravely. I kept quiet for a long while, wondering whether to spin a yarn about my own erotic experiences, but then I began to feel more ill than ever and wondered whether the apple juice was poisoned. I had to lie down on a grassy slope by the road. Fine icy rain started to fall and the river bank opposite disappeared into the mist.

One night it snowed, the river turned blacker than ever and all the greenery and yellow colours vanished. The wind dropped and an overwhelming silence fell. Although it was half-light, the whiteness dazzled because it came from below and struck where the eye was unprotected. We walked along the railway embankment towards the Good Templars' hall. The grey sawmill crouched sagging and abandoned under the weight of all that white, the water in the pool rippled discreetly, and there was a thin layer of ice on the water nearest to the closed hatchways.

We could not speak, nor did we dare look at each other, the pain was too great. We shook hands, said goodbye and maybe we would see each other next summer.

Then she turned quickly away and ran towards the house. I walked along the embankment back to Våroms thinking that if a train came along it might as well run straight over me.

8

Rehearsals of Strindberg's *Dance of Death* were resumed on Friday 30 January 1976. Anders Ek had been ill for a few weeks, but he claimed that he was now fully recovered.

During those unexpectedly free days I worked with Ulla Isaksson, the writer, and Gunnel Lindblom, the director, on the script of *Paradise Place*, based on a novel written by Ulla. The film was to be produced by my company, Cinematograph, and filming was due to start in May. We were all fully occupied with preparations, drawing up contracts and looking for locations. My television series, *Face to Face*, had just been completed and the film version was to be shown at the weekend to visiting American backers. A few months earlier, I had completed the script of *The Serpent's Egg*, which was to be produced by Dino De Laurentiis.

Slowly and with some hesitation, I had begun to turn in the direction of America, the reason being the greater resources there for both myself and Cinematograph. The chances of producing quality films with American money, directed by others, were increasing sharply. I was extremely amused by playing film mogul, a rôle I now think I did not manage particularly well. However, Cinematograph rested on twin pillars who had also been close friends and colleagues for several years: Lars-Owe Carlberg (our collaboration started in 1953 with *Sawdust and Tinsel/The Naked Night*) who saw to our considerable administration; and Katinka Farago (*Journey into Autumn/Dreams*, 1954) who looked after our increasingly lively filming activities. From Sandrew's Film Company we had rented the top floor of a lovely eighteenth-century building, where we had equipped a spacious office with a screening room, editing rooms, a kitchen and a sense of home.

For a month or so, we had been visited by two quiet, courteous gentlemen from the Tax Authority, who had been given a space in our temporarily empty office and were busy going through our accounts. They had also expressed a wish to be allowed to examine my Swiss firm, Personafilm, so we immediately sent for all the books and placed them at the gentlemen's disposal.

No one had the time to bother about these quiet individuals in the empty room. According to my diary notes, I see that a voluminous memorandum from the Tax Authority landed with us on Thursday 22 January. I did not read it but sent it on to my lawyer.

A few years earlier, I think in 1967, when my finances began to get beyond me in what was indeed a pleasant way but an avalanche, I asked my friend Harry Schein to find me an irreproachably honest lawyer who would take over as my financial 'guardian'. His choice fell on the relatively young and highly commended Sven Harald Bauer, who in addition to everything else was a high ranking bigwig in the international scout movement.

We got on very well together and contact with the Swiss lawyer looking after Personafilm was also good. Our activities multiplied: *Cries and Whispers*, *Scenes from a Marriage*, Kjell Grede's *A Madman's Defence*, and *The Magic Flute*.

In my notes on 22 January, I seem to be less worried about the memorandum from the Tax Authority than about a painful eczema that had broken out on the third finger of my left hand.

Ingrid and I had been married for five years. We lived in a newly built apartment house at Karlaplan 10 where Strindberg's House had once stood.

We led a quiet bourgeois life, meeting friends, going to concerts and the theatre, seeing a number of films and working with gusto.

This is a brief background to what happened on 30 January and subsequently.

There are no notes in my diary for the months that follow. I returned to writing them, intermittently, about a year later. So what follows will be what I remember in momentary images, sharply in focus, but blurred at the edges.

We had started rehearsing *Dance of Death* at half-past ten as usual. 'We' were Anders Ek, Margaretha Krook, Jan-Olof Strandberg, the production assistant, the prompter, the stage manager and myself. We were in pleasant, light premises high up under the roof of Dramaten.

We were progressing in a relaxed and easy-going way, as usually happens at the start of rehearsals. The door opened and Margot Wirström, the theatre director's secretary, came in. She said that I was to go immediately to her room where two policemen were waiting to speak to me. I said perhaps they could be given a cup of coffee and then we could meet at one o'clock when we had our lunch break. Margot Wirström said they wished to speak to me at once. I asked what it was all about, but Margot did not know. We laughed in astonishment and I asked the actors to continue the rehearsal and said we would assemble again at half-past one, after lunch.

Margot and I went down to her room, outside the director's office. A gentleman in a dark coat was sitting there. He got up, shook hands and gave his name. I asked him what was going on, why there was so much hurry. He looked away and said something about it being this tax business and I had to come with him immediately for questioning. I stared at him like a madman and said I didn't understand, which was true. Then I suddenly remembered that people in my situation (in Amer-

ican films) usually call up their lawyer. I said that my lawyer
must certainly be present at any questioning and I would
telephone him. Still looking away, the policeman said that was
impossible, as my lawyer was also involved and had himself
been brought in for questioning. I asked hopelessly if I could
go to my room and fetch my coat. 'Then I'll come with you,'
said the policeman. So we went. On the way to my room, we
met several people who looked in surprise at the stranger
walking just behind me. I met a colleague in the producer's
corridor. 'Aren't you rehearsing?' he said in surprise. 'I've
been nabbed by the police,' I said. My colleague laughed.

When I had got my outdoor clothes on, I suddenly had a
violent attack of stomach cramp and said I had to crap. The
policeman inspected the toilet and forbade me to lock the
door. The cramps doubled me up and I defecated lengthily and
noisily. The policeman had sat down just outside the half-
open door.

At last we were ready to leave the theatre. I was feeling ill
and was silently lamenting the fact that I had no talent for
fainting. We met actors and other staff on their way to the
canteen for lunch. I greeted them bleakly. I noticed the
inquisitive face of the girl at the switchboard.

We emerged into Nybrogatan and another policeman came
up and greeted me. He had been posted on the crossroads
between Nybrogatan and Almlöfsgatan to make sure I did not
escape.

Detective Kent Karlsson from the Tax Authority had
parked just outside the theatre. (Or perhaps it was his
colleague. I could never tell the two gentlemen apart, both
were flabby and wore flowered shirts, had grubby com-
plexions and dirty fingernails.) We got into his car and drove
off. I was in the back between two policemen, Detective
Karlsson (or his colleague) at the wheel. One of the policemen
was a friendly soul and made conversation, laughed and told
stories. I asked him if he could possibly be quiet. A little hurt,
he replied that he had only wanted to lighten the atmosphere.

The Police Superintendent was nesting in an office near

Kungsholmstorg, though I am not absolutely certain of that for the images are now growing less clear and the dialogue more and more inaudible.

A pleasant older man came towards me and introduced himself. He had placed a number of papers on the desk and asked me to look at them. I asked for a glass of water, because my mouth, throat and gullet had dried up. I took a drink. My hand was shaking and I found it hard to breathe. Farther away in the room (which suddenly seemed endless) some indefinable people had assembled, five or six in number, possibly more, all seated. The Commissioner said that I had made false declarations and that Personafilm was a 'nullity'. I replied quite truthfully that I never read my declarations and I had never had any intention of withholding money from the state. The Commissioner started to ask me about first one thing then another. I repeated that I had requested other people to see to my finances because I was quite incompetent to deal with such matters, and I would never get involved in any risky undertakings which would be totally alien to my nature. I willingly admitted I had signed papers I had not read. If I had read any, then I had not understood them.

In the whole of this miserable episode – which lasted several years and caused me and mine considerable pain, which cost a fortune in legal fees, which sent me abroad for nine years and finally led to a tax demand for 180,000 kronor – I was guilty of only one thing – that I had signed papers I had not read or had not understood. Thus I had approved financial operations that I had no grasp of. Nor was I capable of supervising them. I had been assured everything was legal and above board and had contented myself with that. If I did not understand, nor did my nice lawyer, international scout leader that he was, know what he had let himself in for. So a number of transactions were dealt with incorrectly or not at all. This in its turn had made the tax authorities suspicious, with good reason. Detective Karlsson and his colleague thought they had a big catch. They had been given a free hand by a puzzled and ignorant prosecutor, frightened that I would probably flee the country and cock a snook at the authorities.

The hours went by. The gentlemen at the other end of that remarkably extended room disappeared one by one. I mostly sat in silence and occasionally said in a distant voice that this was a major catastrophe. I also remarked to the Commissioner that it was a snip for the media. He calmed me down by telling me that our conversation was confidential. They had put him here in Kungsholmstorg, far away from police headquarters, to avoid arousing any unnecessary attention. I asked if I could phone my wife, but I was not allowed to because they were searching our apartment at that very moment. Then the telephone rang. It was *Svenska Dagbladet* who'd had a tip-off. The nice policeman was disconcerted and requested the journalist not to write anything. After that, he told me I could not travel anywhere and that they were confiscating my passport. An interrogation was being arranged. I signed something, I didn't know what, because I no longer understood what anyone was saying to me.

We got up. The policeman patted my back kindly and urged me to go on living and working as usual. I repeated that this was a major catastrophe, couldn't he understand that it was a major catastrophe?

Finally I found myself out on the street again. It was snowing slightly, dusk falling. Everything was very clear, but in black-and-white, no colour, rough like a duplicate. My teeth were chattering and every thought or feeling numbed. I took a taxi to the rear of the theatre where I had parked my car. On my way home, I passed the Life Guards' barracks and great flames were shooting out of the roof into the darkening light. Now, afterwards, I wonder whether I had imagined it. I saw no fire engines or crowds. It was perfectly quiet, snow falling and the Life Guards' barracks on fire.

When I finally got home, Ingrid was there. The search of the apartment had taken her totally by surprise. The police had been polite and not particularly thorough. They had taken away a number of files, mostly for the sake of appearances. Then she had sat down to wait and, when the time dragged, had made some cakes.

I telephoned Harry Schein and Sven Harald Bauer. Both were perplexed and shocked. What happened next that evening I don't know. Did we have dinner? We must have. Did we watch television? Maybe we watched television.

Late that evening after we had already gone to bed, it struck me that the media would besiege Karlaplan 10 the next morning. I packed a few necessities and set off for the little apartment in Grevturegatan that Gun and I had moved into after our flight to Paris in the autumn of 1949. Ever since then, I have always moved to Grevturegatan whenever catastrophes, collapsed marriages and other difficulties have arisen.

I got there at midnight. The room's anonymity gave me a sense of security. I took a sleeping pill and fell asleep.

I have forgotten what happened on the Saturday and Sunday. I shut myself in at Grevturegatan and went home for a few hours in the evening, sneaking through the garage and meeting no one.

The media had a field day on placards, front pages and the television news. My twelve year-old son refused to go to school. Anguish overcame him and he ensconced himself in the projection room of Röda Kvarn cinema with his friend 'Nypan', the projectionist, who was to be a continuous support to him in the difficult times to come. I don't know how my other children reacted because I saw little or nothing of them. Most of them belonged to leftish groups and, as I found out later, thought that it served Dad right. Some were convinced I was guilty.

The breakdown came on Monday morning. I was sitting at home in the big room on the first floor, reading a book and listening to music. Ingrid had gone to a meeting with the lawyers. I felt nothing. I was quite collected but somewhat dopey from sleeping pills, which at that time I was not in the habit of using.

The music ceased and the tape stopped with a small bang. It was absolutely quiet, the roofs on the opposite side of the street white and the snow falling slowly. I stopped reading. Anyhow, I was finding it hard to take anything in. The light in the room was sharp, with no shadows. A clock struck a few times. Perhaps I was asleep, perhaps I had taken that short step from the accepted reality of the senses into the other reality. I didn't know and now I was deep down in a motionless vacuum, painless and free of emotions. I closed my eyes. I thought I had closed my eyes, then sensed there was someone in the room and opened my eyes. In the sharp light, a few metres away, I myself was standing looking at myself. The experience was concrete and incontestable. I was standing on the yellow rug looking at myself sitting in the chair. I was sitting in the chair looking at myself standing on the yellow rug. So far, the I who was sitting in the chair was the one in charge of reactions. This was the end, there was no return. I could hear myself wailing.

I have once or twice in my life toyed with the idea of committing suicide and at one time in my youth I staged a fumbling attempt, but I have never taken these games seriously. My curiosity has been too great, my love of life too robust and my fear of death too childishly solid.

My attitude to life, however, presupposed a proper and continuous control of my relation to reality, imaginings and dreams. When that control did not function – something which had never happened to me before, not even in my early childhood – the machinery exploded and my identity was threatened. I could hear my whining voice. I sounded like an injured dog. I got up out of my chair to leave through the window.

What I didn't know was that Ingrid had come home. Suddenly Sture Helander, my best friend and doctor, was there. An hour later I found myself in Karolinska Hospital psychiatric clinic. I was put by myself into a large room with four other beds in it. A professor doing his rounds spoke kindly to me and I said something about the shame, drawing on my favourite quote about fear manifesting what is feared, petrified by grief. I was given an injection and fell asleep.

The three weeks in that ward passed pleasantly. We were a meek collection of drugged zombies following an undemanding daily routine without protest. I was given five blue Valiums a day and two Mogadons at night. If I felt in the slightest uneasy, I went at once to the nurse and was given an extra dose. I slept heavily and dreamlessly at night and dozed off for several hours a day.

In between times, with what remained of my professional curiosity I explored my surroundings. I was living behind a screen in my large empty room, mostly reading without registering what I was reading. Meals were taken in a small dining room, the conversation polite, putting one under no obligation. No emotional outbursts were obvious, the only exception being a famous sculptor who became disturbed one evening and almost ground his teeth to pieces. Otherwise I can remember a sad girl who continually felt the need to wash her hands, a gentle six-foot young man who had jaundice and was on Methadone. He was taken once a week to Ulleråker Mental Hospital where much-discussed research was being carried out. There was also a silent older man who had tried to commit suicide by sawing at his wrists with a handsaw. A middle-aged woman with a stern lovely face was suffering from motor-anxiety and walked in silence for miles and miles through the corridors.

In the evening, we assembled in front of the television and watched the World Ice Skating Championships on a ramshackle old black-and-white set with fuzzy pictures and bad sound, but that didn't matter, nor did it give rise to any comment.

Ingrid visited me a couple of times a day and we talked calmly in a friendly way. Sometimes we went to a matinée at the cinema, sometimes Sandrews arranged a showing in their screening room. The young man on Methadone was allowed to come to that.

I read no papers, and neither saw nor heard any news

programmes. Slowly and imperceptibly, my anxiety disappeared – my life's most faithful companion, inherited from both my mother and my father, placed in the very centre of my identity, my demon but also my friend spurring me on. Not only the torment, the anguish and the feeling of irreparable humiliation faded, but the driving force of my creativity was also eclipsed and fell away.

I imagine I could easily have become a ward case for the rest of my life, as my existence was so woefully pleasant, so undemanding, so lovingly protected. Nothing was either real or urgent any longer, nothing worrying or painful. I moved with caution, all my reactions delayed or non-existent; sexuality ceased, life became an elegy sung by a madrigal choir far inside under some echoing arch, the rose windows glowing and telling fairy tales no longer any concern of mine.

One afternoon, I asked the friendly professor if he had ever in his life cured anyone. He thought seriously and replied, 'Cure is a big word.' Then he shook his head and smiled encouragingly. Minutes, days and weeks went by.

I don't know what made me break out of this hermetically sealed security. I asked the professor if I could move to Sophiahemmet, on trial. He gave me permission, at the same time warning me insistently not to break off my Valium cure too abruptly. I thanked him for all his kindness, said goodbye to my fellow patients and donated a colour television to our day room.

One day at the end of February, I found myself in a quiet comfortable room at Sophiahemmet. The window faced out onto the garden. I could see the yellow parsonage, my childhood home, up there on the hill. Every morning, I walked for an hour in the park, the shadow of an eight year-old beside me; it was both stimulating and uncanny.

Otherwise this was a time of violent torment. In protest against the professor's instructions, I stopped taking both Valium and Mogadon and the effect was immediate. My suppressed anxiety shot up like the flame of a blowlamp, insomnia was total, my demons raging. I thought I would be torn apart by internal detonations. I started reading the papers, involving myself in all that had happened in my absence, reading kind and unkind letters that had piled up, talking to lawyers and making contact with friends.

This was neither bravery nor desperation, but the instinct for self-preservation which, despite or rather thanks to being unconscious at the psychiatric clinic, had had time to collect itself into some resistance.

I went on to the attack against the demons with a method that had worked well in previous crises. I divided the day and the night into definite units of time, each of which was filled with activities organized beforehand, alternated with periods of rest. Only by rigidly following my day and night programme could I maintain my sanity against torments so violent that they became interesting. To put it briefly, I returned to planning and staging my life with great care.

Through these routines, I quite quickly put my professional ego in order and was able to investigate with interest the torments tearing me to pieces. I started taking notes and soon came close to the parsonage up there on the hill. A calm voice somewhere maintained that my reaction to what had happened to me was exaggerated, that surprisingly enough I had reacted with submission instead of anger, that despite everything I had declared myself guilty without being guilty, craving punishment so that I would receive forgiveness and release as quickly as possible. The voice mocked me kindly. Who would forgive you? The Tax Authority? Detective Karlsson with his flowered shirt and dirty nails? Who? Your enemies? Your critics? Will God forgive you? And give you absolution? What do you think? Will Olof Palme or the King issue a communiqué stating that you have now been punished, asked for forgiveness and been forgiven? (Later in Paris, I switched on the television quite by chance and there was Olof Palme assuring everyone in perfect French that the tax story was exaggerated, not the result of social-democratic tax policies, and that he was a friend of mine. At that moment I despised him.)

A stifled rage, compressed and silenced for some considerable time, started moving down in my darkest corridors. But I mustn't exaggerate! To the outside world I was pitiful. I was whiney and irritable. I took all tenderness and care for granted but grizzled like a spoilt child. Inside my routines and imposed self-discipline, I was perplexed and confused, not knowing one day what the next would bring. I could not plan a week ahead. What would my life be like, my work at the theatre, the filming? What would happen to Cinematograph, the apple of my eye? What would happen to my employees? At night, when I was unable to summon up the energy to read, a whole platoon of demons was there to attack me. In the daytime, within the apparent order, chaos reigned as if in a bombed city.

In the middle of March, we moved out to Fårö, where the long struggle between winter and spring had just started, one day strong sunlight and mild winds, shimmering reflections on the water and newborn lambs scuttling about on the bare thawed-out ground, the next day stormy winds from the tundras, the snow coming in horizontally, the seas raging, windows and roads blocked, the electricity off. Fires, paraffin stoves and battery radio.

All that was calming. I worked hard, writing up my investigation which had been given the working title of *The Closed Room*. I slowly made my way along unfamiliar roads almost always leading to silence and the sensation of having lost my way. But writing was part of my daily discipline.

At night I took Mogadon and Valium when I felt the threat of annihilation was too great. I could at least control my own intake now, though my restored balance was precarious.

Ingrid had to go to Stockholm on urgent business and suggested I should go with her, but I did not want to. She suggested someone should come and keep me company the few days she would be away, but I wanted that even less.

I drove her to the airport. On the way between Fårösund and

Bunge, we met a police car, an unusual sight in northern Gotland. I was seized with panic and thought they had come to fetch me. Ingrid told me I was wrong. I calmed down and left her at Visby airport, but when I got back home to Hammars, a little snow had fallen and there were fresh footprints and tyre-tracks outside the house. I was then utterly convinced the police had been looking for me. I locked all the doors, loaded my rifle and sat in the kitchen where I could keep watch on the road and the parking place. I waited for hours, my mouth and throat dry. I drank some mineral water and, in my mind, I thought calmly but without hope that this was the end. The March twilight descended silently and sharply. No police appeared. Gradually I realized that I was behaving like a dangerous lunatic. I unloaded the rifle, locked it away and cooked dinner.

Writing became more and more difficult. My anxiety persisted, for there were rumours of a charge of tax evasion, the whole matter thus becoming a banal tax affair.

We waited. Nothing happened. I read Selma Lagerlöf's *Jerusalem*, maintaining my routines with some difficulty. Wednesday 24 March was a calm cloudy day, the snow thawing and dripping off the roof. From my room I could hear the telephone ringing and Ingrid answering. She threw down the receiver and came running in, wearing her everyday blue check dress. She slapped her thigh with her right hand and cried, 'Dropped!'

At first I felt nothing, then slowly I felt exhaustion. I broke all my routines and went to bed. I slept for several hours. I hadn't been so worn out since the time I had got out of a plane, the one engine of which had caught fire so the plane had had to fly round over Öresund for several hours to use up its fuel.

Towards evening, there was a knock on the door. A good friend and neighbour was standing outside. She thrust a flower at me and said she just wanted to congratulate me and tell me how pleased she was.

I had a sleepless night, kept awake by an explosion of projects and plans. When neither sleeping pills, music, Selma, chocolate nor biscuits helped, I got up and went to sit at my worktable. I quickly wrote down the action of a film called *Mother and Daughter and Mother*, and noted that Ingrid Bergman and Liv Ullmann were to play the parts.

On 30 March, we returned to Stockholm, where a good deal of work was waiting for me. With a weariness which was hard to bear, I cautiously started to tackle important tasks, primarily all the preliminaries for Ulla Isaksson's and Gunnel Lindblom's *Paradise Place*.

By 2 April, the Tax Authorities had reloaded and fired off a broadside. At one o'clock in the afternoon, we had a meeting with our lawyer, Rolf Magrell, and slowly, with some difficulty, I began to understand the content of the message from the Tax Authority he was putting over. Later, I wrote an article on the whole affair and its consequences:

On Friday April 2nd, my legal representative, Rolf Magrell, was 'invited' to a meeting with Bengt Källén and Hans Svensson, two senior tax officials.

The message these two gentlemen had to convey was very complicated. Despite his patient attempts, Magrell has not been entirely successful in explaining all the details to me, but, on the other hand, I had grasped the main theme.

In order to get in before the National Tax Authority's alert publicity department, which appears to work intimately with the media, my present intention is to reveal what these two tax officials had in mind.

The fact that, in that way, I rob someone of a fee for a good tip to the Press I will have to take with equanimity. As far as I can make out, considerable sums have already been made out of what is called the 'Bergman tangle'. One question in passing – how does the Press account for their expenses in such cases and in what way does the recipient declare his income?

I will now briefly attempt to describe the message brought by Svensson and Källén. I beg the reader to be patient, as the point of it all is really quite interesting.

They explained that the *State* Tax Authority was not entirely satisfied with the failure of the *Local* Tax Authority's previous statement which Tax Superintendent Dahlstrand's new claim involved. Dahlstrand proposed that I should be taxed on two and a half million kronor in 1975 (as my share from my ex-Swiss firm Personafilm). The State Tax Authority now wished to tax my Swedish company, Cinematograph, for the *same* income, as they considered the Swiss company a 'nullity'. The fact that the same income would thus be taxed twice (at 85% plus 24% or all together 109%), was not their concern, as that was Dahlstrand's fault. (I hope you are still with me?)

If, on the other hand, Dahlstrand and I could agree on my being taxed as the State Tax Authority had first wished, then they would desist from taxing my Swedish company.

To put it simply, with threats and blackmail, they wished to get Dahlstrand and me to admit that the State Tax Authority had been right from the start.

It is a pleasure for me to inform Bengt Källén and Hans Svensson, through this newspaper, that I do not accept their methods and I refuse to be involved in any kind of horse-trading.

Naturally I now have to speculate further on the reasons that may lie behind this astonishing action by the State Tax Authority.

Here are a few explanations. A number of people within the State Tax Authority lost face when the Public Prosecutor, Nordenadler, declared the charge dropped. Detective Karlsson of the Tax Authority and his collaborators had worked on this case for many months, culminating in my being fetched from the Royal Dramatic Theatre. When it later turned out that all this work had more or less been in vain, an imperative need was felt to find something else which, anyhow temporarily, would counteract the negative publicity the State Tax Authority had attracted both inside the country and abroad. Presumably it was reckoned that in my fear of having to go on running the gauntlet, I would

submit to this blackmail, at which under any circumstances the State Tax Authority would be seen as the
victor.

I do not accept such games.

At the same time, I wish to say immediately that I would
like to press these two officials to my heart. For they
actually managed to do something neither psychiatry nor I
myself had been able to achieve during my two months'
illness.

To put it simply, I was so furiously angry that I recovered immediately. The horror and sense of ineradicable
humiliation I had been suffering from day and night
evaporated within a few hours and have never been heard
of since. I realised that my opponents were not impartial,
objective and discerning authorities, but a collection of
prestige-seeking poker players.

Naturally I had previously suspected something of the
sort, especially after a closer view of Detective Karlsson of
the Tax Authority, who was present at the police hearing
and was literally trembling with excitement at his approaching triumph. I have to admit that I later hesitated
when Prosecutor Nordenadler had the moral courage to
resist the powerful forces that had already condemned me.
(I decided to forget it all, to return to my activities and
hand over with complete confidence the actual tax case to
the experts. I am indifferent to money and material objects, always have been and always will be. I did not worry
about losing what I possessed, should all eventually go
against me. I do not count assets in money terms. I thought
I had been badly treated, but felt I had to forget it all in
order to return to reality. I also thought that at the end of
this depressing story there would be both decency and
justice.)

But Källén and Svensson, with threats of blackmail, re-
established order and confirmed my most paranoid
thoughts. At the same time, the paralyzing creative crisis I
had suffered for the first time in my conscious life was solved.

Thus, in consultation with myself and some of my closest associates, I had now made a number of decisions and was going to write them down, otherwise a whole garden of speculations, rumours and insinuations would grow and would be hard to control later.

My first decision was that, as I demand a certain security in order to achieve anything in my profession, and as this security clearly would be denied me in the foreseeable future, I would be forced to seek this security elsewhere apart from in this country. It was perfectly clear to me that this would be taking a big risk. The practice of my profession is perhaps so strongly tied to my environment and my language that I might not survive such a change in my fifty-eighth year. Despite this, I would have to risk the attempt, for this paralyzing sense of insecurity had to be brought to an end. If I could not work, my whole life would be meaningless.

My second decision was that, in order for 'right-minded Swedish taxpayers' not to think I was running away because of the tax charge, I left my income in a blocked account at the disposal of the State Tax Authority should I lose my case. A corresponding sum was to be made available if Cinematograph lost its case. Should I owe any more money, I aimed to pay in full. I had had various offers and intended not to owe my native country a single cent.

My third decision was that, as I had paid over two million kronor in tax over recent years and had given employment to various people, I had been anxiously careful to ensure that all transactions should be absolutely honest. As I have never understood figures and am afraid of money, I had requested recognized skilled and honest people to look after these and other relevant matters. Fårö had been my security. I had lain as if in a womb without a thought that I should ever again in my life have to leave. I had always been a convinced Social Democrat. I had embraced with sincere enthusiasm this grey ideology of compromises. I thought my country was the best in the world and I still do, possibly because I have seen so little of other countries.

My awakening came as a shock, partly because of the unendurable humiliation and partly because I realized that anyone in this country could be assailed and degraded by a special kind of bureaucracy that grows like a galloping cancer and is in no way equipped for its difficult and vulnerable task, and which society has given powers the individual exercisers of which are by no means qualified to handle.

When the State Tax Authority's representatives with Detective Kent Karlsson in the lead unexpectedly turned up at the Cinematograph office and demanded to see our accounts, I found their way of going about things a trifle objectionable, but was told that nowadays this was how it was done and all was in order. They informed us they were particularly interested in Personafilm's transactions. Without questioning them, we put Personafilm's books at their disposal.

My lawyer and I waited without anxiety to be summoned to a discussion with the auditors.

Not so.

Detective Kent Karlsson and his lads had other plans. They were going to make a show of strength which would immediately give echo all over the world and bring themselves a number of points in this special points-table of bureaucracy.

In any case, it had not been very well thought out. Several months had gone by between the beginning of the audit and when they came for me and my lawyer 'in order that we should not destroy any evidence'. If we had had anything to hide, we would have destroyed the evidence during those months. Even a village policeman would have been able to think that out. If I had had a guilty conscience, I could have turned myself into a Swede-in-exile during that long period of time. And finally, if I had not been so desperately fond of this country and also not been so criminally honest, I should today have had a considerable fortune at my disposal — abroad.

None of these thoughts crossed the minds of either Detective Karlsson or Prosecutor Dreifaldt. The Karlsson coup was a fact, and precisely fourteen minutes after I had been hustled out of the Dramatic Theatre, the first newspaper telephoned the man conducting the hearing, asking for details of this sensational action.

But then this hugely organized show of strength failed and they turned to extraordinary trench warfare tactics, with ingredients of threats and blackmail. I feared that this strategy would continue into the unforeseeable future.

I had neither the mind nor the nerves to stand that kind of warfare. Nor the time.

So I decided to leave. I was to leave the country to prepare for my first film abroad, and in a foreign language. I could find no reason to be sorry. For everyone apart from myself and those nearest me, this was just a bagatelle, or a 'nullity', as they say at the State Tax Authority.

I have been told I ought to attack *Aftonbladet* for the way it handled my case, but I have said that would be pointless. A newspaper that excels at insinuations, open insults, half-truths and rabble-like personal persecution collects comments with the same delight as an Indian collects scalps. I presume that every society has a use for sewage outlets such as *Aftonbladet*. It has never ceased to surprise me that that particular sewage outlet is the flag-ship of the Social Democrats and that within its collapsing accumulation of cells work several respectable and decent people.

I have also been told that I ought to sue Prosecutor Dreifaldt for damages (two lost productions at forty-five thousand kronor, a cancelled film worth about three million, psychological damage at one krona and tarnished honour at one krona, making a total sum of three million, ninety thousand and two kronor).

I also find this pointless. Amateurishness, a sense of duty and clumsiness had worked hand in hand. One has to understand that. It is very Swedish. Perhaps one day I will write a farce on the subject. I say as Strindberg did when he was angry: 'Watch out, you bastard, we'll meet again in my next play.'

Björn Nilsson of *Expressen* saw to the article. Ingrid and I went to stay with her sister and brother-in-law in Lesjöfors. On our return to Stockholm, we went via Våroms, now silent and closed up in the grey late winter light, the river black and mist lying over the hills. We passed Stora Tuna, where Ingrid's mother is buried. We stopped for an hour or so in Upsala and I showed Ingrid my grandmother's house in Trädgårdsgatan, and we stood by the River Fyris which was in full spate. It was both sentimental and a farewell.

Then we went for a few days to Fårö, which was painful but necessary. I told Lars-Owe Carlberg and Katinka Farago. They promised to keep Cinematograph going as best they could. On Good Friday I wrote the article, then rewrote it and wrote it once again, wondering why the hell I was going to all that trouble, but the rage that had kept me going in recent weeks produced the necessary adrenalin.

On 20 April, Ingrid and her sister went to Paris. I spent the evening with my friend and doctor Sture Helander. We have known each other since 1955 when I was brought crapping and vomiting into his department at the Karolinska Hospital. I weighed only fifty-six kilos and they suspected cancer of the stomach. Although we are very different, we became friends, a friendship that still means a great deal to us both.

On Wednesday 21 April, at 16.50 hours, I left for Paris. As the plane took off, I was seized with a wild euphoria and read stories to a little girl in the seat next to me.

What happened then is uninteresting in this context. My article came out in *Expressen* the day after I had left and caused quite a stir. The media besieged my Paris hotel and a photographer on a motorbike almost killed himself following the car taking us to the Swedish Embassy. I had promised Dino De Laurentiis I would keep quiet because we had planned a press conference in Hollywood a few days later.

It was a tumultuous party. I realized we had won the second round, but at the same time wondered whether the price had not been too high.

Ingrid and I had thought of living in Paris, where we returned about a week later. We were to spend the summer in Los Angeles, as the preparations for *The Serpent's Egg* had been delayed. It was hot in Paris. Our elegant hotel offered air-conditioning which thundered and squeaked, the colossal machine exuding a thin stream of cold air down by the floor. Incapable of movement, we sat naked in front of this little current of air and drank champagne. Two bombs went off in a side street and wrecked some West German offices.

It grew even hotter, so we fled to Copenhagen, where we hired a car and toured the Danish countryside. One evening we chartered a private plane and flew to Visby. We got to Fårö rather late, but it was still light. The huge lilac hedge outside the old house at Dämba Water was in full bloom. We sat on the steps to the house until dawn, enveloped in the heavy fragrance, then early in the morning we flew back to Copenhagen.

Dino De Laurentiis and I had agreed that the film was to be made in Germany, a sensible decision as it is set in Berlin in the 1920s. I went to Berlin to look for locations, but could find nothing except a part of the city close to the Wall, called Kreuzberg, a ghost town where nothing had been repaired since the war. The façades were still pockmarked from grenades and spraying bullets. The ruins of bombed buildings had been removed, but there were empty sites like open infected sores between the grey blocks. The signs above the shops were in a foreign language. Not a single native German lives in this part of what had once been a proud capital. Someone once said that a dwelling can be a dangerous weapon and I suddenly understood the point of this remark. The buildings were overflowing with people, children playing in the courtyards, the garbage stinking in the heat. The streets were badly maintained, the asphalt inadequately patched.

I am sure some authority supervises this cancerous tumour on the wealthy back of West Berlin. It probably has exactly what is required in the way of social institutions and safety arrangements, so that no one will come to any harm and thus embarrass the German conscience and the scarcely concealed racial hatred. In plain language they say: anyhow the bastards are better off here than wherever they come from. Young junkies hang around Bahnhof Zoo, occasionally dispersed by some organized swoop. I have never before witnessed such blatant physical and spiritual misery. The Germans simply don't see it, or they are angry and say there ought to be camps. Nevertheless, the thinking behind Kreuzberg is as simple as it is cynical. If the enemy on the other side of the Wall wants to come in, he must first shoot his way through a barrier of non-German bodies.

The Bavaria Studios in Munich turned out to be a decent establishment with twelve studios and 4000 employees. In the city of Munich, there are two opera houses, thirty-two theatres, three symphony orchestras, innumerable museums, huge parks and neat streets crowded with stores; and the shop windows display a sophisticated luxury which can hardly be matched in any other big city in Europe. The people were friendly and hospitable and we decided to settle in Munich, especially as I had been invited to stage *A Dream Play* at the Residenz Theatre, Bavaria's equivalent of the Royal Dramatic Theatre in Stockholm.

I also received a prestigious award, called the Goethe Prize, to be presented in Frankfurt in the autumn. After some searching we found a light and spacious apartment in an ugly high-rise building bordering on Englischer Garten. From the terrace we could see the Alps and old Munich with all its spires and steeples.

As the apartment would not be free until September, we returned to Los Angeles to spend the summer there. The heatwave of the century had struck California. We arrived two days before midsummer and sat in the tomblike air-conditioned chill, watching boxing on television. We tried walking to a nearby movie theatre in the evening, and the heat hit us like a falling concrete wall.

The next morning, Barbra Streisand telephoned and asked us whether we would like to bring our bathing gear with us for a little party by the pool. I thanked her, put down the receiver, turned to Ingrid and said: 'Let's go back home to Fårö at once and spend the summer there. We'll just have to put up with the scorn and the laughter.'

A few hours later we were on our way.

We arrived in Stockholm on Midsummer Eve. Ingrid phoned her father, who had gathered together friends and relations on his farm near Norrtälje. He insisted that we come at once.

It was past eleven o'clock and a mild evening, everything at its most beautiful and fragrant. And then the Swedish light!

Towards morning, I was lying in a white bed in a room that smelt of summer house and newly scrubbed wooden floor. Outside the window was a tall birch, its shadow drawing a swaying pattern on the light-coloured blind, rustling, whispering and whispering.

The long journey fell away, the catastrophe of my life was a dream someone else had dreamt.

Ingrid and I quietly talked over this new life of ours which we knew was going to be difficult.

I said: 'I'll either die or it'll be hellish stimulating!'

9

I was alone at the parsonage with some insoluble mathematics homework one Sunday afternoon. I was thirteen. The bells of Engelbrekt Church were tolling for a funeral; my brother was at a matinée at the cinema, my sister in hospital with appendicitis, my parents and the maids had gone to the chapel to celebrate the memory of Queen Sophia, founder of the hospital. The spring sunlight was blazing down over my desk, the old nurses from Solhemmet walking in single file through the shade below the trees across the road. I had been forbidden to go to the cinema because I had been to *Götterdammerung* the night before instead of doing my maths homework. Bored and confused, I drew a naked woman in my exercise book. I have always been a hopeless draughtsman. She had colossal breasts and exaggerated genitals.

I knew little about women and nothing whatsoever about sex. My brother had dropped some scornful hints; my parents and teachers had said nothing. Naked women could be seen at the National Museum or in art history books. In the summer, there might be an occasional glimpse of a bottom or a naked breast. This lack of information had not been a problem. I was spared temptations; nor was I tormented by curiosity.

One insignificant episode had left a definite impression. A middle-aged widow called Alla Petréus was a friend of the family. She was of Finland-Swedish origin and took a lively interest in church affairs. Because of some temporary epidemic affecting the parsonage, I had to spend a few weeks with Aunt Alla. She lived in a huge apartment on Strandvägen with a view over Skeppsholmen and innumerable timber boats. The noise from the street did not penetrate up to her quiet sunny rooms, which overflowed with intriguing and exciting art nouveau objects.

Alla Petréus was certainly not beautiful. She wore thick glasses and walked in a mannish way. When she laughed, which she did a great deal, saliva appeared in the corners of her mouth. She dressed elegantly and wore large hats which she had to take off at the movies. She had a fine complexion, warm brown eyes and soft hands. She had several variously shaped birthmarks on her neck and smelt of some exotic perfume. She had a deep, almost mannish voice. I was happy to be staying with her, and my walk to school had been halved. Her maidservant and cook both spoke Finnish, but spoilt me and pinched my cheeks and bottom.

One evening I was to have a bath. The maid filled the bath and poured into it something that smelt good. I got into the hot water and dozed with pleasure. Alla Petréus knocked on the door to ask if I had fallen asleep. When I did not answer, she came in. She was wearing a green bathrobe which she at once took off.

She told me she was going to scrub my back. I turned over and she got into the bath, soaped me and scrubbed me with a stiff brush, then rinsed me with her soft hands. Then she took my hand, drew it towards her and pulled it between her thighs. The pulse in my neck throbbed as she parted my fingers and pressed them further in towards her loins. She enclosed my penis in her other hand and it reacted astonishingly and vigorously. She carefully pulled back my foreskin and poked away a mass of white stuff that had collected round my penis. All this was most pleasurable and not in the least frightening.

She held me firmly between her strong soft thighs and let me be rocked without resistance or fear into a weighty almost painful enjoyment.

I was eight, perhaps nine years old. Aunt Alla and I often met at home at the parsonage, but the matter was never mentioned, though sometimes she looked at me through her thick glasses and laughed slightly. We had a mutual secret.

This memory, five years later, had almost faded, but was in future to be transformed into a painfully enjoyable, guilt-ridden, constantly repeated performance, roughly like the cinematograph's constantly repeated loop, wound on by some demon who hated me and wished me torment and distress.

So I drew a naked woman in my blue exercise book, the light warmed me and the Solhemmet nurses marched on. I rubbed myself cautiously between my legs, unbuttoned my trousers and let my bluish-red and slightly trembling prick stand up, free and large. Now and again I rubbed it carefully, an enjoyable process in an unfamiliar and slightly frightening way. I went on drawing at the same time and another naked woman appeared, rather bolder than the first. I drew a prick for her, cut it out, then cut a hole in between the woman's legs and pushed it in.

I suddenly felt as if my body was going to explode and that something I was incapable of controlling was on its way out. I rushed over to the toilet on the other side of the hall and locked myself in. The enjoyment had now turned into physical pain, my nice little willie, which I had previously regarded with absent-minded interest, had suddenly been transformed into a throbbing demon sending violent sensations of pain up towards my stomach and down my thighs. I didn't know what to do with this mighty enemy. I took a firm hold of him with my hand and the detonation occurred simultaneously. To my dismay, an unknown fluid spurted out over my hands, my trousers, the toilet seat, the net curtain over the window, the walls and the blue towelling mat on the floor. In my horror, I thought that I and everything around me was being soiled by this unfamiliar mess welling out of my body. I knew nothing, understood nothing, had never had any wet dreams and my hard-on had come suddenly and vanished just as quickly.

My sexuality struck me like a clap of thunder, incomprehensible, hostile and tormenting. I still don't know how this happened, why this profound bodily change came so without warning, why it was so painful and from the first moment so guilt-laden. If the fear of sex had penetrated us children through our skin, it was in our nursery like an invisible poisonous gas. No one had said anything, no one had warned us, least of all frightened us.

This illness or obsession afflicted me without pity, the action constantly repeating itself, almost compulsorily.

For lack of anyone better, I asked my brother if he had ever had a similar experience. He grinned amiably and told me that as he was seventeen he lived a sound satisfactory sex life with a teacher who gave him extra lessons in German. He did not want to hear about my sickly filth. If I wanted any more information, I could read about something called masturbation in the family medical book. I did so.

There it stated in plain language that masturbation was called self-abuse and it was a youthful vice that had to be resisted by all possible means, that it led to pallor, sweating, trembling, black rings round the eyes, concentration difficulties and equilibrium disturbances. In more serious cases the disease led to softening of the brain, attacks on the spinal cord, epilepsy, unconsciousness and an early death. With these prospects for the future before my eyes, I continued my activities with terror and enjoyment. I had no one to talk to, nor anyone to ask. I had constantly to be on my guard, constantly concealing my terrible secret.

In desperation I turned to Jesus and asked my father if I could attend confirmation classes a year earlier than planned. My request was granted and through spiritual exercises and prayers I tried to obtain release from my curse. The night before my first communion, I tried with all my might to resist my demon. I fought with him until long into the small hours, but lost the battle. Jesus punished me with a gigantic infected pimple right in the middle of my pallid forehead. When I received the means of grace my stomach contracted and I almost threw up.

Today, all this must seem comical, but at the time it was bitter reality. The dividing wall between my real life and my secret life grew higher and soon became insurmountable. Lying became more and more necessary. My fantasy world suffered a short-circuit and it took several years and many kind tactful helpers to repair it. My isolation became hermetic and I thought I was going mad. I found some consolation in the anarchical bantering tone in Strindberg's *Getting Married* stories. His words on communion were gracious and the story about the happy viveur who survived his respectable brother was reassuring. But how the hell could I get hold of a woman, any woman? Everyone screwed except me; I who masturbated, was pale, sweated, had black rings round my eyes and difficulties in concentrating.

In addition to all that, I was thin, hung my head, was irascible, started rows, shouted and yelled, getting bad marks and my ears boxed. The cinema and the side row in the upper circle of Dramaten were my only refuge.

That summer we did not go to Våroms as usual, but stayed in a yellow house in a thickly wooded bay on the island of Smådalarö, the result of a prolonged and embittered tug-of-war behind the parsonage's increasingly cracking façade. Father hated Våroms, Grandmother and the suffocating heat of inland. Mother loathed the sea, the archipelago and the wind, which gave her pains in her shoulders. For some unknown reason, she had now given up her opposition. Ekebo on Smådalarö was to be our idyllic summer place for many years ahead.

For me, the archipelago was a bewildering revelation. There were summer visitors and their children there, many of them of my age. They were adventurous, beautiful and cruel. I was spotty, dressed wrongly, stammered, laughed loudly and without reason, was hopeless at all sports, dared not dive and liked talking about Nietzsche, a fairly useless social talent on the stony shore where we bathed.

The girls had breasts, hips, bottoms and cheerful mocking laughs. I lay with them all in my hot little attic room, torturing and despising them.

Dances were held on Saturday nights in the manor farm barn, everything there exactly as in Strindberg's *Miss Julie*, the night light, the excitement, the heavy scents of the bird-cherries and lilacs, the squealing fiddle, the rejection and acceptance, the games and the cruelty. Owing to the shortage of male partners at the Saturday dances, I was restored to favour, but dared not touch the girls as I immediately got a hard-on. I also danced badly and was gradually discarded, embittered and furious, hurt and ridiculous, terrified and withdrawn. Puberty, bourgeois style, summer 1932.

I read ceaselessly, often without understanding, but I had a sensitive ear for tone: Dostoevsky, Tolstoy, Balzac, Defoe, Swift, Flaubert, Nietzsche and, of course, Strindberg.

I no longer had any words. I started stammering and biting my nails. My loathing of myself and life itself was suffocating me. I walked hunched up, my head thrust forward, the cause of constant reprimands. The strange thing was that I never questioned my wretched life. I thought it should be like that.

*　　*　　*

Anna Lindberg and I were contemporaries. We were in what was called the ninth grade, which represented the last step before the gymnasium. The school was called the Palmgren-ska Samskola and stood on the corner of Skeppargatan and Kommendörgatan. The three hundred and fifty pupils were accommodated in pleasant but cramped premises in a private house. The teachers were considered to represent a more modern and more advanced education than that practised in the public grammar schools. This was hardly true, because the majority of them were also employed at Östermalm Grammar school, five minutes walking distance away from the Palm-gren's.

They were the same shitty masters and the same shitty crammers in both places. The main difference was probably that the term's fees were considerably higher at Palmgren's, and it was also a mixed school. In our class, there were twenty-one boys and eight girls – including Anna.

The pupils sat in pairs at old-fashioned desks. The teacher occupied a desk on a platform in one corner. The blackboard was out in front of us. It was always raining outside the three windows, the light in the classroom a semi-twilight with six electric bulbs struggling listlessly with the failing daylight. The smell of wet shoes, unwashed underclothes, sweat and urine had forever permeated the walls and furniture. It was an institution, a storage place, based on an unholy alliance between authorities and family. The stink of boredom was sometimes penetrating, sometimes suffocating. The class was a miniature reflection of pre-war society; indolence, indifference, opportunism, sucking-up, bullying and a few confused flashes of revolt, idealism and curiosity. But anarchists were kept in place by society, school and home. Punishments were exemplary and often affected the offender for life. The teaching methods largely consisted of punishments, rewards and the implanting of a guilty conscience. Many of the teachers were National Socialists, Nazi-adherents, some from foolishness or bitterness over their failure to gain academic advancement, others from idealism and veneration of the old Germany, 'a nation of poets and thinkers'.

Naturally there were exceptions; some teachers and pupils were gifted and irrepressible people who opened doors and let in air and light. They were not many. Our headmaster was a fawning, power-mad man and a prominent string-puller in the Mission Society. He liked taking morning prayers, slimy preaching consisting of sentimental lamentations over how Jesus would grieve if he visited the Palmgren's School that very day, or fire-and-brimstone sermons on politics, traffic and the epidemic spread of jazz culture.

Homework not done, humbug, cheating, ingratiation, suppressed rage and stinking farts formed the dreary everyday routine. The girls huddled together in a giggling whispering conspiracy. The boys yelled with breaking voices, fought, kicked a ball, prepared cribs or did neglected homework.

I sat roughly in the middle of the class, Anna diagonally in front of me by the window. I thought she was ugly. Everyone thought so. She was a tall, fat girl with round shoulders, bad posture, large breasts, big hips and a bouncing bottom. Her hair was mousy fair, parted at the side and cut short. Her eyes were askew, one blue, the other brown. She had high cheek bones, swollen protruding lips; her cheeks were childishly round and there was a dimple in her well-shaped chin. From her right eyebrow up to her hairline she had a scar which turned red when she cried or was angry. Her hands were square with short fat fingers, her legs long and shapely, her feet small with high arches, and one of her little toes was missing. She smelt of girl and children's soap. She wore ill-fitting brown skirts and pink or pale-blue silk blouses. She was clever, quick-witted and kind. Malicious rumour had it that her father had run away with someone who was 'not quite a lady'. It was also said that Anna's mother lived with a red-haired travelling salesman, that he maltreated both mother and daughter, and that she did not pay full fees.

Both Anna and I were outsiders. I was peculiar and she was ugly. We were not troubled or bullied by our schoolmates.

One Sunday we met at the Karla cinema matinée. It turned out that we both often went to the cinema and liked it. In contrast to me, Anna had plenty of pocket-money at her disposal, so I let her pay for me. Gradually I was allowed to go back home with her. Her apartment was spacious but shabby, one floor up in a block facing Nybrogatan at the corner of Valhallavägen.

Anna's room was dark and rectangular, containing assorted furniture, a worn rug and a tiled stove, over by the window a white desk which she had inherited from her paternal grandmother. Her bed was of a sofa-bed kind and the coverlet and cushions had Turkish patterns on them. Anna's mother was friendly towards me, but without cordiality.

Outwardly she was like her daughter, but her mouth was bitter, her skin yellowish, her thin hair grey, backcombed and brushed back. There was no sign of the red-haired salesman.

Anna and I began to do our homework together. She was introduced at the parsonage and surprisingly enough was accepted. Presumably she was considered so plain that she would be no threat to my virtue. She was indulgently integrated into the family, had Sunday dinner of roast veal and cucumber with us, was examined with scornfully ironic looks by my brother, replied quickly and openly to questions put to her and collaborated on several toy-theatre performances.

Anna's plump goodness led to a lessening of the tension between me and the rest of the family.

What they did not know, on the other hand, was that Anna's mother was seldom home in the evenings and that our homework activities developed immediately into confused but obstinate exercises on the violently creaking bed.

We were lonely, starved, inquisitive and utterly ignorant. Anna's virginity offered resistance and the hammocklike bed made the operation more difficult. We never dared take our clothes off, but practised fully dressed minus Anna's woollen knickers. We were at once careless and cautious, and I usually ejaculated somewhere between her hard suspender belt and soft stomach. Anna was brave and clever and suggested we should lie on the floor in front of the tiled stove, something she had seen in a film. We set fire to a few sticks and newspapers in the stove and tore off our restraining clothes. Anna squealed and laughed, I sank deeply inward in a secretive way, Anna shrieked, it hurt but she held on to me. I dutifully tried to free myself, she wrapped her legs round my back, I sank even deeper, Anna cried, tears and snot running all over her face. We kissed with lips pressed together: 'Now I'm pregnant,' she whispered. 'I felt I got pregnant.' She was laughing and crying. I was seized with icy terror and tried to bring her back to her senses, she must wash herself and the mat at once. We both had blood on us and some had got on the mat.

At that moment, the hall door opened and Anna's mother appeared. Anna was sitting on the floor trying to get her knickers on and push her big breasts inside her vest. I pulled at my jersey to hide some dark spots round my fly.

Mrs Lindberg slapped my face, took me by the ear and dragged me twice round the room, then stopped, boxed my ears again and said with a menacing smile that I should damned well stop making her daughter pregnant. Otherwise we could do as we liked, as long as she didn't have to slip in it. After saying that, she turned her back on me and slammed the door behind her.

I did not love Anna, as there was no love where I lived and breathed. I had certainly been encased in a wealth of love in my childhood, but I had forgotten what it tasted like. I did not feel love for anyone or anything, least of all for myself. Anna's feelings were not so corroded. She had someone to hug, to kiss, to play with, a troublesome, temperamental, naughty doll, who talked and talked, sometimes amusingly, sometimes just stupidly or so childishly you might wonder whether he really was fourteen. Sometimes he wouldn't walk beside her in the street, maintaining she was too fat and he too thin and they looked silly together.

Sometimes, when the pressure from the parsonage grew too overwhelming, I hit her, and she hit me back. We were equally strong but I was the angrier, so our fights ended with her crying and my exits. We were always reconciled. She once got a black eye, another time a split lip, and it amused her to show off her wounds at school. If anyone asked her who had done this to her, she said her lover had. Everyone laughed, because no one believed that the pastor's skinny stammering son was capable of such outbursts.

One Sunday before morning service, Anna phoned and shouted that Palle was murdering her mother. I rushed to the rescue. Anna opened the hall door and at that moment I received a stunning blow on the mouth and fell backwards against the shelf where the galoshes were kept. The red-haired travelling salesman, in nothing but a nightshirt and short socks, was tumbling around with both mother and daughter, shouting that he would kill them. There would at last be an end to all these damned betrayals. He was sick of keeping a whore and a whore's daughter. He had a hold on the older woman's throat, and her face was dark red, her mouth wide open. Anna and I tried to force open his hands, but in the end Anna rushed out into the kitchen for a carving-knife and screamed that she would stab him to death. He at once let go, hit me again in the face, at which I returned the blow, but missed. Then without a word he got dressed, put his bowler hat on at an angle, thrust his arm into his dark overcoat, flung the porch key on the floor and was gone.

Anna's mother made coffee and sandwiches and a neighbour rang the bell to ask what had happened. Anna dragged me into her room and examined my injuries. A sliver of a front tooth had been knocked out (as I write this I can still feel its absence with my tongue).

To me, all this was interesting but unreal. What was happening around me was like bits of film loosely put together, partly incomprehensible, sometimes simply sad. I found to my surprise that my senses did indeed register the external reality, but the impulses never reached as far as my emotions. They inhabited a closed room and were produced on command, but never rashly. My reality was so profoundly divided that it had lost consciousness.

I have dwelt upon this row in the shabby apartment in Nybrogatan because I remember every single moment of it, every moment, the shouts and remarks, the light of reflections in the windows on the opposite side of the street, the smell of frying and squalor, the man's haircream in his greasy red hair. I remember it all, and each individual item. But there are no emotions linked with these impressions of my senses. Was I frightened, angry, embarrassed, curious or just hysterical? I don't know.

*   *   *

Now that I have the key in my hand, I know that more than forty years were to go by before my emotions were released from that closed room where they had been imprisoned. I existed on the memory of feelings. I knew perfectly well how emotions should be reproduced, but the spontaneous expression of them was never spontaneous. There was always a micro-second between my intuitive experience and its emotional expression.

Today, when I fancy that I have more or less recovered, I wonder whether there are, or ever will be, instruments which can measure a neurosis that so effectively gave the appearance of normality.

Anna was invited to my fifteenth birthday, which we celebrated in the yellow house on Smådalarö. She shared one of the attic rooms with my sister. At sunrise, I woke her and we slipped down to the bay and rowed out towards Jungfrufärden, past Rödudd and Stendörren. We rowed across the bay, straight into all that motionlessness, the glinting of the sun and the indolent waves from Saltsjön soundlessly making their morning way from Utö to Dalarö.

We got back in time for breakfast and the birthday congratulations. Our backs and shoulders were sunburnt, our lips a little stiff and tasting of salt, our eyes half-blinded from all that light.

We had seen each other's nakedness for the first time.

10

In the summer when I was sixteen, I was sent to Germany as an exchange student. This entailed spending six weeks in a German family with a boy of my own age. When his summer holiday started, he went back with me to Sweden and stayed for the same period of time.

I was placed with a pastor's family in Thüringen, in a small town called Haina, halfway between Weimar and Eisenach. The town was in a valley and surrounded by prosperous villages. A muddy slow-moving river wound its way between the houses and the town had an outsize church, a market square with a war memorial and a bus station.

The family was large, six sons and three daughters, the pastor and his wife, plus an old relative, who was a deaconess or *dienende Schwester* [serving sister]. She had a moustache, sweated profusely and ruled the family with a rod of iron. The head of the household was a slight man with a goatee beard, friendly blue eyes, tufts of cotton wool in his ears and a black beret pulled low down over his forehead. He was widely read and musical, played several instruments and sang in a soft tenor. His wife was fat, worn out and submissive; she spent most of her time in the kitchen and patted me shyly on the cheek. Perhaps she was trying to apologize for the house being so humble.

My friend, Hannes, seemed to have been cut out of a National-Socialist propaganda broadsheet, blond, tall and blue-eyed, with a fresh smile, very small ears and the first growth of beard. We made mutual efforts to understand each other, but it was not easy. My German was the result of cramming nothing but grammar, a common practice at the time, when the consideration that a language might possibly be spoken was not part of the curriculum.

The days were tedious. At seven o'clock in the morning, the children of the house went off to school and I was left alone with the adults. I read, roamed about and was homesick. I preferred being in the pastor's study and going with him when he was out visiting in the parish. He drove a ramshackle old car with a high hood, over roads dusty in the still heat and with angry fat geese marching everywhere.

I asked the pastor whether I should raise my arm and say Heil Hitler like all the others. He replied: '*Lieber Ingmar, das wird als mehr eine Höflichkeit betrachtet.*' [My dear Ingmar, that will be regarded as more than mere politeness.] I raised my arm and said 'Heil Hitler', and it felt odd.

After a while, Hannes suggested I should go with him to school and listen in on the lessons. With a choice between the devil and the deep blue sea, I chose the school, which was in a larger town a few kilometres bicycle ride from Haina. I was received with enthusiastic cordiality and allowed to sit next to Hannes. The classroom was spacious, shabby and rather cold and damp, despite the summer heat outside the tall windows. The subject was Religious Knowledge, but Hitler's *Mein Kampf* lay on the desks. The teacher read something out of a paper called *Der Stürmer*. I remember only one phrase that seemed peculiar to me. Again and again, he repeated in a factual tone of voice, *von den Juden vergiftet* [poisoned by the Jews]. I asked later what it meant. Hannes laughed. '*Ach, Ingmar, das alles ist nicht für Auslander.*' [Oh, Ingmar, all that's not for foreigners.]

IB as a baby in the arms of his brother, Dag.

IB's father, Erik, as a boy, with IB's paternal
grandmother.

IB's mother, Karin, as a girl, with IB's maternal grandmother and great grandmother.

IB's maternal grandmother, Anna Åkerblom, a highly important influence on his young life; and grandfather, Johan Åkerblom, a railroad engineer. He built Våroms, the country house which played such a significant part in IB's childhood.

Våroms. The railway ran below the house.

IB's mother, aged twenty.

IB's parents during their engagement. Photographed at Våroms.

Smiling picture of IB's mother. About 1913, when she was newly married; and IB, with his younger sister, Margareta, and older brother, Dag. About 1922.

Inset: the schoolboy. *Above*: the young producer of student theatre, about 1941.

The young film director. A posed publicity photograph.

IB's parents, with Teddy, the poodle.

IB in the late 1940s.

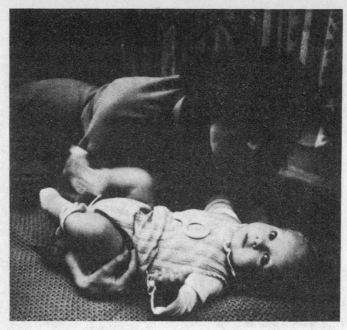

Gun Hagberg, with little Ingmar.

Directing *Summer with Monika*, which starred
Harriet Andersson (*right*).

On Sundays, the family went to morning service, and the pastor's sermon was surprising for his text was not from the gospels but from *Mein Kampf*. After church, coffee was served in the church hall. There were a number of people in uniform, so I had several opportunities to raise my arm and say 'Heil Hitler'.

All the young people in the house were in organizations, the boys in the *Hitler-Jugend*, the girls in *Bund Deutscher Mädel*. There was drilling with spades instead of rifles in the afternoons, or sports at the sports stadium, lectures with film shows in the evenings, or we sang and danced. We could bathe in the river, but with some difficulty, for the river bed was muddy and the water smelly. The girls' sanitary towels, crocheted out of thick white cotton, hung out to dry in the primitive washroom, which had no hot water or other conveniences.

There was to be a party rally in Weimar, a gigantic procession with Hitler to the fore. Everyone bustled around the house, shirts were washed and ironed, boots and straps polished, and the young people set off at dawn. I would go later in the car with the pastor and his wife. The family made quite a fuss about being given tickets near the platform of honour and someone suggested as a joke that my presence might be the reason for their good seats.

That morning, the telephone rang. It was from home, and far away I could hear Aunt Anna's sonorous voice. This expensive call was possible because of her immense wealth. She did not even bother to hurry, but only gradually came to the point. She told me a friend of hers, married to a banker and living in Weimar, had heard from Mother that I was staying nearby, so she had at once telephoned her friend and suggested I should visit the family. Aunt Anna then spoke to the pastor in fluent German, and returned to the conversation with me, pleased that I would be meeting her friend and her lovely children.

We arrived in Weimar at about midday. The parade and Hitler's speech were to begin at three o'clock. The town was already seething with excitement, people in their best clothes or uniforms strolling along the streets. Bands were playing everywhere and the houses were hung with garlands of flowers and banners. The church bells, both gloomy Protestant and cheerful Catholic, were ringing, and a big fair had been set up in one of the old squares. They were advertising Wagner's *Rienzi* at the Opera House as a gala performance with fireworks afterwards.

The pastor's family and I were placed close to the saluting platform. While we were waiting in the sticky heat, we drank beer and ate sandwiches out of the greasy packets the pastor's wife had clutched to her swelling bosom all through the journey.

On the stroke of three, we heard something resembling an approaching hurricane, the sombre frightening sound spreading along the streets and resounding off the walls of buildings. Far away in the extension of the square, a procession of open black cars was crawling along. The roaring sound grew louder and drowned the claps of thunder, the rain falling like a transparent curtain and the crashes detonating above the arena.

No one took the slightest notice of the storm, all attention, all enthusiasm, all this glory centred on one single figure. He stood quite still in the huge black car slowly swinging into the square. He turned and looked at the cheering weeping obsessed crowds, the rain running down his face and dark patches of moisture appearing on his uniform. Then he stepped slowly down on to the red carpet and walked alone towards the platform, his entourage keeping at a distance.

Suddenly silence fell, the rain splashing against the stone-laid streets and balustrades the only sound. The Führer spoke. It was a short speech. I did not understand much, but the voice was sometimes lofty, sometimes bantering, the gestures synchronized and well matched. When the speech was over, everyone shouted his *Heil*, the rain stopped and the hot bright light broke through the blue-black formations of clouds. A huge band played and the parade poured out through the side streets in and across the square round the platform and then on past the theatre and the cathedral.

I had never seen anything like this eruption of immense energy. I shouted like everyone else, held out my arm like everyone else, howled like everyone else and loved it like everyone else.

During our nightly conversations, Hannes had explained the Abyssinian war to me, how important it was that Mussolini was at last paying attention to the natives who toiled in the darkness, and how he was generously giving them the benefit of ancient Italian culture. He had also said that far away up there in Scandinavia we did not understand how, after the collapse, the Jews had exploited the German people. He explained how the Germans had created a bulwark against communism, and how the Jews had consistently sabotaged this bulwark, and how we must all love the man who had shaped our common destiny and decisively welded us together into one will, one strength, one people.

I was given a present by the family on my birthday, a photograph of Hitler. Hannes hung it up above my bed so that 'I would always have the man before my eyes', so that I should learn to love him in the same way as Hannes and the Haid family loved him.

I loved him too. For many years, I was on Hitler's side, delighted by his successes and saddened by his defeats.

My brother was one of the founders and organizers of the Swedish National-Socialist party, and my father voted several times for them. Our history teacher worshipped 'the old Germany', our gymnastics teacher went to officers' meetings in Bavaria every summer; some of the pastors in the parish were crypto-Nazis and the family's closest friends expressed strong sympathies for the 'new Germany'.

*   *   *

When all the evidence from the concentration camps actually hit me, my mind could not at first accept what my eyes were registering. Like so many others, I said the pictures were

prearranged propaganda lies. When the truth finally con-
quered my resistance, I was overcome with despair, and my
self-contempt, already a severe burden, accelerated beyond
the borders of endurance. I did not realize until long
afterwards that I was guilty by association only.

As an '*Austauschkind*', an exchange student, unvaccinated
and unprepared, I fell headlong into an atmosphere glowing
with idealism and hero worship. I was also suddenly exposed
to an aggressiveness which to a great extent was in harmony
with my own. The surface lustre blinded me, and I did not see
the darkness.

When I went to Gothenburg Municipal Theatre the year
after the end of the war, there was a deep rift between, on the
one side, the German Ufa newsreel commentators, the
organizers of the Swedish National Film Chamber and their
usual fellow-travellers and, on the other, the Jews, the anti-
Nazi followers of Segerstedt, the editor of the pro-Allies
Gothenburg newspaper, and the actors with their Norwegian
and Danish friends. They sat in an atmosphere thick with
mutual loathing, munching sandwiches they had brought
with them and drinking the canteen's disgusting coffee.

When the bell rang, they went on stage and became the best
ensemble theatre in the country.

I did not mention my aberrations and despair, but a strange
decision slowly matured. Politics – never again! Of course, I
should have made an utterly different decision.

*   *   *

The festivities in Weimar went on all evening and through the
night. The pastor drove me to the banker's house, a handsome
art nouveau mansion of marble, surrounded by a fragrant
park, the street quietly distinguished with similar buildings
each side of it. I walked up the broad steps and rang the bell. A
maid in black with a lace cap on her elaborate hairdo opened
the door and I stammered out my name. She laughed and
pulled me into the hall.

Aunt Anna's friend was blonde, large and unaffectedly

kind. Her name was Annie, her mother Swedish and her father American. She spoke broken Swedish and was extremely elegant, because she and her husband were to be present at that evening's performance at the opera. I was steered into the breakfast room where they were having tea and a cold meal. The most beautiful people I had ever seen were sitting all round the neatly laid table. The banker was a tall dark gentleman with a well-groomed beard and an amiably ironic expression behind his glasses. The younger daughter, Clara, known as Clärchen, was sitting beside him, very like her father, tall, dark and white-skinned with almost black eyes and a pale full mouth. She had a slight squint which in some inexplicable way increased her charm.

Her brothers were older, dark like Clärchen, but with blue eyes. They were both wearing English blazers with some kind of university badges on the breast pocket.

I sank into a chair beside Aunt Annie, who was pouring out tea and handing round sandwiches. There were pictures everywhere, silver, soft rugs on great stretches of parquet flooring, ornamental marble columns, heavy draperies and lintels. In the outer dining room, a rose window glowed in the light of the setting sun.

When the meal was over, I was taken to my first floor room alongside the boys' two-roomed suites. We shared a bathroom with several basins and a sunken bath. Annie said goodbye after she had shown me all this luxury; the chauffeur was standing to attention in the hall and her husband waiting on the stairs.

Clärchen appeared wearing high-heeled shoes (making her taller than me) and a dull-red informal dress, her hair loose and tumbling down over her shoulders. She put her finger to her lips in a playful conspiratorial gesture.

She took me by the hand and guided me through a long corridor to a tower room that was clearly not used, as the furniture was covered and the crystal chandelier in the ceiling enveloped in tulle. A few lighted candles were reflected in large wall mirrors. Clärchen's brothers were already there, smoking flat Turkish cigarettes and sipping brandy. A portable gramophone stood on a small gilded table, wound up and ready. David, the younger of the brothers, stuffed a couple of socks into the soundbox.

A record with a blue Telefunken label on it lay on the turntable. The needle was dropped into the track and the harsh but subdued notes of the overture of *The Threepenny Opera* rose out of the black box. After the speaker's sarcastic words about why *The Threepenny Opera* was called just that, there followed 'The Ballad of Mac the Knife': *'Und Macheath der hat ein Messer/Doch das Messer sieht man nicht.'* [And Macheath has got a knife/But not in such an obvious place.] and then 'Pirate Jenny' with Lotte Lenya, that wounded voice, that scornfully arrogant tone, and then her gentleness and bantering: *'Und wenn der Kopf fällt, sag ich? "Hoppla!"'* [And as the first head rolls I'll say: 'Hoppla!']

A whole world of which I had never had an inkling, despair without tears, desperation that wept! *'Versuch es nur, von deinem Kopf lebt höchstens eine Laus.'* [Just you try – only one louse at most can live on your head.] I gulped brandy, smoked Turkish cigarettes and felt slightly sick. Why all this secrecy with night-time concerts, closed doors, soft gramophone needles and socks in the soundbox? 'It's banned music,' Horst said. 'Brecht and Weill are banned. We found the records in London and smuggled them over so that Clärchen could hear them too.'

He picked out the next record, Lewis Ruth's band crashing in. *'Was ich möchte, ist es viel? Einmal in dem tristen Leben einem Mann mich hinzugeben. Ist das ein zu hohes Ziel?'* [What I'd like, is that a lot? Once in my miserable life to devote myself to a man. Is that too high an aim?] The tomb-like sonorous bass broke in: *'Ein guter Mensch sein? Ja, wer wär's nicht gern.'* [Being a good person? Yes, who wouldn't like to be that.]

The acrid perfumed cigarette smoke floated round us and the moon shone down on the trees in the park. Clärchen was holding her head half turned away and was staring into the big mirror between the windows, her hand over one eye. David filled my glass. The moment burst like a thin membrane and I floated unresisting on to the next moment, which immediately burst, then on and on.

The Threepenny Opera finale. 'Und man siehet die im Lichte, die im Dunkeln sieht man nicht.' I didn't understand the words, anyhow not many of them, but I have always, like a shrewd animal, understood tone of voice, and I understood this tone of voice. It sank into my deepest consciousness, to remain there as part of me.

Twenty years later I at last had the opportunity to stage The Threepenny Opera in Sweden. What a dreadful compromise, what a parody of great ambitions, what cowardice, what betrayal of monumental insight! All resources, both artistic and material, had been put at my disposal and I failed because I was foolish and vain, an unbeatable combination when you are directing. I did not think about Clärchen's half-illuminated face and the harsh moonlight, the Turkish cigarettes and David leaning over the black portable gramophone. We had had the opportunity to listen to those scratchy Telefunken records, but we had done so absentmindedly, and agreed that the music would have to be reorchestrated. Provincial idiots and village geniuses. That's what it was like then. What's it like now?

The concert went on with Louis Armstrong, Fats Waller and Duke Ellington. I fell asleep with excitement and brandy, but woke a short time later to find myself lying in my big bed, pale dawn outside the window and Clärchen sitting at the end of the bed wrapped in a pleated dressing gown, her hair in curlers. She was looking steadily and curiously at me. When she saw that I was awake, she nodded with a smile and disappeared without a sound.

Six months later, I received a letter with Clärchen's bold generous handwriting on the envelope, franked in Switzerland. She reminded me in a jocular way that we had promised to write to each other but that I had evidently forgotten our agreement. She told me she was back at her boarding school and that her parents had gone to friends in Canada, and that she herself was to start at art school in Paris when she left school. The brothers had been able to return to their university thanks to the intervention of the British Ambassador. She did not think the family would ever return to Weimar.

That was one page of the letter. The other was as follows:

My name isn't really Clara, but Thea. That's not in my passport. My religious upbringing, as I've told you, has been strictly orthodox and I'm sure I correspond to what my mother and father think a good daughter ought to be.

I have suffered a great many bodily ills, the worst an irritation which has persecuted me like a waking nightmare for two years. Another torment is my over-developed sensitivity. I react violently to sudden noises, intense light (I'm blind in one eye) or unpleasant smells. The normal pressure of a dress, for instance, can drive me mad with pain. When I was fifteen, I married a young Austrian actor. I wanted to start in the theatre, but the marriage was unhappy, I had a child who died, and I went back to the school in Switzerland. Now the dry twilight rattles above the child's head. I can't go on. I cry now.

My glass eye also weeps.

I pretend I am a saint or a martyr. I can sit for hours at the big table in the closed room (where we played the forbidden records). I can sit for hours gazing at the palms of my hands. Once a redness appeared out of my left palm, but no blood. I pretend I am sacrificing myself for my brothers. I am saving them from mortal danger. I pretend ecstasy and speak to the Holy Virgin. I pretend faith and disbelief, defiance and doubt. I pretend I am a rejected sinner with an insupportable burden of guilt. Suddenly I reject the guilt and forgive myself. It's all a game. I am pretending.

Within the game, I am the same, sometimes extremely tragic, sometimes boundlessly exhilarated. All with the same small effort. I confided in a doctor (I've been to so many doctors). He told me that my dreaming and idle life were damaging my psyche. He prescribed specific things that would force me to leave the prison of my egocentricity. Order. Self-discipline. Tasks. Corsets. My father, who is so gentle, so wise and coolly calculating, says that I should not worry, that everything exists in all things, and living is a torment that one overcomes with resignation, but preferably without cynicism. I am not keen on that kind of effort, so I'm thinking of going even further into my games, taking them more seriously, if you understand what I mean.

Please write back immediately and tell me all, in whatever language you like except Swedish, which perhaps I shall have to learn one day. Write and tell me about yourself, you, my youngest brother, I yearn for you!

Then followed some instructions about her future addresses and an affectionate but formal ending, signed Clara: *Mein lieber Ingmar ich umarme Dich fest, bist Du noch so schrecklich dünn? Clara.* [My dear Ingmar, I hug you tight. Are you still so terribly thin?]

I never answered her letter. Language difficulties were insuperable and I did not want to make a fool of myself. On the other hand, I have kept her letter. I used it almost word for word in a film called *The Rite* in 1969.

After a few more days in Weimar and a terrible week in Haina, I became involved in a religious dispute with the old deaconess. She had found out that I read Strindberg. She maintained he was a rabid radical, a woman hater and a mocker of God. She scolded me, objected to my reading habits and questioned whether their Hannes should be allowed to stay with a family which permitted such literature. I replied in bad German that in my home country we had hitherto had freedom of religious belief and freedom of expression (democracy was now suddenly fitting). The storm abated. Hannes and I set off for home.

*

We were all to assemble in Berlin, from where a special train was to take us to Stockholm. We stayed in a gigantic youth hostel on the outskirts of the city. Provided with Aunt Annie's discreet reinforcement of my travel funds, I escaped from a planned tour of monuments and other sights.

I took a bus outside the youth hostel and stayed on it until it reached the terminus. It was a hot July afternoon, about six o'clock, and I was bewildered and lost in the roaring rumble and movement which blocked all my senses. I chose a side street at random, encountered an even heavier stream of traffic, followed it and came to a huge bridge called Kurfürstenbrücke, where there was a palace on the other side of the water. I stood for several hours by the balustrade, watching dusk falling and the shadows darken over the rushing, stinking river. The roar increased.

I passed yet another bridge over a narrower river with sunken wooden quays and piles that were being hammered with a hellish noise into the water by a pile-driver. A barge was anchored farther away and two men were sitting in basket chairs on it, fishing and drinking beer. I was drawn even further into the sluggish motion of the city. Nothing happened. I was not even accosted by a prostitute, although they had begun to take up their positions for the evening. I was hungry and thirsty, but dared not go into any eating place.

Night fell. Still nothing happened. Exhausted and disappointed, I took a taxi back to the hostel, the fare swallowing the last of my money. They were just about to telephone the police when I appeared.

The next morning we were taken to Stockholm on an endlessly long special train of old carriages with wooden seats and open platforms. It poured with rain. I stood in the rain and the noise, shouted and played the fool to make someone take notice of me, preferably a girl. I went on like that for several hours. On the ferry, I considered jumping into the sea, but was afraid of being caught up in the propellers. Towards nightfall, I pretended to be drunk, fell down and tried to spew. In the end a plump freckled girl intervened, pulled my hair, gave me a good shaking and said sternly that I should stop making an ass of myself. I stopped at once, sat down in a corner, ate an orange and fell asleep. When I woke, we were in Södertälje.

In my dreams, I have often been in Berlin. Not the real Berlin, but a stage setting, a boundless unwieldy city of smoke-blackened monumental buildings, church towers and statues. I roam through the unceasing flow of traffic, everything unfamiliar and yet familiar. I feel terror and delight and know pretty well where I am going. I am looking for the area beyond the bridges, the part of the city where something is going to happen. I am walking up a steep hill, a menacing aeroplane passes between the houses, then at last I come to the river. They are winching up a dead horse as large as a whale out of which water is pouring on to the pavement.

Curiosity and terror drive me on. I must get there in time for the public executions. Then I meet my dead wife. We embrace each other tenderly and look for a hotel room where we can make love. She walks with quick light steps beside me and I hold my hand on her hip. The street is brightly lit up although the sun is blazing, the sky black and moving jarringly. Now I know I have at last reached the forbidden area. The Theatre is there with that unfathomable production.

Three times I have tried to create the City of my dream. First I wrote a radio play called *The City*, about a large town in decay, its buildings collapsing and streets undermined. A few years later, I made *The Silence*, in which two sisters and a little boy are stranded in a mighty warring city with an incomprehensible language. Lastly, the most recent, I made yet another attempt in *The Serpent's Egg*. Its artistic failure was mainly due to the fact that I called the city Berlin and decided to set it in 1920. That was both thoughtless and foolish. If I had created the City of my dream, the City that is not, never was and yet manifests itself with acuteness, smells and loud sounds, if I had created *that* City, I would not only have been moving in complete freedom and with an absolute sense of belonging but also, most importantly, I would have taken the audience into an alien but secretly familiar world. Unfortunately I allowed myself to be led astray by my excursion into Berlin in the mid-1930s, that evening when absolutely nothing happened. In *The Serpent's Egg*, I created a Berlin which no one recognized, not even I.

11

After a trying battle over the appointment, Father had been put in charge of the Hedvig Eleonora parish in Stockholm, where he had served as curate in 1918. The family moved into the church apartment three floors up in Storgatan 7, opposite the church. I was allocated a large room on Jungfrugatan facing Östermalm Cellar's row of eighteenth century chimneys and a view beyond over Östermalm Square. My walk to school was to be shorter; I had an entrance of my own and more freedom of movement.

Father was a popular preacher and always had a full house. He was a conscientious good shepherd and had an invaluable talent: an unfailing memory for people. Over the years, he had baptized, confirmed, married and buried a great many of his 40,000 parishioners. He knew them all by sight, also their names and circumstances, so each person enveloped by his interest and amiable gravity felt remembered and therefore chosen. Going for a walk with Father was a complicated procedure. He kept stopping, greeting people and talking to them, naming them by name and absorbing information about children, grandchildren and relatives. Long into old age, he successfully nurtured this talent.

He was undoubtedly a much-liked parish priest and, as an administrator and manager, he was decisive but also conciliatory and diplomatic. He had not had the opportunity of choosing the people he worked with. Some of them had competed with him for the post of parish priest, while others were lazy, hypocritical and obsequious. Father managed to keep his activities fairly free of open squabbles and clerical intrigues.

The pastor's home was by tradition open to all and Mother ran a considerable organization. She involved herself in parish work and was a driving force in welfare societies. She was always at Father's side on official occasions and loyally sat in the front pew regardless of who was preaching. She also took part in conferences and arranging dinner parties. My brother was twenty and away at university in Upsala, my sister twelve and I sixteen. Our relative freedom was entirely due to our parents' excessive burden of work, but it was poisoned freedom, the tensions great and the knots impossible to unravel. What was outwardly an irreproachable picture of good family unity was inwardly misery and exhausting conflicts. Father undoubtedly possessed considerable acting ability, but off stage he was nervous, irritable and depressive. He worried about being inadequate, he agonized over his public appearances, kept writing and rewriting his sermons and was very uneasy about many of his administrative duties. He was always fretting and given to violent outbursts of temper, picking heavily on minor matters. We were not allowed to whistle, or go around with our hands in our pockets. He would suddenly decide to test our homework and anyone who stumbled was punished. He also suffered from over-sensitive hearing and loud noises enraged him. The walls of his bedroom and study were insulated, but he complained bitterly about what was then only minor traffic in Storgatan.

Mother carried a double work load and was always tense, so slept badly and used strong remedies which had side effects causing restlessness and anxiety. Like Father, she was haunted by a sense of inadequacy when faced with exagger-

ated ambitions. Her worst torment was probably the feeling
that she was slowly losing contact with us children. In her
desperation, she turned to my sister who was well-behaved
and compliant. After an attempt at suicide, my brother had
been sent to Upsala. I retreated deeper and deeper into my
own world.

It is more than possible that I am exaggerating the blackness
of the scene. No one questioned our allocated rôles or the
absurd intrigues. This was our allotted reality, life. There were
no alternatives, nor were any considered. Father occasionally
said he would have preferred to be a pastor in the country, and
that kind of challenge would probably have suited him better.
Mother wrote in her secret diary that she wanted to break up
her marriage and go to live in Italy.

One evening I was allowed to accompany Mother to see an
old friend who was head of the church publishing house, a
man called Uncle Per. He had been married, then divorced and
lived in a large dark apartment in Vasastaden. To my surprise,
Uncle Torsten, a childhood friend of Mother's and Father's,
now a bishop and married with many children, was also there.

I was given the task of working Uncle Per's big gramophone
in the echoing dining room where the music was loud, mainly
Mozart and Verdi operas. Uncle Per disappeared into his study.
Mother and Uncle Torsten stayed by the fire in the salon. I
could see them through the half-open sliding doors, each in an
armchair, faintly lit by the firelight, and Uncle Torsten was
holding Mother's hand. They were talking quietly and
because of the music I could not hear the words. I could see
Mother was crying and Uncle Torsten leaning forward, still
holding her hand.

A few hours later, Uncle Per drove us back home in his big
black car with its leather seats and dark panels of wood.

Summer and winter, we had dinner at five o'clock. When
the dining-room clock struck, we would be there, hands
washed and hair brushed, standing by our chairs. Grace was
said and we sat down, Father and Mother at either end of the
table, my sister and I on one side, my brother and Miss Agda

on the other. Miss Agda was a gentle, tall, so somewhat unsteady woman, who was really a primary schoolteacher and for many summers she had been our patient tutor and had become an intimate friend of Mother's.

The little electric bulbs in the bronze chandelier spread a murky yellow light over the table. The heavy sideboard, overloaded with silver objects, was by the pantry, with a pianoforte on the other side, the hateful music-lesson score left open on the stand. Heavy curtains at the windows, dark Arborelius pictures on the wall.

The meal started with pickled herring and potatoes, or pickled Baltic herring and potatoes, or ham-au-gratin and potatoes. Father drank schnapps and beer with this. Mother pressed an electric bell hidden under the table and the parlour maid dressed in black appeared. She cleared away the plates and cutlery, and then the main dish was served, at best meat balls, at worst macaroni pudding. Cabbage rolls or pork sausages were all right, fish loathsome, but we were careful about expressing dissatisfaction. Everything had to be eaten. Everything *was* eaten.

When the main course was over, Father finished off his schnapps, his forehead by then somewhat red. We all ate in silence. Children don't speak at table. They reply if spoken to. The obligatory question was asked. 'How did it go at school today?' followed by the obligatory answer, 'Well.' 'Have you had to do any of your essays again?' 'No.' 'What questions were you given? Could you answer them?' 'Yes, of course I could.' 'I phoned your class teacher. You've passed in maths.' 'Fancy that.'

Father smiled sarcastically. Mother took her medicine. She had recently undergone a major operation and constantly had to take medicine. Father turned to my brother. 'Imitate that idiot Nilsson.' My brother had a talent for imitating people and at once let his jaw drop, rolled his eyes, pinched his nose, and mumbled incoherently in a thick voice. Father laughed and Mother smiled reluctantly. 'Prime Minister Per Albin Hansson should be shot,' Father suddenly said. 'That whole socialist pack should be shot.' 'You mustn't say that,' said Mother, her voice controlled. 'What mustn't I say? Can't I say that we're governed by rabble and bandits?' Father's head shook very slightly. 'We must do the agenda for the church council meeting,' Mother said to distract him. 'You've already said that several times,' Father replied, his forehead now scarlet. Mother lowered her eyes and poked at her food. 'Is Lilian still ill?' she asked softly, turning to my sister. 'She's coming back to school tomorrow,' Margareta replied in a small voice. 'She can come to dinner with us on Sunday, can't she?'

Silence fell over the table; we ate, knives and forks screeching against porcelain; yellow light, the silver on the sideboard shining, the dining-room clock ticking. 'They've appointed Beronius despite the cathedral chapter's recommendation to Algård,' said Father. 'That's how it is and that's how it'll go on. Incompetence. Idiocy.' Mother shook her head, her expression slightly contemptuous. 'Is it true Arborelius is going to preach on Good Friday? No one can hear what he's saying.' 'Perhaps that's just as well,' said Father, and laughed.

*　　*　　*

Immediately after our final exams at school, my first love, Anna Lindberg, went to France to improve her French. She married there a few years later, had two children and caught polio. Her husband was killed on the second day of the war. We lost contact. Instead I courted another school friend.

Cecilia von Gotthard was red-haired, clever, quick-witted and considerably more mature than her admirer. Why she had chosen me from among all the beaux was a mystery. I was a useless lover, an even worse dancer and a conversationalist who talked ceaselessly about himself. We later became engaged and immediately were mutually unfaithful. Cecilia broke off our relationship saying that I'd never get anywhere, a judgement shared by my parents, by me and by all those around me.

Cecilia lived with her mother in a desolate show apartment in Östermalm. Her father had been an important man in the administration, then one day he had come back early from work, gone to bed and refused to get up again. He spent some time in a mental hospital, then had a child by a young nurse and moved to a small farm up in Jämtland.

Cecilia's mother was so ashamed of this social disaster she had moved into the dark maid's room behind the kitchen, and seldom showed herself, then only at dusk, her thickly painted face below her wig a cold draught of suffering and passion. She clucked as she spoke, so quietly it was hard to hear what she was saying, and she made sudden involuntary movements of her head and shoulders. Within Cecilia's young beauty glimpses of shades of her mother's behaviour could be seen. Later, this led me to the conclusion that the Mummy and the Young Lady in Strindberg's *Ghost Sonata* ought to be played by the same actress.

*   *   *

Freed from the iron restrictions of school, I bolted like an insane horse and did not stop until six years later, when I became director of Helsingborg Municipal Theatre. I learnt some history of literature from Martin Lamm, who lectured on Strindberg in a bantering tone that caught the audience and offended my uncritical admiration. I realized only later that his analysis was brilliant. I joined a youth organization in the Old City called Mäster-Olofsgården and had the great privilege of taking charge of the lively and expanding drama activities. Then there were student dramatics. I soon started a course at the university in Stockholm for the sake of appearances, but student drama took up all the time not spent sleeping with Maria. She played the Mother in *The Pelican* and was famous within the student unions. She had a thickset body with sloping shoulders, high breasts and big hips and thighs. Her face was flat with a long well-shaped nose, broad forehead and expressive dark blue eyes. She had a thin mouth, the corners sophisticatedly drawn down. Her hair was thin and dyed very red. She had a considerable gift for language and had published a collection of poems praised by Artur Lundkvist. In the evenings, she held court at a corner table in the student café, drank brandy and chain-smoked American Virginian cigarettes called Goldflake, packed in a dark yellow tin with a blood-red seal.

Maria gave me all kinds of experiences, and became a splendid antidote to my intellectual indolence, my spiritual sloppiness and confused sentimentality. She also satisfied my sexual hunger, opening the prison bars and letting out a raving lunatic.

We inhabited a cramped one-room apartment on the South Side of Stockholm, containing a bookshelf, two chairs, a desk with a reading lamp and two mattresses plus bedclothes. Cooking was done in a cupboard and the basin was used for both dishes and washing. We sat and worked, each of us on a mattress, Maria smoking incessantly. In self-defence, I fired off a counterattack and was soon a chain-smoker.

My parents immediately discovered I was spending my nights away. Investigations were made, the truth revealed and I was asked to explain myself, with the result that I had a violent altercation with my father. I warned him not to hit me. He hit me and I hit him back. He staggered and ended up sitting on the floor while Mother alternately wept and appealed to the remnants of our commonsense. I pushed her aside and she screamed loudly. That same evening I wrote a letter to say we would never see one another again.

I left home with a sense of relief and stayed away for several years.

My brother tried to commit suicide, my sister was forced into an abortion out of consideration for the family, I ran away from home. My parents lived in an exhausting, permanent state of crisis with neither beginning nor end. They fulfilled their duties, they made huge efforts, appealing to God for mercy, their beliefs, values and traditions of no help to them. Nothing helped. Our drama was acted out before everyone's eyes on the brightly lit stage of the parsonage. Fear created what was feared.

* * *

I was offered a few professional commissions. The stage producer Brita von Horn and her Playwrights' Studio let me work with professional actors. The public parks committee asked me to produce performances for children. I started a small theatre in the Civic Centre. We played mostly to children, but also tried to stage Strindberg's *Ghost Sonata*. The actors were professionals and were to be paid ten kronor a night. The venture came to an end after seven performances.

A touring actor sought me out, wanting me to produce Strindberg's *The Father* with himself in the main part. I was to go on tour with them in charge of props and lighting. My intention had actually been to take a postponed exam in the history of literature, but the temptation was far too great. I gave up my studies, broke with Maria and set off with Jonatan Esbjörnsson's company. The première took place in a small town in southern Sweden. Seventeen people bought tickets in response to our call. The reviews in the local paper were scathing and the company dispersed the next morning, each one of them having to find his and her own way home as best they could. I myself possessed a hard-boiled egg, half a loaf of bread and six kronor.

My retreat could not have been more ignominious and Maria, who had advised me against going, did not attempt to conceal her triumph. Neither did she keep her new lover a secret. All three of us lived for a few nights in the cramped apartment, before I was thrown out with a black eye and a sprained thumb. Maria had wearied of our improvised ménage and my rival was stronger than me.

During the same period, I was employed at the Opera House as a virtually unpaid production assistant. A nice girl in the ballet provided me with my keep and houseroom for a few weeks. Her mother cooked our food and washed my under-clothes, my stomach ulcer healed and I was given the job of prompter in *Orpheus in the Underworld* for thirteen kronor a night. I was able to move into a rented room at Lill-Jansplan and could afford a proper meal once a day.

Then I suddenly wrote twelve plays and an opera. Claes Hoogland, director of the Student Theatre, read them all and decided we would put on *The Death of Punch*, a play which is an audacious plagiarism of *Punch's Shrove Tuesday* by Strindberg and *The Old Play of Everyman*, a fact that did not embarrass me in the slightest.

The première was a success and was even reviewed in *Svenska Dagbladet*. On the last night, Carl Anders Dymling, recently appointed head of Svensk Filmindustri, and Stina Bergman, Hjalmar's heir and head of the screenplay department, were in the audience. The next day I was summoned to Stina and given a year's employment, my own office, desk, chair, telephone and a view over the roofs around Kungsgatan 30. The salary was 500 kronor a month.

I was now respectable and in permanent employment, a person who sat at a desk every day and edited scripts, wrote dialogue and did drafts for films. We were five 'script slaves' working under Stina Bergman's competent and motherly guidance. Occasionally a producer put in an appearance in our locality, often Gustaf Molander, who was always remote if friendly. I had submitted a screenplay about my schooldays. Molander read it and recommended that it should be filmed. Svensk Filmindustri bought it and paid me 5000 kronor, an immense sum of money. Alf Sjöberg, whom I admired, was to direct it. I managed to argue my way into the studio crew.

My suggestion was that I should function as some kind of script boy. It was generous of Alf Sjöberg to accept my offer, as I had never been involved in filming and did not know what a script boy was supposed to do. Naturally I was a nuisance and a burden to them. I often forgot my professional rôle and interfered with the work of the director. I was reprimanded and shut myself into a cubbyhole and wept, but I did not give up. The opportunities for learning from a master were unlimited.

I had married Else Fisher, a playmate from my recent touring days. She was a dancer and choreographer, and considered very talented. She was kind, clever and funny. We lived in a two-room apartment in Abrahamsberg. A week before our wedding, I ran away, but I came back. A daughter was born the day before Christmas Eve in 1943.

*　　*　　*

During the filming of *Frenzy*, I was offered the post of director of the Municipal Theatre in Helsingborg. This town in south west Sweden ran one of the oldest municipal theatres in the country and it was now to be closed, the grants to be transferred to the newly built theatre in Malmö. This provoked the patriotic locals into deciding to carry on if at all possible. Several theatre people were approached, but they declined as soon as they found out about the premises and financial circumstances. In their need, the management turned to the renowned drama critic on *Stockholms Tidningen*, Herbert Grevenius, who replied that if they wanted a theatre maniac who was also talented and had some administrative skills (I had run the children's theatre in the Civic Centre for a year), then they should speak to Bergman. After some hesitation, they took his advice.

I bought the first hat of my life to give an impression of stability I did not possess, went to Helsingborg and looked at the theatre. It was in an appalling state, the premises shabby and dirty. The company performed twice a week on average and the statistics revealed an audience of twenty-eight paying people per performance.

I loved the theatre from the very first moment.

I made a number of demands. The company should be changed. The theatre should be re-equipped. The number of plays put on should be increased. A subscription scheme should be started. To my surprise, the management agreed. I was now the country's youngest theatre director of all time and could choose my own actors and other staff. Our contract ran for eight months, so for the rest of the year we would have to manage as best we could.

There were fleas in the theatre. The old company must presumably have been immune, but the new members with their young blood were severely bitten. The plumbing from the theatre restaurant ran past the men's dressing room and urine dripped on to the radiator by the wall. The old building was draughty, and a faint moaning of the lost souls of demons came from the lofty flies. The heating functioned badly and, when they ripped up the floor of the auditorium, they found hundreds of rats dead from coke fume poisoning. The living rats were robust, unafraid and enjoyed appearing. The theatre engineer's fat cat went into hiding when attacked.

I do not wish to become nostalgic, but for me this was paradise on earth. There was a spacious stage, draughty and dirty, true, but the stage floor sloped gently down towards the footlights, the curtain was patched and worn but painted red, white and gold. The dressing rooms were primitive, cramped and equipped with four washbasins. There were two toilets for eighteen people.

We were constantly performing and rehearsing. The first year we did nine plays in eight months, the second year ten. We rehearsed for three weeks, then had a première.

No play ran for more than twenty performances, except our New Year revue, which was a huge success and ran for thirty-five shows. Our daily life belonged to the theatre from nine in the morning until eleven at night. We did quite a bit of revelling, but festivities were drastically limited by our disastrous finances. We were banned from the Grand's elegant dining room, but welcome at the rear where the restaurant keeper had arranged a special hash with beer and schnapps. Credit was generous, not to say indulgent. After rehearsals on Saturday, we were given hot chocolate with genuine (war-time) whipped cream and fine cakes at Fahlman's patisserie café in Stortorget.

Helsingborgians received us with overwhelming friendliness and hospitality. We were often invited back for late-night food at the homes of important citizens. When members of the company appeared after the performance, the other guests had already eaten, and found amusement in watching the starving actors helping themselves from the relaid and groaning tables. A wealthy grocer had a shop diagonally across the street from the theatre, where a dish-of-the-day cost one krona and rooms and apartments were rented out in a decaying eighteenth-century building inside the courtyard. The virginia creeper had grown right through the window-frames and walls, the toilet was in the stairwell and water had to be fetched from a pump in the cobbled yard.

The highest salary was 800 kronor, the lowest 300. We managed as best we could, borrowed and took out advances. No one thought of protesting about our wretched conditions. We were grateful for our incredible good fortune at being able to play every night, and rehearse every day. Our industry was rewarded. The first year a total of 60,000 people came, and we also recouped our grant, undoubtedly a great triumph. The Stockholm newspapers began to notice our performances and our morale rose. Spring came early that year and we went on an excursion to Arild, where we settled down on the edge of a beechwood with a view over the mild spring sea, ate our packed food and drank bad red wine. I got drunk and made a confused speech in which I pointed out in obscure terms that we theatre people lived in God's open hand and were especially chosen to endure pain and joy. Someone played Marlene Dietrich's *Wenn Du Geburtstag hast, bin ich bei Dir zu Gast die ganze Nacht*. [When it's your birthday, I'll be your guest the whole night long.] No one listened to me and gradually everyone began to talk, a few to dance. I felt misunderstood, went aside and threw up.

I had gone to Helsingborg without my wife and child. It had been established in the spring that both Else and our infant daughter had tuberculosis. Else was admitted to a private sanatorium near Alvesta, where the fees were the same as my monthly salary, and Lena ended up in the Sachska children's hospital. I went on editing scripts for Svensk Filmindustri, so could just support them.

I was also alone in the sense that I was the director and in charge, but I did have a financial director alongside me, a remarkable man who owned a number of haberdashery shops in Stockholm. For several years, he had run the Boulevard Theatre on Ringvägen, where I had put on a few plays. When I asked him to come with me to Helsingborg, he had at once accepted. He was a good amateur actor and liked playing minor rôles. He was a bachelor, loved young women and had a repellent appearance which almost hid the good man beneath. He ensured there was money in the house. When funds were low, he mortgaged his haberdashery shops. He considered me insane, but smiled and said: *You* must decide. I did so, often brutally and ruthlessly. So I became rather lonely.

Else, who was to have been the theatre's choreographer and dancer, recommended as a replacement a friend from her days with Mary Wigman. Her name was Ellen Lundström and she had just married the then fairly unknown photographer Christer Strömholm. She came to Helsingborg and he went to Africa. Ellen, a strikingly beautiful girl who radiated erotic appeal, was talented, original and highly emotional.

A mild promiscuity spread through the company. For a short period everyone had crablice and there were occasional outbreaks of jealousy. The theatre was indeed our home, but otherwise we were all fairly confused and hungry for companionship.

Without really giving it much thought, Ellen and I had started a relationship which soon resulted in pregnancy. At Christmas, Else was allowed out of the sanatorium and we met in Stockholm at her mother's. I told her what had happened and said that I wanted a divorce, and that I was going to live with Ellen. I registered Else's face turning rigid with pain. She was sitting at the dining table in the kitchen, her cheeks red from her illness and her childish mouth tight shut. Then she said quite calmly: 'You'll have to pay maintenance. Can you afford that, you poor thing?' 'If I've been able to pay 800 kronor a month for your damned private sanatorium,' I replied bitterly, 'no doubt I'll be able to scrape up something for maintenance too. Don't worry.'

I do not recognize the person I was forty years ago. My distress is so profound and the suppression mechanism functions so effectively, I can evoke the picture only with difficulty. Photographs are of little value. They simply show a masquerade that has entrenched itself. If I felt attacked, I snapped like a frightened dog. I trusted no one, loved no one, missed no one. Obsessed with a sexuality that forced me into constant infidelity, I was tormented by desire, fear, anguish and a guilty conscience.

So I was alone and raging. My work at the theatre provided some alleviation of a tension which only let go for brief moments in orgasm or drunkenness. I knew I had persuasive powers, that I could make people do what I wanted them to do, that I had some kind of surface charm which I could switch on and off at will. I was also aware that I had a talent for being frightened and acquiring a guilty conscience, because ever since childhood I had known a great deal about the mechanics of fear. In brief, I was a man with power who had not learnt to enjoy power.

We were dimly aware that a world war was raging on our doorstep. When the American squadrons flew over the Sound, the actors' words were drowned by the noise of the engines. We industriously read the increasingly black headlines, then turned eagerly to the theatre reviews, giving the stream of refugees across the Sound from Denmark an absentminded momentary interest.

I sometimes wonder what our productions looked like. As a guide I have nothing but a handful of photographs and a few yellowed cuttings. Our rehearsal time was short, our preparations nonexistent. What we managed to achieve was a hastily assembled artifact. I think that was good, in fact useful. Young people should be constantly faced with new tasks. The instrument has to be tried and hardened. Technique can be developed only through uninterrupted and sturdy contact with the audience. I staged five plays that first year. Even if the results were dubious, it was salutary. Neither I nor my friends, understandably enough, had sufficient human experience to go into the profundities of the problems in the drama of *Macbeth*.

One night on my way home from the theatre, I was suddenly aware of how I would handle the witches when they appear in the latter part of the play. Macbeth and Lady Macbeth are lying in bed, the wife fast asleep, the husband half-asleep, half-awake, feverish shadows flitting across the wall. The witches appear out of the floor at the foot of the bed, whispering and tittering, closely linked together, their limbs moving like plants in running water. Behind the stage someone is hammering on the wires of an untuned piano. Macbeth is kneeling up in bed, semi-naked, his head turned away, unaware of the witches.

I stopped in the quiet street and stood quite still for several minutes, repeating silently to myself, 'Damn it, I've got talent, I'm probably brilliant,' an outburst that made me feel hot and dizzy. In all my misery, a well-regulated self-confidence existed, a steel column right through the ramshackle ruins of my soul.

To a great extent I tried to imitate my masters, Alf Sjöberg and Olof Molander, stealing what can be stolen and patching it with something of my own. I had little or no theoretical training. I had read some of Stanislavsky, who was fashionable among young actors, but I hadn't understood or even wanted to understand him. Neither had I any opportunity to see theatre abroad. I was self-taught and a village genius.

If anyone had asked me and my friends the reason for our nonstop activity, we would have had no answer. We made theatre because we made theatre. Someone had to stand on the stage turned towards some people out there in the darkness. That it happened to be just us standing there in the light was a stroke of luck. As a schooling, it was all splendid;

the actual results were probably highly dubious. I wanted so very much to be Prospero, and I mostly behaved like Caliban.

After two years of thrashing wildly around, I was summoned to Gothenburg. I departed with enthusiasm and an unshakable self-confidence.

12

Torsten Hammarén was sixty-two and had been the director of Gothenburg City Theatre since its inception in 1934. Before that he had been director of the Lorensberg Theatre, and he was also a distinguished character actor.

Torsten was highly regarded and his company was considered the best in the country. Knut Ström, the theatre's first producer, was an old revolutionary who had trained under Reinhardt. Helge Wahlgren preferred producing on the Studio Stage and was taciturn, sharp and precise. His actors had played together for decades, but that did not mean they liked one another.

Early in the autumn of 1946, Ellen and I moved to Gothenburg with our two children. I was twenty-eight. The dress rehearsal of Strindberg's *Ghost Sonata* was taking place at the theatre. The guest-producer was Olof Molander. I crept into the back of the huge stage, which was in darkness. Far far away out in front, I could hear the actors' voices and occasionally catch a glimpse of them in the circle of the spotlights. I stood quite still and listened. A large theatre contains every possibility, great actors and great demands. I would not like to say I was frightened, but I did quake.

Suddenly, I was no longer alone. At my side was a tiny little creature, or possibly a ghost, the grand old lady of the theatre. Maria Schildknecht, dressed up in the parrot dress and hideous mask of the Mummy. 'I assume you are Mr Bergman,' she whispered, smiling kindly but terrifyingly. I confirmed my identity and bowed awkwardly. We stood in silence for a few moments. 'Well, what do you think of this then?' said the little ghost, her voice stern and challenging. 'To me it's among the greatest works in the history of drama,' I replied truthfully. The Mummy looked at me with cold contempt. 'Oh,' she said. 'This is the kind of shit Strindberg knocked up so that we should have something to play at his Intimate Theatre.' She left me with a gracious nod. A few minutes later, she went on stage, out of the greenroom, startled by the sunlight, shaking her trailing dress in the way a parrot ruffles its feathers. Imperishable, in a rôle she hated under a producer she hated.

I was given a generous debut, *Caligula* by Camus. Anders Ek, a friend and contemporary from our frantic Stockholm days, made his debut in the title rôle.

The whole corps of eminent actors stood around looking on us beginners with suspicion and no goodwill. All the theatre's technical and material resources had been put at my disposal.

One afternoon in the middle of rehearsals, Torsten Hammarén came unannounced into the auditorium and sat down to scrutinize our efforts. It was an unfortunate moment. Anders Ek was marking out, the other actors reading their parts. From lack of experience, I had lost control over developments and I could hear Hammarén groaning and recrossing his legs. In the end, he could stand it no longer and shouted: 'What the hell are you up to? Is this private prayers? Or a private wank? Playing marbles? What the bloody hell are you doing?'

Cursing and swearing, he rushed up on to the stage and started remonstrating with the nearest actor because he had not let his book go. The accused man stammered something about new methods and improvisations, squinting in my direction. Hammarén interrupted him briskly and started making changes in the set. I was furious and yelled from the auditorium that I was not going to stand for this, that this was an intrusion and the language of force. Hammarén answered with his back turned to me. 'Sit down and shut up, then perhaps you'll learn something at last.' I burst a blood vessel and yelled back that I wasn't going to stand for this. Hammarén laughed, in a not unfriendly way, and called out: 'Then you can go to hell, you provincial little genius!' I rushed to the door and, after a struggle to get it open, stormed out of the theatre.

Early next morning there was a telephone call from the theatre director's secretary. She told me that if I was not present at the day's rehearsal, my contract would be cancelled.

My anger had cooled, but now it gathered momentum again and I tore down to the theatre to kill Hammarén. We met unexpectedly in an angle of the corridor, literally bumping into each other. We both found this extremely comical and started to laugh. Torsten embraced me and I at once appointed him in my heart the father-figure I had lacked since God had abandoned me. He took on the rôle and played it conscientiously during the years I stayed in his theatre.

Kaj Munk's *Love* starts with a cocoa party.

The pastor has invited his parishioners back home to discuss how to build embankments against the sea. Twenty-three actors are sitting on the stage drinking hot chocolate, some with a few lines, others just sitting. Hammarén had good actors for all the parts, even those with nothing to say. His instructions were murderously detailed and a trial to one's patience. When Kolbjörn says his line about the winter weather, he takes a cake, then stirs his chocolate. Now please rehearse that. Kolbjörn practises. The director changes it. Wanda serves chocolate from the left-hand jug and smiles kindly at Benkt-Åke as she says: 'You certainly need it.' 'Carry on now!' The actors rehearse it. The director corrects them.

I think impatiently that the director is a gravedigger. This is the decay of the theatre.

Hammarén goes on unmoved.

Tore stretches out for a bun and shakes her head at Ebba. They have said something to each other which we haven't caught. Please find some appropriate subject of conversation. Ebba and Tore make suggestions. Hammarén approves. They rehearse.

I think: This gummed-up old dictator has managed to squeeze all enjoyment and spontaneity out of the scene and has killed it stone dead. I might as well leave the churchyard. For some reason I stay on, perhaps from spiteful curiosity. Pauses are marked or eliminated, movements weighed up against tone of voice and tone of voice against movements, breathing is fixed. I yawn like a malicious cat. After endless hours of repeats, interruptions, corrections, pushing and shoving, Hammarén considers the time is ripe to play the scene from start to finish.

Then the miracle occurred.

An easy, relaxed and amusing conversation broke out, with all the social gestures, looks, hidden meanings and consciously unconscious behaviour of a cocoa party. The actors, secure in their thoroughly rehearsed territories, felt a freedom to create the characters. They fantasized unexpectedly and humorously. They were not doing down their fellow-players, but respecting the whole, the rhythm.

My first lesson was Hammarén's intervention in *Caligula*.

Staging must be clear and directed. Haziness in emotions and intentions must be eliminated. Signals from all actors to the audience must be simple and lucid. Always one at a time, preferably rapid; one suggestion may contradict the next but *intentionally*, then an illusion of simultaneousness and depth-effect arises, a stereo-effect. Events on the stage must reach the spectator at every moment, truth in the expression coming second; good actors always have resources to act as intermediaries for the reflected truth.

My second lesson was the cocoa party in Kaj Munk's *Love*.

True freedom is dependent on mutually drawn patterns, thoroughly penetrated rhythms. Acting is also the act of repetition. So every contribution must be based on voluntary co-operation between the parties concerned. If a director forces an actor, he can get his own way during rehearsals. When the director leaves the acting space, the actor consciously or unconsciously starts correcting his activities according to his own lights. His fellow player at once changes for the same reason. And so on. After five performances, a 'tamed' performance has fallen apart, unless the director continues to watch closely over his tigers. On a surface level, Hammerén's cocoa party appeared to be a 'tamed' number. But that was not the case. The actors saw their opportunities only within clearly drawn limits. They were pleased and waited for the moment when they could insert their own creativity. The cocoa party never fell apart.

One day I caught Torsten Hammarén looking through my producer's notebook. There was not a single note or sketch of a set in it. 'So you don't draw your scenes,' he said sarcastically. 'No, I prefer to create directly on the stage together with the actors,' I said. 'It'll be interesting to see how long your nerves can take that,' said Hammarén, slamming the book shut.

He was soon proved right. Now I make my preparations down to the very last detail and force myself to draw every single scene. When I start rehearsing, every moment of my performance is ready. My instructions are clear, practicable and preferably stimulating. Only he who is well prepared has any opportunity to improvise.

*   *   *

My family had expanded. In the spring of 1948, the twins were born and we moved into a five-room apartment in a new area outside Gothenburg. I also had a spartan little room right at the top of the theatre and spent the evenings there editing scripts, writing plays and films.

Ellen's stepfather killed himself, leaving large debts. My mother-in-law and her small son moved in with us. They settled in my study next to Ellen's and my bedroom. Newly widowed,

Ellen's mother often cried at night and, in addition to that, Lena, my elder daughter, lived with us because Else was still ailing. The family was completed by a kindly but gloomy person who was to help in the household. We were ten people in all. Ellen had so much to do, she could only occasionally devote time to her profession. Marital complications became more and more infected by all this. Our sex life, which had been our deliverance, ceased because of the proximity of my mother-in-law and her little son through the thin wall.

I was thirty and had been kicked out of Svensk Filmindustri after the fiasco of *Crisis*. My domestic finances were stretched. Added to our other troubles were bitter quarrels about money. Both Ellen and I were careless and extravagant.

My fourth film became a modest success, thanks to Lorens Marmstedt's wisdom, thoughtfulness and patience. He was a genuine producer, who fought and lived for his films from script to release.

It was he who taught me how to make films.

I started commuting between Gothenburg and Stockholm and rented a room in Miss Nylander's boarding house on the corner of Brahegatan and Humlegårdsgatan. Miss Nylander was an aristocratic old lady, a tiny little creature with glossy white hair and dark eyes, very pale and well made-up. A great many actors lived in her boarding house and were maternally looked after. I had a sunny room facing the courtyard, my refuge and security. Miss Nylander benevolently closed her eyes to the irregularities of life and finances which often afflicted the troubled inhabitants of her establishment.

I was not happy in Gothenburg. The city was in many ways cut off, the theatre a limited world in which no one talked about anything except the profession. Home seethed with crying children, damp washing, weeping women and raging scenes of jealousy, often perfectly justified. All escape routes were closed and betrayal became obligatory.

Ellen knew I was a liar. Her despair was corrosive. She begged me to tell the truth just once, but I was incapable of doing so and no longer knew where the truth lay. For brief moments between battles, we felt a profound fellowship, the sympathy and forgiveness of the body.

Ellen was actually a good and strong friend. In different, less dire, circumstances, we would certainly have enjoyed living together, but we knew nothing about ourselves and thought life was supposed to be as it was. We never complained about our circumstances or expressed regret over our condition. We were fighting chained together and were drowning.

Torsten Hammarén gave me the chance of putting on two of my own plays in the Studio, a brave and not entirely uncomplicated decision. Some of my other plays had already been staged and critics had been pretty well in agreement. Bergman is a good, even talented producer, but he is a bad writer. By bad, they meant pretentious, immature, spotty, sweaty, sentimental, silly, ridiculous, wretched, humourless, unpleasant and so on.

Olof Lagercrantz, who had been much admired by me, started persecuting me. When he finally became the cultural guru of the newspaper *Dagens Nyheter*, his attacks took on grotesque proportions. About *Smiles of a Summer Night*, he wrote in 1955: 'The poor imagination of a spotty youth, the insolent dreams of an immature heart and a boundless contempt for artistic and human truth are the forces which have created this "comedy". I am ashamed to have seen it.'

Today this is a comic curiosity. At the time, it was a poisoned pill that caused much damage and suffering.

Torsten Hammarén, a brave and amusing man, was persecuted for several years by one Gothenburg critic. When he had put on a much appreciated and amusing performance of *Bichon*, he saw his chance. In the interval when the audience, exhausted by laughter, was on its way out into the foyer, Hammarén appeared in front of the curtain and asked for a few moments' attention. Then slowly, with unexpected pauses for thought and suitable facial expressions, he read out the scathing review. He was rewarded with expressions of tremendous sympathy. The open persecution ceased, to be replaced by a more sophisticated kind. The offended critic proceeded to profane Hammarén's actress wife and his closest friends in the theatre.

Today I take a polite almost fawning attitude to my judges. I once very nearly hit one of the most damaging critics. Before I had had time to strike, he sat down on the floor among a number of music stands. I was fined 5000 kronor, but considered it worth the money, as I thought the newspaper would never again allow him to review my productions. I was wrong of course. He was absent for a few years, and is now back spreading his stultifying bile over the efforts of my old age.

He even travelled to Munich in order to fulfil his executioner's task. I saw him one spring evening in Maximilianstrasse, extremely drunk, in a thin tee-shirt and pair of far too tight velvet trousers. His shaven head was rolling about disconsolately and he was trying to make contact with passers-by, but was scornfully rejected. He was clearly cold and ill.

On a momentary impulse, I thought of going over to the poor man and shaking him by the hand. After all these years, surely we can be reconciled? We're quits now, aren't we? Why should we go on hating each other so long after all that uproar? I at once regretted the impulse. There goes a Deadly Enemy. He should be destroyed. True, he was destroying himself through his deteriorating writing, but I shall dance on his grave and wish him many eternities in hell, where he can sit and read his own reviews.

As life consists of nothing but contradictions, I should at once add that Herbert Grevenius, another theatre critic, is one of my dearest friends. We meet nearly every day at the Royal Dramatic Theatre. At the time of writing, he is eighty-six years old and always equally amiably mocking, smoking one of his daily fifty cigarettes.

When I was green and unformed, Torsten Hammarén and Herbert Grevenius stood like two stern and incorruptible angels. I learnt my craft from Hammarén and a certain orderliness of thought from Grevenius. They pinched me, kneaded me and put me right.

Bad reviews and other public humiliations tormented me out of all proportion. Grevenius once said to me: 'Imagine a chalk line. You're on one side of the line, your critics on the other. Both of you perform tricks for the public.' That helped. I was working on a production with an alcoholic but brilliant actor. Hammarén blew his nose and said: 'To think that lilies so often grow out of the arses of corpses.' Grevenius saw one of my earlier films and complained that it had a hole in the middle. I defended myself by saying the actor was supposed to represent a mediocrity. Grevenius said: 'A mediocrity must never be played by a mediocrity, a vulgar woman never by a vulgar woman, a conceited primadonna never by a conceited primadonna.' Hammarén said: 'Actors are the devil. As soon as they've drunk a face on to themselves, they lose their memories.'

13

I had never been abroad except for those six weeks in Germany. Neither had Birger Malmsten, my friend and companion in film work. Now it was going to happen. We settled in Cagnes-sur-Mer, a small town tucked away high in the mountains between Cannes and Nice, at that time unknown to tourists but visited regularly by painters and other artists. Ellen had an engagement as choreographer at the Liseberg Theatre in Gothenburg, her mother was looking after the children, and all was fairly calm. Our finances had temporarily improved, as I had just finished a film and had a contract for another during the late summer. I arrived in Cagnes at the end of April and was given a sunny room with a red tiled floor. There was a view over fields of carnations in the valley, towards the sea, which was occasionally the colour of wine, as Homer says.

Birger Malmsten was immediately gobbled up by a beautiful but consumptive Englishwoman, who wrote poetry and lived a rather hectic life. I was left to my own devices and sat on the terrace writing the film we were to start making in August. Decision-making and preparation times were brief in those days. There was never time to be really frightened, an invaluable advantage The film, entitled *To Joy*, was to be about a couple of young musicians in the symphony orchestra in Helsingborg, the disguise almost a formality. It was about Ellen and me, about the conditions imposed by art, about fidelity and infidelity. Music would stream right through the film.

I was left completely alone, speaking to no one and meeting no one. I got drunk every night and was helped to bed by *la patronne*, a motherly woman who worried about my alcoholic habits. Every morning, however, at nine o'clock, I was sitting at my worktable, allowing my hangover to help intensify my creativity.

Ellen and I started writing careful but tenderhearted letters. Under the influence of a dawning hope of a possible future for our tormented marriage, the portrayal of the film's leading female character turned into a miracle of beauty, faithfulness, wisdom and human dignity. The male part, on the other hand, became a conceited mediocrity; faithless, bombastic and a liar.

I was being courted, shyly but intensively, by a Russian-American painter. She was athletic but well-proportioned, dark as night with bright eyes and a generous mouth, a statuesque Amazon radiating uninhibited sensuality. My fidelity to my marriage stimulated us both. She painted and I wrote, two loners in unexpected creative fellowship.

The end of the film became terribly tragic. The female character was blown up by a paraffin stove (possibly secret wishful thinking), the last movement of Beethoven's Ninth Symphony was shamelessly exploited and the main character realized that there was 'a joy greater than joy'. (A truth I did not understand until thirty years later.)

I extracted Birger Malmsten from the lap of Venus, took a tearful farewell of *la patronne* and returned home. After some hesitation the screenplay was accepted.

My reunion with Ellen was hurried and not entirely successful. I was terribly jealous, because I had discovered my wife was mixing with a lesbian artist, but we were reconciled to some extent. I went to Stockholm. Filming began, my companion Birger Malmsten and Stig Olin playing two wimps of men. Maj-Britt Nilsson succeeded in making the desperately idealized wife almost believable, which was as good evidence as any of her brilliance.

The exteriors were filmed on location in Helsingborg. One day at the beginning of August, we filmed the couple's marriage at the Town Hall. Ellen and I had been married there a few years before. Journalists from a weekly magazine called *Film-journalen* came to see us, to do a feature article. The magazine's charming chief editor, Gunilla Holger, had done us this honour. She brought with her a colleague called Gun Hagberg. The management, in the person of myself, realizing its obligations and also violently attracted to the chief editor, scraped the barrel of the film's insignificant expense account and invited them to dinner at the Grand.

After dinner, Gun and I went for a walk beside the Sound. It was a warm and windless night. We kissed with delight; and agreed, rather absentmindedly, to meet when the filming returned to Stockholm. *Filmjournalen* left and I forgot the whole thing.

I returned home in the middle of August. Gun phoned and suggested we should have dinner together at the Cattelin and go to the cinema. With a stab of panic, I thanked her and accepted with all my heart.

Then everything went very quickly. The following weekend Gun and I went to Trosa, booked in at a hotel, went to bed and stayed there until Monday morning. By then we had decided to run away to Paris, separately, but secretly together. My friend Vilgot Sjöman was there on a grant. His first novel was to be filmed by Gustaf Molander and several scripts had been rejected. The board of SF ordered me, as a last resort, to drop the final work on my just-completed film and go at once to Paris and the unruly Vilgot. Gun would cover fashion shows for some weekly magazine. She entrusted her two small sons to their Finnish nurse's competent care. Her husband had been on the family rubber plantation in South-East Asia for six months.

I went to Gothenburg to talk to my wife. It was late in the evening and Ellen had already gone to bed. She was pleased at my unexpected visit. I sat on the edge of the bed without taking off my raincoat and told her everything.

Anyone interested can follow the events in the third part of *Scenes from a Marriage*. The only difference is the depiction of Paula, the lover. Gun was more like her opposite. She had always been an A-1 girl, beautiful, tall, athletic, with intensely blue eyes, a large laugh, lovely full lips, openness, pride, integrity, womanly strength, but a sleepwalker.

She knew nothing about herself, wasn't interested, had faced her life openly with no defences or subsidiary intentions, truthfully and unafraid. She ignored the stomach ulcer which periodically flared up; simply stopped drinking coffee for a few days and took medicine, then it soon improved. She didn't mind her poor relationship with her husband; all marriages become dull sooner or later and a little salve rescues sex life. Nor did she reflect on her recurring anxiety dreams; perhaps she had eaten something that didn't agree with her or drunk too much. Life was matter of fact and magnificent. She was irresistible.

Our love tore our hearts apart and from the very beginning carried its own seeds of destruction.

We left on 1 September 1949, early in the morning, and were in Paris by midday. We booked in at a reputable family hotel on rue Ste-Anne, a narrow turning off Avenue de l'Opéra. The room was rectangular like a coffin, the beds not alongside each other but in single file, the window facing out on to a cramped courtyard. If one leant out, one could see a patch of the white-hot summer sky six floors up. The air in the courtyard was musty, cold and damp; there were some windows in the asphalt to let light into the hotel kitchen, where one could see numerous white-clad people moving about like maggots; out of this chasm rose the stench of refuse and cooking smells. For further details, please refer to the lovers' room in *The Silence*.

Exhausted and appalled, we sat on our beds, I at once

realizing this was God's punishment for my ultimate betrayal. Ellen's delight at my unexpected homecoming, her smile – that mercilessly clear picture kept appearing. It was to return again and again, and still does.

The next morning Gun spoke in French to the all-powerful hotel porter. A 10,000 franc note changed hands (a thousand francs was then 10 kronor) and we moved into a comfortable room facing the street, with a bathroom as large as a church, coloured windows, heating pipes in the floor and huge handbasins. At the same time, I rented a tiny hovel under the roof with a rickety desk, a squeaky bed, a bidet, and a handsome panorama over the roofs of Paris with the Eiffel Tower in the background.

We stayed in Paris for three months. In every way, it was a crucial time in both our lives.

I had my thirty-first birthday during that summer of 1949. Hitherto I had worked hard and relentlessly in my profession. So coming to this autumn-warm Paris was an experience which had the effect of knocking down barriers. Love had both time and opportunity to grow freely, opening closed rooms and knocking down walls. I could breathe. My treachery to Ellen and the children existed somewhere in a mist, ever-present but strangely stimulating. For a few months, there lived and breathed a bold production that was incorruptibly true, so therefore priceless, although it turned out to be horribly expensive when the bill came.

Letters from home were not encouraging. Ellen wrote to say that the children were ill and she herself had eczema on her hands and feet and she was losing her hair. On my departure, I had given her what at that time was a very large sum of money. She complained that it had almost all gone. Gun's husband had hurriedly returned to Stockholm and his family sent a lawyer, who was now threatening a lawsuit; a family fortune was partly in Gun's name.

We let almost nothing disturb us. A flow of rich impressions and experiences was flooding over our heads.

Greatest of all was discovering Molière. I had plodded

through some of his plays in history of literature seminars, but had understood nothing and considered him musty and unexciting.

So now the village genius from Sweden was sitting at the Comédie Française watching *The Misanthrope* in a youthful, beautiful and emotional performance. The experience was indescribable. The dry alexandrines blossomed and thrived. The people on the stage stepped through my senses into my heart. That was what it was like. I know it sounds ridiculous, but that's what it was like. Molière stepped into my heart to remain there for the rest of my life. The spiritual circulation of my blood, previously linked to Strindberg, now opened an artery to Molière.

One Sunday afternoon we went to the Odéon, the annexe of the Comédie Française, where they were playing *L'Arlésienne*, with Bizet's music. The operetta is a French equivalent of *Värmlänningarna* (The Värmlanders), but worse.

It was a full house, parents with their children, grandmothers, aunts and uncles, all murmuring with expectation, newly-washed round faces, decent people with Sunday's *coq-au-vin* in their stomachs, the French petit-bourgeoisie on an excursion into the world of theatre.

The curtain went up on a dreadful set of the nineteenth-century Grabow era. The young girl was played by one of the famous *Sociétaires* who was well past pensionable age. She acted with brittle intensity, her wig brutally yellow, accentuating her sharp nose and painted little old woman's face. They all declaimed at walking pace or at a gallop, the heroine throwing herself down on the boards at the very bright footlights. A thirty-five man orchestra played the vigorous sensual music without exerting themselves, skipping repeats, people went in and out of the orchestra pit, talking unconcernedly, and the oboist drank a glass of wine. The heroine screamed in heart-rending tones and yet again fell to the floor.

A strange sound then welled up from the darkness of the auditorium. I looked round and discovered to my astonishment that everyone was crying, some rather discreetly into their handkerchiefs, others openly and with pleasure. Monsieur Lebrun at my side, with his well-brushed and parted hair and well-groomed moustache, was shaking as if with fever, and out of his round black eyes clear tears were running down his well-shaven rosy cheeks, his little fat hands moving helplessly over the sharp creases of his trousers.

The curtain fell to resounding applause. The ageing girl came up front stage, her wig crooked, placed a small hand on her bony chest and stood quite still, regarding her audience with a dark unfathomable gaze. She was still in a trance, then allowed herself to be woken slowly by the jubilant cries of the faithful, all those people who had lived a life with *L'Arlésienne*, all those people who again and again had gone on a pilgrimage to a Sunday performance at the theatre, first with grandmother holding their hands and now with their own grandchildren, secure in the fact that Madame Guerlaine, eternally on the same stage, at a definite time, year after year, would throw herself down headlong by the footlights, lamenting her grief over the cruelty of life.

Everyone was shouting. The little old woman up there on the mercilessly illuminated stage had once again touched the hearts of the faithful. *Theatre as a miracle*. I stared with young and relentlessly curious eyes at this spectacle within a spectacle. 'Cold people easily grow sentimental,' I said to Gun. Then we went up the Eiffel Tower so that at least we had been up it.

Before the theatre, we had had lunch at a distinguished restaurant just opposite the Odéon. Over the next few hours, the kidneys *flambé* we had eaten had passed through various stages. Now as we stood at the very top of the Eiffel Tower, gazing over that famous panorama, countless colon bacilli struck. We were both afflicted with terrible internal spasms and rushed for the lifts, where large notices stated that they were closed for two hours in sympathy with the protracted strike of the workers in the public cleansing department. We made our way down the winding staircase with no possible chance of preventing a catastrophe. An incredibly obliging taxi driver spread his newspapers out on the back seat and conveyed this semi-conscious stinking couple to their hotel, where for the next twenty-four hours, crawling from the bed across the floor, we alternately and jointly embraced the lavatory bowl. Until then, shyness in our love had prevented us from using the bathroom's convenience, and when in need we had pattered off to the considerably less luxurious arrangement in the corridor. At one blow, all discretion was swept away. Our physical misery undoubtedly brought us closer to each other.

Vilgot Sjöman's screenplay was finished. He went home, much missed by us both, and now we were left to ourselves; there was no longer any excuse to remain in Paris. Days with a chill in the air arrived. The mist rolled in from the plains and removed the Eiffel Tower from my view under the hotel roof. I wrote a play called *Joachim Naked*. He is a maker of silent films in imitation of Méliès. A bottomless canal runs below his dilapidated studio. He catches a talking fish, breaks up his marriage and tells a story about how the Eiffel Tower one day grew tired of being the Eiffel Tower, left its post and removed itself to the English Channel. Later, the Tower gets a guilty conscience and returns. Joachim ends up in a religious brotherhood, in which suicide has been turned into a meaningful rite.

The one and only copy of this play was submitted, in insane hope, to the Royal Dramatic Theatre, where it disappeared without trace; perhaps just as well.

We roamed aimlessly around the city, lost our way, found our way, got lost again. We wandered down to the sluice gates in Marne, Port-Auteuil and La Pie. We sought out the Hôtel du Nord and the little amusement park on the outskirts of the Bois de Vincennes.

The exhibition of Impressionists at the Jeu de Paume. Roland Petit's *Carmen*. Barrault as K. in *The Trial*, anti-psychological acting style, alien but enticing. Serge Lifar, the ageing monster in *L'Après-midi d'un faun*, a fat whore with moist open lips, shamelessly radiating all the vices of the

1920s. Ravel's *Concerto for the Left Hand* one Saturday morning in the Théâtre de Champs Elysées. I can go on forever. Racine's *Phèdre*, unobtrusive and furious. *The Damnation of Faust*; Berlioz at the Grand Opéra with all its apparatus. Balanchine's ballets. La Cinémathèque: the bizarre Monsieur Langlois with a dirty streak round his blindingly white collar. They had shown *Frenzy (Torment)* and *Prison (The Devil's Wanton)*. I was received kindly and saw films by Méliès as well as silent French farces, Feuillade's *Judex* and Dreyer's *Leaves from Satan's Book*. Experiences piled on experiences. My hunger was insatiable.

One evening, we went to the Athénée to see Louis Jouvet in a play by Giraudoux, and Ellen was seated in the row diagonally in front of us. She turned round and smiled. We fled. A lawyer in a pale blue suit and red tie arrived, dispatched by the relations to put Gun to rights. They were to have lunch together. I stood at the hotel window watching them walking side by side down rue Ste-Anne. Gun was wearing shoes with very high heels and was taller than the small gesticulating lawyer. Her thin black dress was stretched tight over her hips and she was running her hand through her short ash-blond hair. I thought she would not come back. When she appeared in the evening, shaken and tense, I had only one single question which I kept repeating furiously and manically: 'Did you sleep with the lawyer? Did you sleep with him? Admit that you slept with him. You know you slept with him.'

Fear would soon create what was feared.

* * *

One icy December day, we booked in at a boarding house in Stockholm's Strandvägen where we were not allowed to share a room, as that was against Swedish hotel regulations.

Gun had quickly broken down under the threat of losing her children. She returned to the house in Lidingö and a husband who had had plenty of time to think out some subtle ways of taking revenge. I was to go to Gothenburg to complete one last production under my contract.

We were not allowed to meet, to talk on the telephone, to write to each other. Every attempt at contact increased the risk of Gun having the children taken away from her. In those days, the laws against a mother who had 'run away' from home were strict.

I managed to get hold of a small apartment (which I still rent) and moved in with four gramophone records, dirty underclothes and a cracked teacup. In my grief, I wrote a film script which was given the title of *Summer Interlude*, and a synopsis for another film as well as a play which has been lost. There were rumours that all film production would be halted by the producers' protest against the government's entertainment tax. For me, such an action would entail financial disaster as I was supporting two families.

One day after Christmas, Gun stepped out of her humiliation and refused to play games under male rules any longer. We paid an exorbitant rent for a furnished four-room apartment right at the top of a lovely old Östermalm house and moved in with Gun's two small boys and the Finnish nurse.

Gun had no work, and I now had three families to support.

What happened after that can be told briefly. Gun became pregnant. At the end of the summer, all film production ceased. I was dismissed from Svensk Filmindustri and became artistic director for Lorens Marmstedt's newly launched theatre, but failed with two productions and got the sack from there too.

Gun's husband telephoned one autumn evening and suggested a reconciliation and an agreement instead of a court case. He asked to see her alone. When they had come to terms, they would go to a lawyer together to draw up a legal agreement. I forbade her to meet her husband alone. She was implacable. He had sounded soft and compliant on the phone, almost crying. After dinner, he came to fetch her in his car. At four in the morning, she came back, her face rigid and her tone of voice evasive. She wanted to sleep. We could talk tomorrow and all the other days. I refused to leave her in peace and demanded to know what had happened. She told me he had driven her out to Lill-Jansskogen and raped her. I left the apartment and ran through the streets.

I have never found out what really happened. There was probably no question of rape in the physical sense, but she may well have been subjected to physical violence: if you sleep with me you can have the children.

I didn't know what was happening. Gun was four months' pregnant. I behaved like a jealous child. She was alone, deserted. There are moving pictures with sound and light which never leave the projector of the soul but run in loops throughout life with unchanging sharpness, unchanging objective clarity. Only one's own insight inexorably and relentlessly moves inwards towards the truth.

In under an hour, all our chances of getting through the crisis together expired. The beginning of the end was a fact, although we clung together in a desperate attempt at reconciliation.

The court case would proceed. That same morning, it was cancelled when Gun's lawyer threatened to make her husband's financial manipulations public. I do not know the detailed circumstances, but the divorce went through fairly painlessly and, after a humiliating investigation, the Child Care Commission recommended that Gun should have the custody of the children.

The drama was over. But our love was so wounded that it bled to death and financial problems overshadowed everything.

No money, no filming, and every month considerable sums to be found for the maintenance of two ex-wives and five children. If maintenance was two days late, a furious Child Care official materialized and remonstrated with me about my dissolute life. Every visit to the family in Gothenburg started with formal courtesy and ended in savage scenes, blows, and the children's anguished screams.

I finally ate humble pie and turned to Svensk Filmindustri for a loan. I was given a loan, but at the same time had to sign a contract for five films for which I would receive two-thirds of my normal fees for both script and direction. In addition, I had to repay the loan within three years, including interest, the sum to be automatically deducted from my income from the company. I was temporarily saved from financial disaster, but tied hand and foot for the foreseeable future.

Our son — Gun's and mine — was born on Walpurgis Night [at the end of April] in 1951. To get the contractions going, we drank champagne and drove in my ramshackle Ford round the hilly Ladugårdsgärdet area. After I had left Gun in the care of the midwife and had been pushed out of the ward, I went home, got even more drunk, unpacked my old toy train set and obstinately played with it in silence until I fell asleep on the floor.

The ban on filming came to an end and Gun got a locum job as a journalist on an evening paper as well as some translation work. I was to make two films immediately, one after the other, *Waiting Women*, from my own script, and *Summer with Monika*, from a novel by Per Anders Fogelström. A young actress playing in a Scala Theatre review in fishnet stockings and an eloquent décolletage was chosen as Monika. Her name was Harriet Andersson, and she had some film experience and was engaged to a young actor. At the end of July, we went on location in the outer archipelago.

I was at once overcome with euphoric light-heartedness. Professional, financial and marital problems fell away over the horizon. The film crew lived a relatively comfortable outdoor life, working days, evenings, dawns and in all weathers. The nights were short, sleep dreamless. After three weeks' endeavour, we sent our results for developing but, owing to a defective machine, the laboratory managed to tear thousands of metres of film and nearly all of it had to be shot again. We cried a few crocodile tears, but were secretly delighted at our extended freedom.

Film work is a powerfully erotic business; the proximity of actors is without reservations, the mutual exposure is total. The intimacy, devotion, dependency, love, confidence and credibility in front of the camera's magical eye become a warm, possibly illusory security. The strain, the easing of tension, the mutual drawing of breath, the moment of triumph, followed by anticlimax: the atmosphere is irresistibly charged with sexuality. It took me many years before I at last learnt that one day the camera would stop and the lights go out.

Harriet Andersson and I have worked together all through the years. She is an unusually strong but vulnerable person, with a streak of brilliance in her gifts. Her relationship to the camera is straight and sensual. She is also technically superb and can move like lightning from the most powerful empathy to conveying sober emotions; her humour is astringent but never cynical; she is a lovely person and one of my dearest friends.

When we returned from our archipelago adventures, I told Gun what had happened and requested a few months' respite, for both Harriet and I realized that our relationship would be limited in time. Gun was furious and told me to go to hell. I was amazed at her splendid rage, which I had never seen before, and greatly relieved.

I packed a few possessions and moved again into my one-room apartment.

We were able to meet again with neither bitterness nor accusations a few years later. After Gun and I divorced, she started reading Slav languages. She gained a doctorate; her translation assignments became more and more sophisticated, and she won a reputation for herself. She gradually created an independent life of her own, with friends, lovers and foreign travel.

Our joy over our renewed closeness was considerable but selfish. We hardly noticed that our son reacted with pain and jealousy.

When Gun was killed in a road accident, Ingmar junior and I arranged to go to the funeral together. We met beforehand in my one-room apartment in Grevturegatan. He was nineteen years old, a tall handsome young man, taller than me, and we had not seen one another for many years. He was wearing a rather tight suit he had borrowed from his half brother. We sat in silence, hoping the time would go a little faster. It did not. He asked me whether by any chance I had needle and thread, because he had to sew on a button. I hunted them out. We sat down opposite each other by the window, Ingmar junior bent over his sewing, his thick fair hair falling over his forehead, strong red hands busy with needle and thread. Occasionally he sniffed with embarrassment. He was surprisingly like the photograph of his paternal grandfather as a student, the same dark-blue eyes, the same coloured hair, the same forehead and sensitive mouth. The same distant Bergman stance: don't touch me, don't come near me, don't hold on to me, I'm a Bergman, for Christ's sake.

I made a clumsy attempt to say something about his mother, but he made a violently dismissive gesture and, when I persisted, he suddenly looked at me with a cold contempt that silenced me.

Gun was the model for many women in my films: Karin Lobelius in *Waiting Women*, Agda in *Sawdust and Tinsel*, Marianne in *A Lesson in Love*, Susanne in *Journey into Autumn* and Desirée Armfeldt in *Smiles of a Summer Night*.

In the incomparable Eva Dahlbeck, I found her interpreter. The two women together succeeded in materializing my often obscure texts, thus demonstrating indomitable femininity in a way I had never dared imagine.

14

I have recurring dreams. The most usual is a professional dream. I am standing in the film studio and am about to stage a scene. They are all there, actors, cameramen, assistants, electricians, extras. For some reason I can't remember the day's script. I have to keep looking in my producer's logbook in which there are incomprehensible lines. I return to the actors and bluff, saying something about pauses. Take out that pause and turn towards the camera, then say the line, wait, say it again quietly.

The actor looks at me incredulously, but obediently follows my instructions. I look at him through the camera, getting half his face and one staring eye. This can't be right. I turn to Sven Nykvist, who is looking through the viewfinder, focussing and zooming in. The actor has meanwhile disappeared. Someone says he's gone for a smoke.

The problem is getting the scene out on to the floor. Owing to my incompetence, I have a whole lot of actors and extras squashed into a corner, pressed against light but strongly patterned wall surfaces. I realize the scene will be extremely difficult to light and notice Sven's politely dissatisfied face. He hates bright overhead lights and double shadows.

I order the wall to be taken away. In that way, we free ourselves and can take the scene from the other side. An assistant says in an aside that moving the wall will certainly be possible, but will take two hours, for that wall in particular happens to be a double wall, linked to another which is heavy and almost immovable. If the wall is removed, the rendering will collapse. I grumble *sotto voce*, with an unpleasant feeling that I myself had insisted on the linking of interior to exterior.

I order the cameras to move to a doorway, and then look through the viewfinder. The extras are hiding the actor. To be seen, he must turn to the right. The script girl tactfully points out that he had moved to the left in the previous take.

It is very quiet in the studio. They are all waiting patiently but without hope. I stare desperately into the viewfinder, where I can see half the actor's face, his eye staring. For a moment I think this will be remarkable, appreciated and described by international critics, but then reject the thought as dishonest.

Suddenly I have the *solution*, a tracking shot. A tracking shot round the actors, past the extras, tracking. Tarkovsky is always tracking round in every scene, the camera flying in all directions. I actually think it an objectionable technique, but it solves my problem. Time passes.

My heart trembles and I find it hard to breathe. Sven Nykvist says tracking is impossible. Why does Sven have to be so awkward? Of course, he's afraid of difficult camera movements and is growing old and cowardly. I look at him in despair. He points behind my back and looks sad. I turn round and there's no scenery there, just the studio wall. He's right, tracking is impossible.

In my desperation, I decide to make a short speech to the assembled personnel. I want to say that I have worked in films for forty years, that I have made forty-five films and I am seeking new ways and want to renew my imagery. One must constantly question one's results. I want to state that I have the capacity, am a man of great experience, that the present problem is a mere bagatelle. If I wanted to, I could move backwards and take a long shot from diagonally above. That would be an excellent solution. I don't believe in God, I know, but it isn't that simple. We all carry a god within us. Everything is a pattern of which we occasionally catch a glimpse, especially at the moment of death. That is what I want to say, but it's not worth it. The people have retreated, assembled deep inside the murky studio, and are standing close together, arguing. I can't hear what they're saying and can see nothing but their backs.

I am being transported in a large aeroplane and am the only passenger. The plane takes off from the runway but can't gain height, so is roaring along wide streets, keeping at the height of the top floors of the buildings. I can see through the windows, people moving, gesticulating, the day heavy and thundery. I trust the pilot's skill, but realize the end is approaching.

Now I'm floating with no aeroplane, moving my arms in a special way and rising easily from the ground. I am surprised that I have never tried to fly before, when it is so simple. At the same time, I realize this is a special gift, and not everyone can fly. Some who can fly a bit have to strain to the point of exhaustion, their arms bent and the sinews in their necks tense. I float unhindered like a bird.

I find myself above a plain, a steppe presumably. It's bound to be Russia. I float over a huge river and a high bridge. Below the bridge, a brick building protrudes out into the river and clouds of smoke are billowing out of the chimneys. I can hear the roar of machinery. It's a factory.

The river now curves around in a great bend, the banks wooded, the panorama infinite. The sun has gone behind the clouds, but the shadowless light is strong. The water flows along green and transparent in a wide furrow. Sometimes I see shadows moving over stones in the depths and there are huge shimmering fish. I am calm and full of confidence.

When I was younger and slept well, I was tormented by loathsome dreams: murder, torture, suffocation, incest, destruction, insane anger. In my old age, my dreams are escapist, but friendly, often comforting.

Sometimes I dream a brilliant production with great crowds of people, music and colourful sets. I whisper to myself with extreme satisfaction: 'This is my production. I have created this.'

15

I had been promised a post at the Royal Dramatic Theatre during the early 1950s, something that made me happy, but then there was a change of regime. The new director did not consider himself tied to any promises, but told me in humiliating terms that I hardly came up to the standards of our national stage. To console myself, I wrote a number of plays which were not accepted. Harriet continued in fishnet stockings and décolletage at the Scala Theatre and had to sing a couplet with the refrain: 'I don't mind being wild and free if Ingmar Bergman fancies me.'

Meanwhile, our relationship was becoming less promising, the demons of my retrospective jealousy poisoning us. I moved into a little hotel at the top of the South Theatre building with a view over Ladugårdsland and Lil-Jansskogen. In a burst of unusually profound misanthropy, I wrote a film that was baptized *Sawdust and Tinsel*.

As no theatre director in the capital wanted my services, I accepted an offer from Malmö City Theatre. Harriet was also engaged. With no regrets, we moved into a three-room apartment in a new residential area on the road to Limhamn. I bought some furniture and we dumped it in the apartment.

Then we dived into the theatre.

On the surface, Malmö Municipal Theatre was a generous establishment in which opera, ballet, operetta and plays shared two stages. One stage was too big (1700 seats) and was called the Big Boo, the other too small (200 seats) and was called the Little Squeak. The project was a result of an insoluble collision between Per Lindberg's monumental people's theatre, with an arena stage and democratic seating, and Knut Ström's dream of visual theatre, created for stage design visions à la Meyerhold and Reinhardt. The acoustical problems were intractable. Orchestral concerts were plagued by the total lack of resonance, the theatre stage by the twenty-two metre proscenium arch, opera and operetta by the distance from the audience, the ballet by the stage floor's sunken iron rails. A relatively large but wretchedly paid staff serviced this monster and managed to put on about twenty productions a year. The autocratic theatre director, Lars-Levi Laestadius, was descended in a direct line from a great revivalist preacher. He was well read, reckless and manically vain, a combination not to be despised in a theatre director.

My eight years with the Malmö City Theatre turned out to be the best of my life so far. I did three productions each winter, and one or two films each summer. I had a free hand, and my private life had virtually ceased to exist. I lived enclosed in a collective effort to provide our monster with theatrical performances which worked and, as I was not burdened with administrative worries, I could devote myself freely to exploring my profession.

Our theatre increasingly became a centre of interest, prominent actors realizing the advantages of performing good theatre in the winter and collaborating in Bergman films in the summer. Our ensemble began to work really well and we had the courage to venture further and further into world drama.

If anyone had thought of asking what aims we had in mind, we would probably not have been able to answer.

I cannot remember any political, religious or intellectual aims whatsoever in my thirteen productions in Malmö. I knew that theatre needed programmes and that it was meaningless, as Shakespeare says in *Hamlet*, to serve 'caviare to the general' on the big stage. It was a matter of putting on an effective, convincing repertoire.

It was also important to make the actual premises possible to act in. By experimenting, we discovered that the stage had one point, roughly one metre from the prompter's box, which it was possible for the audience to hear and see properly. From this point, we could move a few metres sideways and a few metres back, so we had a rectangle barely six metres wide and four metres deep. Outside this acting area, the actor's chances of affecting the audience rapidly decreased. On a stage twenty-two metres wide and thirty-six in depth ('the revolving stage goes halfway to Ystad'), there was a playable space of barely twenty-four square metres.

We were also forced to reduce the sides of the auditorium with mobile screens, so that it seated fewer than a thousand people. The stage machinery turned out to be inferior and worn out, and the modern lighting installations lay at the bottom of the Baltic Sea in a torpedoed German merchant ship, so had provisionally been replaced with a 1914 apparatus. The technical staff were overworked, few in number and fairly heavy drinkers. Naturally there were exceptions who worked themselves to the bone to get our Golem to function.

I arrived every morning at the theatre on the dot of nine, had breakfast consisting of six biscuits and a cup of tea in the canteen, rehearsed from half-past ten until one, had ham and eggs and drank a cup of strong coffee, went on until four, meetings, teaching in the theatre school, writing scripts, taking a nap in my anatomical folding chair, ate dinner in the canteen, always a piece of red meat and a potato, preparing for the next day, doing my homework and checking on the performance.

When Harriet had taken off her make-up and changed, we went home to sleep, neither of us having much to say to the other any longer. I quite often travelled to Stockholm to work on finished or planned films, and lived in my one room apartment in Grevturegatan, had lunch at the studio and dinner at my regular haunt. I owned two pairs of trousers, a number of flannel shirts, disintegrating underwear, three jerseys and two pairs of shoes. It was a practical and undemanding life. I had decided that a guilty conscience was an affectation, because my torment could never make up for the damage I had done. Presumably some inaccessible process went on inside. I had all kinds of gastric flu and ulcers, I vomited often and had troublesome stomach cramps followed by diarrhoea. In the autumn of 1955, after filming *Smiles of a Summer Night*, I weighed fifty-six kilos and was admitted to Karolinska Hospital with suspected cancer of the stomach. I was thoroughly examined by Dr Sture Helander. He came into my room one afternoon bringing the x-rays with him. He sat down and patiently explained them. He described my ailments as 'psychosomatic' and told me I would have to start looking seriously into this dimly-lit area, the border country between body and soul. He advised me to take a yoghurt-like soured milk, a recommendation I have followed ever since. He considered I suffered from certain allergic reactions and would have to feel my way with them to establish what I could stand and what not. He radiated competence, friendliness and wisdom.

*　　*　　*

I persuaded the veteran director and actor, Victor Sjöström, to take on the main role in *Wild Strawberries*. We had worked together before in *To Joy* without feeling any irresistible need to do so again. Victor was tired and ill, and his work had to be fenced round with various considerations. Among other things, I had to promise he would be back home with his habitual whisky punctually every day at half-past four.

Our collaboration began appallingly. Victor was nervous and I was tense. He overacted and I drew his attention to the fact that he was playing to the gallery. He at once shrouded himself in surly withdrawal, then said there was sure to be someone else who could play the part according to my wishes, and that his doctor would give him a sick note any day.

When the girls put in an appearance, the situation brightened. The old charmer delighted in the affectionate bantering attentions of the ladies, flirted with them and bought them flowers and small presents. Unnoticed and privately, I had filmed Bibi Andersson in a slightly décolleté turn-of-the-century dress sitting on a meadow bank feeding Victor with wild strawberries. He snapped at her fingers and both of them laughed, the young woman clearly flattered, the old lion obviously delighted.

In the breaks between takes, we formed a circle round Victor. Like inquisitive children, we demanded that he should talk about the old days, about his work, about other producers, about his colleagues from the silent era, Mauritz Stiller and Charles Magnusson, about actors, about the old Film Town. He talked willingly and amusingly. He admitted he often found he could not utter a word and then he went away on his own and hit his head against some wall. When the tension had lessened, he went back to the set, frequently with a bump on the back of his head or his forehead. He had never thought *Give us this Day*, *The Phantom Carriage* or *He Who Gets Slapped* were especially remarkable. He mostly saw the failings and was annoyed by his own sloppiness and lack of skill. He often marvelled at Stiller's insolent brilliance and never dreamt of comparing himself with his colleague. He also told us that he was very particular that actors in silent film should speak the words that later appeared in the text panels. Lip-reading deaf-mutes had been irritated by the texts saying one thing and the actors something different.

He spoke openly about his love for his late wife, Edith Erastoff, and the drama behind the drama of *The Outlaw and his Wife*, one of his classic movies. He suddenly fell silent, went into retreat and became distant, his face a mask of pain.

Filming progressed and then one day we were to shoot the final scene. Isak Borg's great love of his youth takes him to a sunny hillside. Far away, he can see his parents beckoning to him. We had chosen a place in the area around Film Town. At five in the afternoon, the sunlight shone low over the grass and made the forest dark. Victor was angry and spiteful. He reminded me of my promise – on the dot of half-past four, home, his whisky. I appealed to him. Nothing helped. Victor stumped off. Quarter of an hour later, he was back. Aren't we going to take those damned scenes?

He was by no means in a better mood, but he did his duty. As he walked through the sunlit grass with Bibi in a long shot, he was grumbling and rejecting all friendly approaches. The close-up was rigged up and he went to one side and sat with his head sunk between his shoulders, dismissing scornfully the offer of a whisky on the spot. When everything was ready, he came staggering over, supported by a production assistant, exhausted by his bad temper. The camera ran and the clapper clacked. Suddenly his face opened, the features softening, and he became quiet and gentle, a moment of grace. And the camera was there. And it was running. And the laboratory didn't muck it up.

It struck me much later that the fuss Victor created around my promise of whisky at half-past four and his senile anger were nothing but an ungovernable fear of finding himself inadequate, of being too tired or indisposed or simply not good enough. I don't want to. They've no right to demand it. I never wanted the part. I was deceived, persuaded. Not again, not the terror, the inadequacy, not all that again. I've refused once and for all, I don't want to any more. I don't have to, no one can make me. I'm old and tired. It's all meaningless. Why this torment? To hell with you all, I want to be alone. I've done my bit. It's ruthless to bully a sick man. I won't be able to cope, not again, to hell with your damned filming. And yet. I'll go and try. They've no one to blame but themselves. It won't be good, it can't be good. I'll go on and put in an appearance to show them I can't any longer, haven't the energy. I'll show that damned snotty little pup that you can't treat sick old people any old how. He will have definite confirmation of my inability which, in his opinion, I demonstrated on the very first day.

Perhaps that was what he was thinking, the histrionic old fellow. I did not understand the content of his rage until now, when I find myself in almost exactly the same predicament. All light-hearted games are irretrievably at an end and boredom stares me in the face. Fear of inability attacks and sabotages ability. In the past, I flew unhindered and lifted others. Now I need others' credence and appetite, others will have to lift me for me to wish to fly.

*   *   *

The second time we started on *The Dance of Death*, in 1978, Anders Ek's leukaemia had been confirmed. It caused him considerable pain which he eased with powerful drugs. Every moment distressed him and the high point of the play, the dance with the sabre, proved impossible to perform, so was put off into the future, as his doctor had made vague promises that the pains would recede as the treatment progressed. Our rehearsals were extraordinary, the hours dragging along. We all realized that the whole project was simply not feasible, but for obvious reasons I did not want Anders Ek to quit. Nor did he.

We had worked side by side since the beginning of the 1940s. We had quarrelled and insulted each other, had been reconciled, squabbled again, parted in anger, regretted it and started again from the beginning. *The Dance of Death* was to be the high point of our collaboration. The others in the cast were of top quality, especially Margaretha Krook and Jan-Olof Strandberg.

With discomfort and grief, I was now watching Anders Ek investing his own fear of death in the Captain's, identifying with him. Strindberg's words, which provide the outline of a deplorable, somewhat comical hypochondriac, became in Anders Ek's interpretation the stoically controlled but obtrusive horror of a Samurai. It was ghastly, shameless, hopeless; it made our work in the theatre seem ridiculous.

One morning, I was summoned to Anders Ek's dressing room. He was sitting at his make-up table, his hands spread flat, his face grey with pain and fatigue, brightly illuminated by the autumnal light. He told me he was giving up, that his constant consumption of pain killers was confusing his judgement and that he realized he had been using his own mortal dread to portray the Captain's.

He reproached me for saying nothing.

* * *

The cast and I assembled in the Cinematograph office at the top of the old building inside the courtyard. We were to go through *Autumn Sonata*. Ingrid Bergman read her part in a sonorous voice with gestures and expressions. She had already rehearsed it all and decided in front of a mirror how she would play it. This was a shock. I got a headache and the script girl went out into the corridor and wept with dismay. So many false intonations had not been heard since the 1930s. The star had made her own deletions and refused to say nasty words.

She said the story was rather dull and ought to be cheered up with a few witticisms. 'Why are you such a bore when you write, Ingmar? Otherwise you can be really funny.' She listened to the Chopin prelude, which was to be a culmination of the first act of the film. 'God in heaven, is that dull bit of music to be played *twice*? Ingmar, you're *crazy*. The audience will fall *asleep*. You might at least have chosen something *beautiful* and a little shorter. That bit's so *tedious*, it makes me yawn my head off.'

Ingrid Bergman was portraying a famous pianist. All pianists have had backache, except possibly Rubinstein. A pianist with backache likes to lie down flat on the floor. I wanted Ingrid to lie on the floor in one of her scenes. She laughed. 'You're quite *crazy*, Ingmar dear. This is a *serious* scene. I can't very well act a *serious scene lying on the floor*. It'd be *silly*. The audience will *laugh*. Of course I know there's not much to laugh at in this dreadful story, but why do you *have* to make people laugh in the wrong place, just tell me that?'

Filming began uncomfortably.

The insurance company refused to insure Ingrid because she had had an operation for cancer. A week after filming started, we heard from London, where Ingrid had gone for a routine check, that they had found more metastases and that she should be admitted immediately for further surgery and radiation treatment. She said she intended to finish the film first, and then asked matter-of-factly whether we could compress her contribution by a few days. If that proved impossible, she would stay for the agreed time.

She went on working as if nothing had happened. The fuss of the first days became a courageous professional assault. She accused me of a lack of honesty and forced me into speaking my mind. I told her exactly what I thought. We quarrelled, and looked through the takes as far as she wished to.

At the same time, Ingrid discovered a phenomenon she had never met before in her professional life. Between the many women in the whole troop, strong, independent, professionally and privately experienced women, there was a solidarity, a sisterhood. Katinka Farago, head of production, Inger Persson, responsible for costumes, Cilla Drott, make-up, Sylvia Ingmarsson, our editor, Anna Asp, the set designer, Kerstin Eriksdotter, the script girl, my wife and office manager, and Liv Ullmann, the actress. Ingrid Bergman was drawn into this sturdy solidarity with gratitude, and for short spells could settle into an unsentimental sisterly attachment.

She kept some strips of film from her childhood and upbringing in a rusty tin she had taken with her all over the world. Her father had been a photographer and had occasionally hired a film camera. In the course of fourteen minutes, her home movie showed a little toddler on her lovely mother's knee, a young girl in mourning clothes at her mother's grave, a thin girl laughing and singing at a piano and a young woman smiling charmingly as she watered roses by a greenhouse. Ingrid treasured her film and I, after some difficulty, was allowed to borrow it to make new negatives and new copies of the worn and dangerous nitrate strip.

IB with his daughter, Lena.

IB on the set of *The Seventh Seal*, talking to Death; and (*right*)
Victor Sjöström, the grand old actor and producer of the silent film
era, who starred in *Wild Strawberries*.

Writing, about 1960.

With Käbi Laretei. From a record sleeve.

Toy train. On the set of *The Silence*.

IB's own photograph of the merged faces of Liv Ullmann and Bibi Andersson; and IB shooting *Persona* with Liv Ullmann and Bibi Andersson.

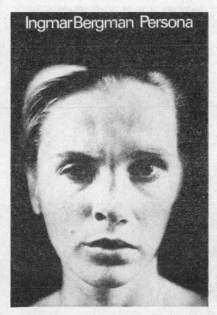

Liv Ullmann in *The Hour of the Wolf*.

Ingrid Thulin in *Cries and Whispers*.

The Magic Flute. Tamino and the Three Ladies.

Sven Nykvist (*left*), the famous cameraman who worked on numerous films with IB, won an Academy Award for Cinematography for *Cries and Whispers*.

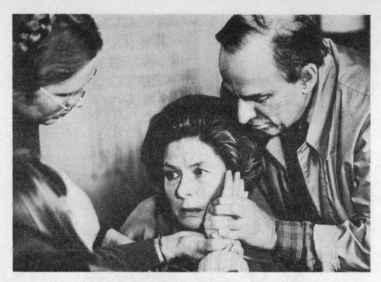

Directing Liv Ullmann and Ingrid Bergman in *Autumn Sonata*.

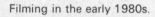

Filming in the early 1980s.

The magic lantern: IB directing young Bertil Guve in
Fanny and Alexander, the film which most directly
draws on his own childhood memories and which
won four Academy Awards in 1984.

IB's father in the pulpit of the Hedvig Eleonora Church, Stockholm; and (*right*) the passport photograph of his mother, about 1963, probably the last picture taken of her.

On the island of Fårö (Sheep Island), where IB built his favourite home.

Ingrid faced her illness with anger and impatience, but her strong body was broken, her senses eroded. She was extremely disciplined in the studio. Once she had made her opposition known, she usually yielded and found it stimulating that someone else made the decisions. One morning she turned round violently and slapped my face (in fun?) and said she would smash me to pieces if I didn't at once tell her how the scene was to be done. Furious at her astonishing attack, I replied that I had asked her a hundred times not to do anything at all and that only bloody amateurs think they have to do something every single moment. She jokingly but sharply mocked my fame as a director of actors. I replied in the same tones that I was sorry for producers who had to work with her during the days of her fame. We went on swapping exchanges in this style, then we started to laugh and went into the studio, where they had been waiting with some curiosity. Ingrid quietened down, her eyelids swollen as if with held-back tears; the rigid mask fell and the camera registered the face of a suffering human being.

A documentary was made of the filming and ran almost five hours when complete. Six months later, Ingrid came to visit us in Fårö. She insisted on seeing the documentary, which was not entirely flattering. When it was over, she sat for a few moments saying nothing – very unusual for Ingrid. Then she said in her inimitable tone of voice: 'I should have seen this before I started filming.'

One afternoon we were sitting in the studio waiting for the setting of the lighting to be completed. It was semi-dusk and we were each in a corner of a shabby old leather sofa. Ingrid made a gesture very rare for an actress – she ran her hand over her face, several times. Then she drew a deep breath and looked at me, without friendliness or trying to make contact. 'You know I'm living on borrowed time.' Sudden smile. Borrowed time.

*　　*　　*

One of the greatest actors of all time, a brilliant portrayer of innumerable kings, heroes, rogues, livers of lies, comical fools, Strindberg characters and more kings, a procession of mighty shadows behind him, was suffering in his seventy-seventh year from circulation trouble in his left leg. An operation would be necessary. He refused and was seized with mortal dread.

For him, the theatre had been Life and Dramaten had been Security. Now there was nothing but Emptiness between him and Death. Despite considerable pain, he went on acting his rôles. After one première, I thanked him for a remarkable performance. He sat in a dirty bathrobe in his dressing room, his make-up still on and his bad leg up on a chair.

He looked at me in the mirror with cold contempt and said: 'To hell with your damned ingratiation. I know what you're up to.'

The kings, the villains, the Strindberg characters, the livers of lies and the comic fools were standing in silence all around him. I had seen them since I was a child. The actor's hatred was as clear as crystal. I was by no means the theatre director bringing my praises, but a hypocritical bastard who had turned his artists' foyer into a lunch room, who had banished him from the Big Stage to the Small Stage, who had refused him *King Lear*. I was to blame for his black and blue foot. I was the person who had let Death out of the props cupboard.

When parts and performances gradually ceased altogether, he dragged himself along to the theatre and took up his post by the noticeboard which everyone passed. He raged away like Philoctetes, unshaven, unwashed and drunk. With terror shining out of his hypnotically blue eyes, he grabbed passers-by, held them by the collar and spurted out his hatred of Hitler-Bergman. The silence grew more profound, the shadows had no eyes, the mirror was shattered, the fragments reflecting emptiness. The familiar veiled voice echoed through the stairwell, everyone was distressed, struck dumb, no one answered him. Day after day he stood there in his last terrible performance in the theatre where he had been king of all kings, the procession of shadows surrounding him, mute but discernible: The Stranger. Hamlet. Richard the Third. Olander. Hickory. The Father. Brendel. Captain Edgar. Orin. James Tyrone. Oedipus. Pius the Seventh. The Officer. Gustav Vasa. Göran Persson. Old Man Hummel. Gustav the Third. Charles the Twelfth.

16

I went to Dramaten – the Royal Dramatic Theatre in Stockholm – direct from Malmö City Theatre and, despite a magnificent cast, I managed to do a bad production of *The Sea Gull*, and requested leave to devote my time to film. I had suddenly become successful, earning money, and my neurosis about financially supporting my various families relaxed its hold.

I had wearied of my bohemian existence and married Käbi Laretei, an up and coming pianist. We moved into a handsome villa in Djursholm, where I intended to live a well-organized bourgeois life. It was all a new and heroic production which rapidly turned into a new and heroic disaster, two people chasing after identity and security and writing each other's parts, which they accepted in their great need to please each other. The masks quickly cracked and fell to the ground in the first storm and neither had the patience to look at the other's face. Both shouted with averted eyes: look at me, look at me, but neither saw. Their efforts were fruitless. Two lonelinesses were a fact, failure, an inadmissible reality. The pianist went on tour, the producer produced and the child was entrusted to competent hands. Outwardly, the picture was of a stable marriage between successful contracting parties. The décor was tasteful and the lighting well arranged.

One afternoon, the Minister of Education telephoned the editing room and asked me if I would like to be the director of the Royal Dramatic Theatre. We met and he briskly explained his request. He wanted me to make a modern theatre out of Dramaten. True, it was magnificent, but its organization and administration were out of date. I pointed out that this would cost money. The Minister replied that if *I* took on the job, *he* would pay. Ignorant of the extremely relative loyalty of politicians to their word, I did not ask for written confirmation of this promise, but assured him I would do my best and that there was sure to be a good deal of fuss. The Minister thought this sounded an excellent description of my programme, so I became the director of the Royal Dramatic Theatre.

I imagine the very first reaction within the theatre was rather favourable. It is true that the board were ungracious, for they, together with the outgoing director, had proposed someone else, but they swallowed their annoyance and received me with impenetrable courtesy.

For tactical reasons, the outgoing director had kept his retirement secret as long as possible, so I had a mere six months to prepare my first season. I was also tied to a large production for television in the spring as well as a film in the summer.

The organization at my disposal at the theatre didn't function. There was virtually no *dramaturg* (artistic adviser) department and the six permanent producers decided on a wait-and-see policy. So reading plays, deciding on the repertoire, drawing up contracts and planning proved to be a tough and lonely business.

One of my first official measures was to 'democratize' the decision-making processes. With the Vienna Philharmonic as a model, we set up an elected representative body consisting of five actors; together with the theatre director, they were to run the theatre, be responsible for the repertoire, engage the actors and take part in casting. They were to be fully informed of the theatre's finances and administration. Should there be controversy, a ballot would be taken in which everyone, including the director, had a vote. This representative body would in its turn be responsible to the company. In that way backroom politics, false rumours and intrigues would be eliminated.

The actors received my suggestions with some hesitation. It is always more comfortable to remain passive and complain about decisions being taken over one's head. Many of them expressed apprehension about our actors' assembly, apprehensions which soon dissolved. It turned out that the representative body shouldered its responsibilities and took a serious part in the running of the theatre. In a surprisingly objective way, it was possible to disregard one's own advantage and narrow egoistic viewpoint and look at one's colleagues with balanced acuteness and insight. A director strong enough to work with the representatives had their invaluable support – or criticism.

Meanwhile, the administration was understaffed and overworked. The theatre director's secretary was also the press officer. The costume studios were disintegrating and the permanent stage designers were ill or alcoholics. Communication was an unknown concept.

The large restaurant in the theatre was notorious for its ghastly food and dubious clientele. Together with the Minister, we inspected the premises. In the meat-cutting room, the drain was blocked: there were several inches of water on the floor and fat grey wormlike encrustations of a repulsive consistency on the tiled walls.

We moved the restaurant out and we moved ourselves in.

Everything was run down, dirty, unmanagable. Previous renovations had barely improved things. When the money had run out, the building committee had ceased working, so ventilation pipes from the dress circle lavatories came out just behind the foyer of the upper circle instead of being equipped with suction fans up to the outer roof. The stench when the wind was in certain directions was more than noticable.

From the artistic viewpoint, there were also painful difficulties. One of the most acute problems was Olof Molander. For decades he had been the theatre's grand master in perpetual rivalry with Alf Sjöberg. He was now over seventy. Ageing had accentuated his unease, his perfectionism, his demands on actors and colleagues. He had become a tormented man who tormented others.

His productions exceeded all the schedules and, because of his temper, he threw the theatre into a state of fevered confusion which was not creative but destructive. No one disputed his brilliance, but more and more people refused to cooperate.

The board gave me the task of telling Molander that his activities at the theatre were to cease.

I had asked by letter for a meeting. He chose to come to my office.

As always, he was elegantly dressed in a well-pressed suit, dazzling white shirt, dark tie and polished shoes. He had broken a finger nail on his beautiful white hand and this was irritating him slightly. His icy clear gaze was fixed on a point somewhere beyond my right ear, the heavy Caesarlike head inclined slightly to one side, and he was smiling almost imperceptibly.

The situation was grotesque. Molander was the man of the theatre who had shown me the innermost magic of drama; and through him I had received my first and strongest impulses. The board's assignment suddenly struck me as being impossible to carry out. Besides, he began to talk about his plans for the next season: all three parts of *To Damascus* on the Small Stage, with a few actors and a bench as the only décor. As he spoke, he fingered his broken nail. He smiled, his eyes fixed on the wall. It suddenly struck me that he had some idea of what was to come and was acting a scene which would make it even more painful.

'Doctor Molander, I am speaking on behalf of the board,' I said.

He looked at me for the first time and interrupted me. 'On behalf of the board, you say? Don't you think anything for yourself?'

I replied that I shared the board's view.

'And what may I ask is the board's view, Mr Bergman?' His smile grew a trifle more cordial.

'I have to tell you, Doctor Molander, that you will not be putting on any productions in this theatre next season.'

The smile faded, the big head turned to the right, the very white hand still occupied with the broken fingernail.

'Oh, is that so?' Then silence fell.

I thought: This is preposterous and I'm making a terrible mistake. This man will remain at the Dramatic Theatre, even if it breaks us. I'm doing wrong. This is wrong, a frightful mistake.

'Your decision will cause you some unpleasantness. Have you considered that, Mr Bergman?'

'You've been a theatre director yourself, Doctor Molander,' I said. 'From what I know of the history of the theatre, you yourself have taken a great many unpleasant decisions.'

He nodded and smiled. 'The press won't approve of your new initiative, Mr Bergman.'

'I'm not scared of the press,' I said. 'In fact, I am not particularly scared at all, Doctor Molander.'

'Oh, aren't you?' he said calmly, looking at me. 'Congratulations. In that case your films are very clever inventions.'

He got up quickly. 'We have nothing else to say to each other, have we?'

I wondered whether I could start again from the beginning and ignore the damage. No, it was too late now, and I had made my first terrifying mistake as theatre director.

I held out my hand to say goodbye. He did not take it. 'I'll be writing to the board,' he said, and left.

Traditionally, the director of the Dramaten is involved in all decisions from major to microscopic ones. It had always been like that and remains so still, despite joint decision-making and a permanent hurricane of meetings. The Dramaten is a hopelessly authoritarian establishment and the director has great opportunities to shape its external and internal activities. I liked the power. It tasted good and was stimulating. On the other hand, my private life developed into a sophisticated catastrophe, but I avoided even contemplating it by being at the theatre from eight in the morning until eleven at night. During my forty-two months as director, I did seven productions, two films and wrote four scripts.

We all threw ourselves into the work. We put on twenty-two plays during the year, nineteen on the Big Stage and three in the China Theatre, the theatre for young people.

The actors' salaries were poor. I increased them by an average of 40 per cent, as I considered an actor to be at least as useful as a curate or a bishop. I instigated one week off, during which rehearsals and performances were prohibited. The hard-working actors were pleased and used those days for moonlighting.

To start with, my measures were met with a confused silence, but the opposition organized itself in a sullen and Swedish way, theatre directors elsewhere in the country meeting at the Golden Otter restaurant to discuss what I was up to. A fast-expanding theatre brings criticism on itself for obvious reasons, and someone started leaking information to the evening papers. Our school theatre was criticized for performing in the China Theatre and our children's theatre because it was performed on the Big Stage. We did too much, too little, too often, too seldom, too many classics, too much that was new. We were accused of not putting on enough modern Swedish drama, and when we put on more modern Swedish drama, it was torn to shreds. All this has beset our national theatre throughout the centuries, and nothing can be done about it.

I don't really know what it was like. I think it was fun in an insane way, both awful and fun. I remember often feeling ill with anxiety, but at the same time I felt a burning curiosity for each new day. I remember climbing up to my command bridge, the narrow wooden stairs up to the secretary's and director's room, with a mixed sense of panic and cheerfulness. I learnt that everything was a matter of life and death, but not particularly important, that reason and misunderstanding went hand in hand like Siamese twins, that in adversity the ordinary fixed proportion of failure predominates and lack of self-confidence is the most dangerous thing in the world, that the desire to give up affects even the strongest, and that the daily grumbling which runs like a humming note through ceilings and walls represents a kind of security. We scream and complain and moan, but we often laugh.

From a strictly professional point of view, my years as theatre director were wasted. I did not develop nor did I have any time to think, and I was always reaching backwards for already proven solutions. When I got to the stage at half-past ten, my head was full of the theatre's morning problems. After the rehearsal, appointments and meetings could be expected until long into the evening.

I think Ibsen's *Hedda Gabler* was the only one of my productions that gave me any satisfaction. Everything else was patchwork, done in too much of a hurry. The real reason why I concerned myself with *Hedda* was that Gertrud Fridh, one of Swedish theatre's many brilliant women, had no leading part that autumn. With a certain reluctance, I set about the play. While I was working on it, the face of its weary supreme architect was unmasked and I realized Ibsen lived desperately entangled in his furnishings, his explanations, his artistic but pedantically constructed scenes, his curtain lines, his arias and duets. All this bulky external lumber hid an obsession for self-exposure far more profound than Strindberg's.

Towards the end of our first season, adversities began to make themselves felt. Our world première of Harry Martinson's *Three Knives from Wei*, put on during the somewhat diffuse Stockholm Festival, was a total failure. The première of my film comedy *Now About These Women* came a few days later and was a convincing and well-deserved fiasco.

The summer was hot. Neither my wife, Käbi, nor I felt like hunting for a holiday house, so we stayed in Djursholm, paralyzed by the heavy thundery heat and our own despondency.

I noted in my intermittent diary: 'Life has precisely the value one puts on it,' undoubtedly a banal way of putting things but, to me, such insight was so breathlessly new I could not implement it.

My permanent assistant, Tim, had a difficult summer. He had been a dancer in the Malmö Theatre Ballet. Because of his small stature and in spite of his skill, he never achieved any of the major rôles, so when he was forty he retired on a pension. I employed him as an assistant, for life had become very complicated after my international breakthrough as a film-maker. Someone had to answer the phone and write letters, someone had to see to payments and accounts, someone had to look after the basic organization, and someone had to take the trouble to be my right hand.

He was a neat person with a high forehead, dyed hair, an elegant thin nose and wide-open childlike blue eyes with long eyelashes. His mouth was a pale line, but not bitter. He was courteous, swift-tongued and good-humoured, obsessed by theatre, but disgusted by mediocrity.

He lived happily with a male friend who was married and had several children. The wife, a wise woman, permitted and encouraged the relationship. To me, Tim was indispensable and our relationship remained relatively uncomplicated. Tragedy descended suddenly and unexpectedly. His friend fell in love elsewhere and Tim was excluded from the secure fellowship of family and regular companionship. He hurtled headlong into a swamp of alcoholism, drug abuse and sexuality of the most brutal kind. Love and closeness turned into lechery, prostitution and undisguised exploitation. This neat, punctual, dutiful man started neglecting his work and turned up openly with peculiar characters who maltreated him.

Sometimes he would be away for several days, sometimes he phoned pleading gastric 'flu, always gastric 'flu. I tried to persuade him to seek psychiatric help, but he wouldn't. The wide-open eyes turned lifeless and red-rimmed, the narrow mouth more and more bitter, his make-up more and more sloppy; his hair-dye peeled off and his clothes stank of cigarette smoke and perfume. 'Gays have no loyalty because we can't have children. Don't you think I'd have made quite a good mother? We're forced to live with our noses shoved so far down in the shit, we choke. Not exactly love and closeness, or what do you think? I don't believe in salvation. No, a full mouth and a bit up the arse, that's my gospel. Maybe it's better for us both that we've never had any kind of physical friendship. That would only create jealousy and enmity, but it's a pity you never want to try in the very slightest. Anyhow, I'm the better off of the two of us because I'm both woman and man. And I'm damned well much brighter than you are.'

Tim died one Sunday morning while making his breakfast, dressed in a play suit, with Donald Duck on his kitchen apron. He fell and lay there, presumably dead within seconds. A good death for a brave little man who was much more afraid of merciful death than bestial life.

Alf Sjöberg had chosen tall young women for the chorus in *Alcestis*, among them the promising Margaretha Byström who had just graduated from our drama school. Another producer wanted her in a major part. I arbitrarily transferred her, without asking Sjöberg; the decision was approved by the representative body, the cast list pinned on the notice board. A few hours later, there was a roaring sound which penetrated right through the double doors as well as the well-insulated metre-thick walls of the director's room. Then came another crash and a bellow. In came Alf Sjöberg, white with rage, demanding that I immediately reinstate Margaretha Byström. I said that was impossible, that she was to have a real chance at last and also that I did not give way to bullying. Sjöberg said he would now at last punch my nose. I retreated behind the board table and said something about bloody peasant manners. The furious producer responded that I had worked against him since the very first day and the limit had now been reached. I went up to him and asked him to hit me at once if he thought that sort of argument was any use. I managed to achieve a frightened smile. Sjöberg's face was trembling, his whole body shaking, and we were both breathing heavily. He said that now I would have to dance so that my shirt flew. At that moment, we both realized how insanely comic the situation was, but it was a long way from laughter.

Sjöberg sat down on the nearest chair and asked how two relatively well brought-up men could behave so idiotically. I promised I would give him back Margaretha Byström if the representative body permitted the change. He made a contemptuously dismissive gesture and left the room. The next time we met, we did not mention the matter. After that we had violent disagreements, both artistic and personal, but we always treated each other with courtesy and without rancour.

I went to the Royal Dramatic Theatre for the first time in my life at Christmas in 1930. They were doing Geijerstam's fairy-tale play *Big Klas and Little Klas*. The producer was Alf Sjöberg, then twenty-seven years old, and it was his second production. I remember every detail, the lights, the set, the sunrise over the small elves in national costume, the boat on the river, the old church with St Peter as doorkeeper, the cross-section of the house. I was sitting in the second row of the upper circle, nearest to the exit door. Occasionally, over the years, in the quiet hour at the theatre between rehearsals and the evening performance, I used to go and sit in my old seat and give in to nostalgia, feeling with every beat of my pulse that this impractical and faded place was really my home. This great auditorium lying in silence and semi-darkness was – after great hesitation, I think of writing 'the beginning and the end and almost everything in between'. It looks silly and exaggerated in print, but I can't find a better way of putting it – the beginning and the end and almost everything in between.

Alf Sjöberg once told me that he never needed a ruler when he was measuring stage surfaces to draw a sketch of a scene. His hand knew the exact scale.

So he stayed on at Dramaten from his début as a passionate young actor (his teacher, Maria Schildknecht said: 'He was a very gifted young actor, but he was so damned lazy he became a producer'). He remained until he died, only two or three times going to other theatres as guest producer, but lingering on at Dramaten, where he became its prince and prisoner. I don't think I've ever met anyone with such obvious violent contradictions within himself. His face was a puppet's mask, controlled by will and ruthless charm. Behind that determined front, social insecurity, intellectual passion, self-knowledge, self-deception, courage and cowardice, black humour and deadly seriousness, gentleness and brutality, impatience and endless patience fought each other or blended in harmony. Like all producers, he also acted the part of a producer; as he was a gifted actor, the performance was convincing.

I never tried to compete with Sjöberg. In the theatre he was my superior, a fact I accepted without rancour. To me, his interpretations of Shakespeare covered everything and I had nothing else to add. He knew more than I did and had looked more deeply, then recreated what he saw.

His generosity often gave rise to mean and petty-minded criticism. I had no idea he was hurt by such grey whimpering.

He was probably most deeply affected by our provincial cultural revolution during the international wave of student unrest. Unlike me, Sjöberg was politically committed and spoke passionately about theatre as a weapon. When the movement blew in over Dramaten, he wanted to man the barricades together with the young. His bitterness was great when he found himself reading that the Dramaten should be burnt to the ground and Sjöberg and Bergman should be hanged from the Tornberg clock outside in Nybroplan.

It is possible some brave researcher will one day investigate just how much damage was done to our cultural life by the 1968 movement. It is possible, but hardly likely. Today, frustrated revolutionaries still cling to their desks in editorial offices and talk bitterly about 'the renewal that stopped short'. They do not see (and how could they!) that their contribution was a deadly slashing blow at an evolution that must never be separated from its roots. In other countries where varied ideas are allowed to flourish at the same time, tradition and education were not destroyed. Only in China and Sweden were artists and teachers scorned.

I myself, under the eyes of my own son, was driven out of the state drama school. When I maintained that young students had to learn their trade to enable them to go out with their revolutionary message, they waved the little red book and whistled, ingratiatingly cheered on by Niklas Brunius, the principal of the school at the time.

The young rapidly and skilfully organized themselves, attracted the mass media and left us, the old and exhausted, in cruel isolation. I personally was not really obstructed in my work. My public was in other countries and earned me a living as well as keeping me in a good mood. I despised a fanaticism I recognized from my childhood, the same emotional sludge, only the content different. Instead of fresh air, we had distortion, sectarianism, intolerance, anxious toadying and a misuse of power. The pattern is unchanging: ideas become institutionalized and corrupted. Sometimes it happens quickly, sometimes it takes hundreds of years. In 1968, it happened at furious speed and the damage done in a short time was both astonishing and hard to repair.

During his last years, Alf Sjöberg did several great things. He translated and adapted Claudel's *The Annunciation to Mary*, an imperishable performance. He put on Brecht's *Galileo [Das Leben des Galilei}* constructed with massive blocks. And lastly he directed *School for Wives*, playful, reserved, obscure and unsentimental.

We had rooms in the same corridor off the upper circle and

often met hurrying to and from rehearsals or meetings. Sometimes we sat down on rickety wooden chairs and talked, gossiped or complained. We seldom went further and never met privately, but simply sat on wooden chairs, sometimes for several hours. It became a ritual.

Years later, as I hurry to my room along that windowless, reeking, drowsily-lit corridor, I think: Perhaps we'll run into each other.

* * *

Örebro, a town west of Stockholm, had built a new theatre and the Royal Dramatic Theatre was invited to celebrate the formal opening. We had chosen a previously unpublished play by Hjalmar Bergman, the town's famous problem son. The play was called *His Grace's Mistress* and elegantly but with little originality made use of characters from *His Grace's Will*, plus the lovable apparition of this mistress. I asked the His Grace of all time, Olof Sandberg, to deck himself out once again in the uniform and nose. He was amused. But just before rehearsals started, Olof Sandberg fell ill and had to turn down the part. I asked Holger Löwenadler to take over. He did so without enthusiasm, because he knew Sandberg was incomparable in the rôle, and that our inventive critics would apply themselves to unfavourable comparisons. A few days before going to Örebro, Per-Axel Branner, the producer, went down with lumbago and was unable to go. I had had a very bad cold for some weeks, but felt I ought to be at the festivities to make a speech and distribute gifts.

The new theatre turned out to be a hideous concrete monster with a fundamental contempt for the art of acting. (Örebro owned one of the most beautiful theatres in the country which, with Swedish indifference to cultural tradition, they had allowed to fall into decay.)

The day before the première, we were rehearsing and setting the lighting. Anders Henrikson, who was playing Wickberg, suddenly succumbed to severe attacks of dizziness and blackouts. He refused to call a doctor and decided to go on, for otherwise the whole ceremony would come to nothing. On the morning of the première, I had a temperature of forty degrees and kept throwing up. I gave in and asked our financial director to take the wheel.

The solemn opening was launched. Lars Forssell had written a masterly prologue which was read by Bibi Andersson, dressed in her star rôle as Sagan in Hjalmar Bergman's play of the same name. She had just started when a man in the second row collapsed and died. He was carried out and the prologue was repeated in an increasingly bizarre atmosphere. Anders Henrikson was feeling even worse, but insisted on going through with it. It became a macabre performance with the prompter in one of the main parts. The critics were scathing and Anders Henrikson received nothing but spite for his courage.

It is understandable that everyone in theatre is superstitious, for our art is irrational, to some extent inexplicable and constantly exposed to chance events. We asked ourselves (jokingly, of course) whether Hjalmar Bergman had been interfering with our efforts, to stop us performing his play.

I have had several similar experiences. Strindberg has been showing his displeasure with me in recent years. I was to do *Dance of Death* and the police came and took me away. I was again to do *Dance of Death* and Anders Ek fell seriously ill. I was rehearsing *A Dream Play* in Munich and the Advocate went mad. We were working on *Miss Julie* a few years later and Julie went crazy. I was planning *Miss Julie* in Stockholm and my intended Julie became pregnant. When I started to prepare for *A Dream Play*, my stage designer grew depressed, Indra's Daughter fell pregnant and I myself contracted some mysterious infection which proved hard to overcome and finally put paid to the project. That number of misfortunes is no coincidence. For some reason, Strindberg did not want me. The thought saddened me, for I love him.

One night, however, he telephoned and we arranged a meeting in Karlavägen. I was jittery and deferential, but remembered how to pronounce his name properly: Ågust (August, as in English, not Owgust). He was friendly, almost cordial. He had seen *A Dream Play* on the Small Stage but said not a word about my affectionate parody of Fingal's Cave.

The next morning I realized that one had to reckon with periods of disgrace if one involves oneself with Strindberg, but the misunderstanding was cleared up on that occasion.

I tell all this as an amusing story but, deep down in my childish heart, naturally I do not consider it as such. Ghosts, demons and other creatures with neither name nor domicile have been around me since childhood.

*   *   *

When I was ten, I was shut inside the mortuary at the Sophiahemmet. There was a caretaker at the hospital by the name of Algot, a clodhopper of a man with cropped yellowish-white hair, a spherical head, white eyebrows and narrow bright blue eyes. His hands were fat and bluish-red. He was responsible for the transport of corpses and liked talking about death and the dead, about death throes and apparent death.

The mortuary consisted of two rooms, a chapel where relatives could say farewell to their dear ones and an inner room where the corpses were tidied up after autopsies.

One sunny day in late winter, Algot lured me into the inner room and pulled the sheet off a corpse that had just arrived. It was a young woman with long dark hair, a full mouth and round chin. I gazed at her for a long time while Algot was busy doing something else. Suddenly I heard a crash. The outer door had slammed shut and I was alone with the dead, the beautiful young woman and five or six other corpses stacked on shelves along the walls and barely covered with yellow-spotted sheets. I banged on the door and shouted for Algot, but it was no use. I was alone with the dead or those in suspended animation. At any moment, one of them might rise up and grab hold of me. The sun shone through the milky white window-panes, above my head accumulated the stillness, a dome that reached the sky. My pulse was thumping in my ears. I found it hard to breathe and was freezing cold right down inside my stomach and on the surface of my skin.

I sat down on a stool in the chapel and closed my eyes. That gave me the horrors. I needed to check what might be happening behind my back or wherever I couldn't see. The silence was broken by a subdued growling. I knew what it was. Algot had told me that the dead farted like hell, a sound that was not immediately frightening. Then some figures passed outside the chapel and I could hear their voices and just see them through the frosted windows. To my own surprise, I didn't call out, but sat in silence and quite still. They gradually disappeared and their voices died away.

Overcome by a violent urge which seared and titillated, I got up and was compelled towards the room of the dead.

The young girl who had just been treated lay on a wooden table in the middle of the floor. I pulled back the sheet and exposed her. She was quite naked apart from a plaster that ran from throat to pudenda. I lifted a hand and touched her shoulder. I had heard about the chill of death, but the girl's skin was not cold, but hot. I moved my hand to her breast, which was small and slack with an erect black nipple. There was dark down on her abdomen. She was breathing. No, she wasn't breathing. Had her mouth opened? I saw the white teeth showing just below the curve of her lips. I moved so that I could see her sex, which I wanted to touch but did not dare.

Then I saw that she was watching me from under her half-lowered eyelids. Everything became confused, time ceased to exist and the strong light grew brighter. Algot had told me about a colleague of his who had wanted to play a joke on a young nurse. He had placed an amputated hand under the covers on her bed. When the nurse did not appear for morning prayers, they had gone to her room, where she was found sitting naked, chewing on the hand. She had torn the thumb off and stuck it into her hole. I was now going to go mad in the same way. I hurled myself at the door, which opened by itself. The young woman let me escape.

I tried to portray this episode in *Hour of the Wolf* but failed and cut it out. It recurs in the prologue of *Persona* and receives its final form in *Cries and Whispers*, in which the dead cannot die but are made to disturb the living.

Ghosts, devils and demons, good, evil or just annoying, they have blown in my face, pushed me, pricked me with pins, plucked at my jersey. They have spoken, hissed or whispered. Clear voices, not particularly comprehensible but impossible to ignore.

Twenty years ago, I underwent an operation, a minor one, but I had to be anaesthesized and, due to an error, was given too much anaesthetic. Six hours of my life vanished. I don't remember any dreams; time ceased to exist, six hours, six micro-seconds – or eternity. The operation was successful.

I have struggled all my life with a tormented and joyless relationship with God. Faith and lack of faith, punishment, grace and rejection, all were real to me, all were imperative. My prayers stank of anguish, entreaty, trust, loathing and despair. God spoke, God said nothing. Do not turn from me Thy face.

The lost hours of that operation provided me with a calming message. You were born without purpose, you live without meaning, living is its own meaning. When you die, you are extinguished. From being you will be transformed to non-being. A god does not necessarily dwell among our increasingly capricious atoms.

This insight has brought with it a certain security that has resolutely eliminated anguish and tumult, though on the other hand I have never denied my second (or first) life, that of the spirit.

*   *   *

When I returned home from Örebro, I had a temperature of forty-one degrees and was more or less unconscious. My doctor confirmed double pneumonia. Stuffed with antibiotics, I lay in bed reading plays.

I gradually got back on my feet but was not entirely

recovered as I still had a temperature which lasted for several days. I was finally admitted to Sophiahemmet Hospital for investigation. My room faced the park, the yellow parsonage on the hill and the hospital chapel, where figures in black marched in and out, with or without coffins.

I was back to square one.

As often as I could, I made my way to the theatre to dispel the rumour of my approaching demise. Otherwise I grew worse, troubled by bouts of dizziness. I had to stand quite still and fix my eyes on a point in the room. If I moved, walls and furniture fell on top of me and I vomited. I looked like an old man, carefully putting one foot in front of the other, holding on to doorposts and speaking slowly.

On certain days, my symptoms eased and I became almost normal. Ingrid von Rosen, a dear friend, bundled me into her car and took me to Smådalarö one windy sunny April day, when there were patches of snow still on the northern slopes and warmth in the lee of the wind. We sat down on the steps of the summer house under the old oak tree, ate sandwiches and drank beer. Ingrid and I had known each other for seven years. We hadn't very much to say to each other, but we liked being together.

I stuck to hospital routines, getting up early, having breakfast, trying a short walk in the park, telephoning the theatre to discuss the latest disasters, reading the papers and sitting down at my desk to see whether I could achieve anything creative.

I had to wait a month or so before images, ceaselessly if reluctantly, freed themselves from my consciousness and gradually took shape as hesitant words and fumbling sentences.

I was contracted with SF to make a film which was to go into production in June. It was to be a tolerable affair called *The Cannibals*. I realized by the end of March that the project was unrealistic and so suggested a *small* film with two women. When the firm's managing director politely asked what the whole thing would be about, I replied evasively that it was about two young women sitting on a shore in large hats, absorbed in comparing hands. The managing director kept a straight face and said enthusiastically that that was a brilliant idea.

So at the end of April, I sat at my desk in my sick room registering the arrival of spring around the parsonage and the mortuary.

The two women were still comparing hands. One day I found that one of them was mute like me, the other voluble, officious and caring, also like me. I hadn't the energy to write in ordinary screenplay form. The scenes were born with infinite labour. I found it almost impossible to shape words and sentences. Contacts with the machinery of the imagination and the cogwheels of invention had been broken off or severely damaged. I knew what I wanted to say but couldn't say it.

Work crawled forward day after day at a snail's pace, interrupted by attacks of fever, disturbances of equilibrium and the fatigue of hopelessness. Time was beginning to run out. The actresses had to be engaged. I knew what to do. I had dinner once or twice a week with my friend and doctor Sture Helander, who was also an enthusiastic amateur photographer. They were filming Hamsun's *Pan* up in Lofoten, under the promising pseudonym of *Summer is Short*. Helander and his wife went to see the filming, as they were close friends of Bibi Andersson's. The doctor photographed a number of things and, as I liked looking at photographs, he showed me his crop, mostly of his wife and the mountains, but also two which especially captivated me. Bibi Andersson was sitting against a dark-red wooden wall, at her side a young actress who was both like and unlike her. I recognized the actress. She had been one of a Norwegian delegation who had previously visited Dramaten. She was considered very promising and had already played Shakespeare's Juliet and Goethe's Margareta. Her name was Liv Ullmann.

After filming the two women had gone off on holiday to Jugoslavia with their husbands, but eventually we tracked them down.

When the season at Dramaten was over, I at last got the script of *Persona* off my hands and met my actresses, who were both amused and scared by the task before them.

At the press conference for *Persona*, my dizzy spells persisted and, when the photographer insisted on photographing me with the ladies beneath some birch trees, I had to refuse. I couldn't move. The photograph he eventually produced shows three pale, somewhat worried people, all inclining their heads to the left. When Kjell Grede saw it, he laughed and said: 'The old diva taking her greyhounds for an airing.'

The start of filming was fixed and the location became Fårö. The choice was easy. Fårö had for many years been a secret love of mine. I had grown up in Dalarna; its landscape – the river, the hills, the forests and heathlands – were deeply engraved on my conciousness. And it became the island of Fårö.

It so happened that, in 1960, I was to make a film called *Through a Glass Darkly*, about four people on an island. In the opening shot, they appear at dusk out of a rolling sea. Without ever having been there, I wanted the filming to take place in the Orkneys. The board of the film company wrung their hands when faced with the expense and put a helicopter at my disposal to explore the Swedish coast. I returned even more determined to do the filming in the Orkneys. One almost desperate executive suggested Fårö. Fårö was supposed to be like the Orkneys. But cheaper. More practical. More accessible.

To settle the argument we set off one stormy April day for Gotland, to reconnoitre Fårö and then definitely decide on the Orkneys. A ramshackle taxi met us at Visby and took us through rain and snow to the ferry. After a rough crossing, we landed on Fårö, then rattled along the slippery winding coastal roads.

In the film, there is a stranded wreck. We swung round a corner of a cliff, and there was the wreck, a Russian salmon cutter, just as I had described it. The old house was to be in a small garden containing ancient apple trees. We found the garden. We would build the house. There was to be a stony shore. We found a stony shore facing infinity.

The taxi finally took us to the steles, the weathered columns of rock off the north side of the island. We stood leaning against the wind, staring with watering eyes at those secretive idols raising their heavy foreheads against the waves and the darkening horizon.

I don't really know what happened. If one wished to be solemn, it could be said that I had found my landscape, my real home; if one wished to be funny, one could talk about love at first sight.

I told Sven Nykvist I wanted to live on the island for the rest of my life and that I would build a house just where the film's stage house stood. Sven suggested I should try a few kilometres farther south. That is where my house stands today. It was built between 1966 and 1967.

My ties with Fårö have several origins. The first was intuitive. This is your landscape, Bergman. It corresponds to your innermost imaginings of forms, proportions, colours, horizons, sounds, silences, lights and reflections. Security is here. Don't ask why. Explanations are clumsy rationalizations with hindsight. In, for instance, your profession you look for simplification, proportion, exertion, relaxation, breathing. The Fårö landscape gives you a wealth of all that.

Other reasons: I must find a counterweight to the theatre. If I were to rant and rave on the shore, a gull, at most, would take off. On the stage, such an exhibition would be disastrous.

Sentimental reasons: I would retreat from the world, read the books I hadn't read, meditate, cleanse my soul. (After a month or two I was hopelessly involved in the islanders' problems, something which resulted in the 1969 *Fårö Document*.)

Further sentimental reasons: during the filming of *Persona*, Liv and I were overwhelmed by passion. With monumental lack of judgement, I built the house with the idea of a mutual existence on the island. I forgot to ask Liv what she thought. I managed to find out later from her book *Changing*. On the whole her testimony is, I think, affectionately correct. She stayed a few years. We fought our demons as best we could. Then she got the part of Kristina in *The Emigrants*. That took her far away. When she left, we knew.

Self-imposed solitude is all right. I entrenched myself and established machine-like routines. I got up early, went for a walk, worked and read. At five o'clock, the wife of a neighbour came and cooked dinner, washed up and left. At seven o'clock, I was alone again.

I had cause to dismantle the machine and examine the parts. I was dissatisfied with my latest films and productions, but dissatisfied *after* the event. While the work had been going on, I had protected myself and my doings from destructive criticism, and could not identify failings and weaknesses until later.

17

In the spring of 1939, I went to see Pauline Brunius, director of the Royal Dramatic Theatre. I asked to be allowed into the theatre to do anything, as long as I could be there and learn the profession. Mrs Brunius, a slender, beautiful woman with a pale face, large rather protruding clear blue eyes and a well-modulated voice, declared in three minutes that she would *terribly* like to have me when I had passed my academic exams. She went on at length about education being the best way into the art of theatre, especially for anyone bold enough to want to be a producer. When she saw my genuine despair, she patted my arm and said, 'We've got our eye on you, Mr Bergman.' I was out on the street within four minutes, my dreams shattered. There was no limit to the hopes I had pinned on my interview with Mrs Brunius.

I did not realize until long afterwards that Father had been in touch with Mrs Brunius, whom he knew in some official capacity. He had told her of his wishes regarding my studies. Maybe that was all for the best.

In my desperation, I applied to the Opera House as an unpaid anything. Harald André had just become director, a tall man with a reddish complexion, snow-white hair and moustache. He viewed my anguish through narrow peering slits of eyes and muttered something benevolent which I didn't hear. I was suddenly employed as a production assistant. According to some mid-nineteenth century decree, this entailed remuneration of ninety-four *riksdaler* a year.

Harald André was a prominent producer and a skilful director; Leo Blech, Nils Grevillius and Issay Dobrowen were his conductors. The opera house had a permanent professional company, a fairly good chorus, a dreadful *corps-de-ballet*, a seething mass of stage hands and a Kafka-like administration. The repertoire was extensive, ranging from *Mignon* to *The Ring*, the audience small, faithful and conservative. They loved their favourites and constantly returned.

The Stage Office formed the hub of the wheel, run by a little man resembling Dr Mabuse who was always in place.

The stage was spacious but heavy going, the floor sloping towards the footlights, no space in the wings, but four traps and huge flies.

The ballet rehearsal room sloped in the same way as the stage, was badly ventilated, draughty and dirty. The dressing rooms at stage level were spacious and equipped with windows, but higher up they became worse and the sanitary arrangements were extremely limited.

Thorolf Jansson had created an enormous number of sets, grandiose scenery-painting of the old school, including an unforgettable living birch in the middle of Arnljot's Jämtland landscape, a dangerous forest with a waterfall and a barn for Strindberg's *The Virgin Bride* and a springlike meadow for the competition in *The Mastersingers*. Inspiration and knowledge. Backdrops and side-flats. Acoustically advantageous and well-made scenery, practical to change and store.

In contrast to this mildly ageing beauty was Jon-And's humorous, German-inspired expressionism in *Carmen*, *Tales of Hoffmann*, *Otello*.

The lighting was an incomprehensible antiquity from 1908 in the hands of an aged nobleman with the title of Fire Master and his son, a taciturn middle-aged youth. They worked in a narrow corridorlike space to the left of the stage, where their chances of seeing what was going on were almost non-existent.

A considerable work force constructed the scenery, took it down, loaded it, transported it, and unloaded it. The whole arrangement was a mystery. Today's computerized electronic sophistications function far worse than that clumsy machinery of the 1930s.

The mystery had only one explanation. Day and night, a permanently employed, somewhat elderly, somewhat drunken army of determined individualists and discerning old-hands worked on the stage. They were responsible. They knew what they were doing. They knew the scene changes. It is possible they worked in shifts, but I don't know. I probably thought the same old men held the same ropes, day and night, year in and year out. Sobriety may have been somewhat affected by Wagner's long notes and Isolde's long-winded dying, but the sets came in and out at the right moments, the backcloth was raised and lowered at the right speed, the curtain rose or fell with an artistic finesse which can never be replaced by a mechanical arrangement with graded speeds. The Flying Dutchman's ship sailed, the Nile glittered in the moonlight, Samson pulled down the temple, the gondola of the Barcarole glided through the canals of Venice, Puccini's witches in *Le Villi* flew, the spring storm ripped the walls off Hunding's house leaving free passage for the incestuous sibling couple sixteen bars before the end of the act.

Sometimes things went wrong. One evening *Lohengrin* was being performed with Einar Beyron and Brita Hertzberg. I was doing the lighting. Everything went smoothly until the finale. Lohengrin had sung his Grail story. The chorus on the narrow headland out into the river sang resoundingly that the swan harnessed to a handsome shell was approaching to fetch our blond hero. Elsa was broken-hearted and clad in white. (I loved Brita Hertzberg ardently and secretly.) The swan was an extraordinarily beautiful creation mutually inspired by Thorolf Jansson and the head of the technical staff. It glided, swam, moved its slender neck and could ruffle its wings.

The swan had now jammed a few metres from the landing stage. It jerked and tugged but refused to budge. The shell was stuck, had gone off the rails. The swan nevertheless moved its long neck and ruffled its wings as if unmoved by its carriage's catastrophic situation. Wagner's instructions involve the bird diving on a given bar. Elsa's younger brother, whom the malicious Ortrud has bewitched but who is now released, ascends in its place and throws himself into his dying sister's arms. As the swan was stuck, it couldn't dive, but Elsa's brother ascended all the same. Panic broke out among the stage hands serving in the first trap. Where the hell is the swan? We've sent the boy up too soon. Let's bring him down again.

Elsa's brother disappeared before he had even left the trapdoor floor. Now they were a long way behind in the score and the boy was once again delivered, but lost his footing and stumbled over Elsa, who was thrown into disarray. According to Wagner, a dove is now lowered from the flies and fastens a golden ribbon to the shell. When Lohengrin has stepped aboard during the elegiac farewell, the shell should be towed away by the dove and disappear into the left-hand wings. As the swan was stuck and the shell stranded, a desperate Lohengrin grabbed the golden cord and marched out to a more and more stifled farewell. The swan swung its beautiful neck and ruffled its wings. Elsa collapsed and lay trembling in her brother's arms. The curtain fell slowly, slowly.

For several weeks I sauntered around as though invisible. No one took the slightest notice of me. I made a few cautious contacts, but was coldly rebuffed. At night, I sat in a corner of the stage office, a large room with a low ceiling and a vaulted window down near the floor. Telephones rang, people came and went, messages were brought and sent, and occasionally some celebrity towered in the doorway. I got up and greeted whoever it was. Someone glanced absently at me, the bell rang to indicate the interval was over, cigarettes were stubbed out and they all took up their places.

One evening, Dr Mabuse took me by the lapels and said: 'The others don't like you sitting in here during the intervals. You can stay in the passage behind the stage.' I hid myself behind the door of the ballet room and swallowed my tears of humiliation. A beautiful dancer with an Italian name found me when she unexpectedly turned on the light in the ballet room. 'You're much too interested in ballet,' she said. 'We don't like you staring when we're working.'

After a few months of floating around in this no man's land I was sent to Ragnar Hyltén-Cavallius, who was producing Gounod's *Faust*. Nicknamed Fiametta, he was a tall gangling person with far too noble features.

To me, he was someone to be reckoned with. I knew he had directed a great many films, written a great many scripts and produced innumerable operas. I had seen him working on the stage with singers and chorus. His voice was hoarse and he lisped slightly, his head thrust forward, his shoulders hunched up, his long hands fluttering. I realized he was knowledgable, temperamental and old-fashioned. To the stars he was gentle, benevolent and playful; to the others sarcastic, malicious and ruthless. His thin lips were always smiling, whether he was amiable or angry.

He quickly saw my total ignorance and reduced me to an ill-treated errand boy. Sometimes he would pinch my cheek, but I was mostly a grateful victim of his ironies. Despite my contempt and fear, I learnt a great deal from his thorough and always practical instructions. Together with the Dramaten's brilliant stage designer, Sven Erik Skawonius, he painstakingly created an atmospheric performance of Gounod's popular old opera.

Leon Björker, the great bass singer, who could not read music, said: 'Why do you look so arrogant? Are you a bum boy, too?' I stared at him, not understanding. Arrogant? Björker went on: 'We usually say hello in this theatre. We've passed each other every day and you've declined to say hello to me. *Are* you a bum boy?' I couldn't answer. I didn't understand and had no inkling of the gossip about Fiametta's new faggot.

Fiametta was audacious, ironic, hurtful, but never importunate. I liked him, really, and admired his devotion and indefatigable obstinacy. An affected, malicious, bitter and mediocre old gentleman for whom, in youth, a brilliant future had been predicted.

One afternoon after rehearsal, he stayed behind on a wooden chair, overcome with sorrow, leaning against the table where I was sitting making stage notes in the score. He said in a quiet and pleading voice: 'Mr Bergman, what shall I do? Hjördis insists. She is determined to have long blonde plaits. It'll be grotesque. She's got a swollen head even in private life!' He sat in silence, rocking his chair. 'You've chosen a peculiar métier, Mr Bergman. When one is getting on in years, it can seem extremely frustrating.'

Issay Dobrowen was to conduct and produce Mussorgsky's *Khovanshchina*. He brought his own assistants and was always surrounded by a cloud of camp followers. I stole opportunities to watch him working – a fundamental experience.

Dobrowen was a Russian Jew, originally from Moscow. His record was good, but rumour had it that he was difficult. We found an impressive and courteous little man, becoming grey at the temples, with a handsome face. When he stepped on to the conductor's podium, he was transformed, and we saw an outstanding European, no respecter of persons, determined to raise the artistic level of theatre. Reactions ranged from straight surprise ('How can he say such things to anyone? I'm worth just as much as he is, aren't I!'), suppressed rage ('I'll give the bastard one on the jaw!'), to submission ('He's a devil but he's a Satan!') and finally devotion ('The best thing that has ever happened to us and the theatre!')

With quiet pleasure, I watched this little man chase the voluminous Björker all over the stage, not once or twice, but thirty times. Our great alto singer, the lovely swarthy Gertrud Pålson-Wettergren, fell headlong in love and had never sung so beautifully. Einar Beyron was insulted daily, with some justice. Slowly the drastic approach began its work and out of a nasty provincial primadonna was born not a singer (there were limits to all miracles) but a fine actor. Dobrowen soon saw the chorus was badly trained but excellent material, which he took in hand with love and thoroughness. Some of his very best moments were with the chorus.

I had a few opportunities to talk to him, though my respect and language difficulties posed major obstacles, and some things were comprehensible. He said he was afraid of *The Magic Flute*, both scenically and musically. He complained about the stage designer's weighty and overloaded sets. The world première stage couldn't have been so large. Just think of Tamino and the Three Gates. The music states the number of steps from gate to gate, the scene changes are swift and simple, backcloth and wing sets changing places, no pauses for rebuilding. *The Magic Flute* had been born in an intimate wooden theatre with the simplest equipment and matchless acoustics. The chorus sings *pianissimo* behind the stage. *Pamina lebt noch* [Pamina is still alive]. Dobrowen wanted *young* singers, *young* virtuosi. The great arias – the medallion aria, the D-minor aria, the Queen of the Night's coloraturas – were fired by far too middle-aged cannons. Young fire, young passion, young playfulness. Otherwise it becomes merely silly.

* * *

In my film *Hour of the Wolf*, I later tried to create the scene that had moved me most profoundly. Tamino is left alone in the palace garden. He cries: 'Oh, dark night! When will you vanish? When shall I find light in the darkness?' The chorus answers *pianissimo* from within the temple: 'Soon, soon or never more!' Tamino: 'Soon? Soon? Or never more. Hidden creatures, give me your answer. Does Pamina still live?' The chorus answers in the distance: 'Pamina, Pamina still lives.'

These twelve bars involve two questions at life's outer limits – but also two answers. When Mozart wrote his opera, he was already ill, the spectre of death touching him. In a moment of impatient despair, he cries: 'Oh, dark night! When will you vanish? When shall I find light in the darkness?' The chorus responds ambiguously. 'Soon, soon or never more.' The mortally sick Mozart cries out a question into the darkness. Out of this darkness, he answers his own questions – *or does he receive an answer?*

Then the other question: 'Does Pamina still live?' The music translates the text's simple question into the greatest of all questions. 'Does Love live? Is Love real?' The answer comes, quivering but hopeful in a strange division of Pamina's name: 'Pa-*mi*-na still lives!' It is no longer a matter of the name of an attractive young woman, but a code word for love: 'Pa-*mi*-na still lives.' Love exists. Love is real in the world of human beings.

In *Hour of the Wolf*, the camera pans across the demons, which through the power of the music have come to rest for a few moments, then stops on Liv Ullmann's face. A double declaration of love, tender-hearted but hopeless.

A few years later, I suggested to Swedish Radio that we should do *The Magic Flute* for television. I was met with some hesitation and confusion. If Magnus Enhörning, head of broadcast music at the time, had not intervened with energy and enthusiasm, the project would never have materialized.

During my professional life, I have not done a great many music-drama productions. The reason is embarrassing. My love of music is scarcely reciprocated, for I am plagued by a total inability to remember or repeat a sequence of notes. I quickly recognize them, but have difficulty placing them, and I can neither sing nor whistle a tune. For me, learning a musical work more or less by heart is a laborious process. Day after day, I sit with the tape-recorder and the score, sometimes paralyzed by my lack of skill.

My embittered struggle may contain some positive features. I have to spend an inordinate amount of time on the work, as I have to listen to every bar, every beat of the pulse, every single moment.

My productions stem from the music. I cannot go in any other direction. My disability prevents me.

*   *   *

Käbi Laretei loved the theatre, I loved music. Through our marriage, we destroyed each other's loves, once so naively and spontaneously emotional. At a concert, I would turn to Käbi, filled with happiness. She would look at me sceptically. 'Did you *really* think *that* was good?' The same misery at the theatre. What she liked, I disliked and vice-versa.

Nowadays we are the best of friends and have returned to our amateurish judgements of each other's art. However, I cannot deny that during my life with Käbi, I learnt a great deal about music.

18

Andrea Corelli came from a wealthy upper-class family in Turin. Brought up according to the conventions of the day, she went to a convent school, was thoroughly educated in the classics and languages and won a place at the Academy of Music in Rome. She was considered a promising pianist and lived near her family. Deeply religious, she was entirely protected within the conventions of the Italian upper classes.

She was a beautiful, happy and somewhat romantic young woman, with great intellectual curiosity, much courted and surrounded by admirers. Not only was she very attractive, she was also what was called a good match. A middle-aged virtuoso violinist, Jonathan Vogler, used to visit the Academy to give lessons. Rather flabby, going grey at the temples and with unusually large black eyes that squinted violently, he came from Berlin. He aroused passions with his playing and his demonic radiance.

Andrea was chosen to accompany him at some Academy concerts. She fell in love with him, left family and the Academy, married him and joined him on his extensive journeys. Vogler later formed a string quartet which became internationally famous, Andrea playing when the ensemble was performing piano quintets. She gave birth to a daughter, who was left with relations and later went to boarding school.

Andrea soon found out that Vogler was being unfaithful to her. His appetite for women of all kinds turned out to be considerable. This short pot-bellied man with a squint, with heart trouble and always short of breath, was a gargantuan pleasure lover and a brilliant musician. Andrea left him and he swore he would take his own life. She returned and everything went back to normal.

She realized now that she loved him without reservations, so cast aside all conventions and not only became the quartet's administrator and manager, but also managed her husband's love affairs with firmness and humour. She made friends with his mistresses, supervised the erotic traffic like a station-master, and became her husband's confidante. He did not stop lying, because he was incapable of telling the truth, but he no longer had to camouflage his lechery. With determination and a talent for organization, Andrea piloted her musicians through endless tours, both at home and abroad.

Every summer during the inter-war period, they were invited to stay at a *schloss* near Stuttgart. This castle lay in beautiful countryside with wide vistas over mountains and rivers. Its chatelaine was a somewhat eccentric elderly lady called Mathilde von Merkens, the widow of an industrial magnate. Both she and the *schloss* had decayed.

Despite this, she went on year after year, bringing together some of Europe's most distinguished musicians, including Casals, Rubinstein, Fischer, Kreisler, Furtwängler, Menuhin and Vogler. Every summer, they obeyed the call, ate at her widely praised table, drank her fine wines, covered their own and other men's wives and made great music.

Andrea still retained her talent for vulgar Italian story telling. She had a hearty laugh. Her mad, bizarre, obscene and comical stories were material that positively demanded a film. I decided to make a comedy of it all.

Unfortunately I missed the point, a fact I realized only when the film had been irretrievably made.

Andrea came to see Käbi and me in Djursholm, bringing with her some photographs from a summer at Mathilde von Merken's *schloss*, among them a picture that made me wail with misery. The picture is of the company on the terrace after what has clearly been a splendid dinner. The greenery has overflowed all over the balustrade and stone steps, cracked the mosaics and climbed up statues and ornaments. Scattered around the damaged floor of the terrace, a handful of Europe's musical geniuses relax in battered basket chairs. They are smoking cigars, perspiring and looking a trifle unshaven. Someone is laughing, so he is blurred. That's Alfred Cortot. Jacques Thibault is leaning forward to say something and has tipped his hat down over his nose. Edwin Fischer is propping his stomach on the balustrade. Mathilde von Merkens is holding a cup of coffee in one hand and a cigarillo in the other. Vogler has closed his eyes and his waistcoat is unbuttoned. Furtwängler has seen the camera and managed to arrange a demonic smile. A few women's faces can just be seen behind the tall windows, ageing, swollen, careworn. A young woman, exquisitely dressed and coiffed, is standing a little to one side, her beauty oriental. That is Andrea Vogler-Corelli. She is holding her five-year-old daughter by the hand.

The stucco is flaking off the wall, a windowpane has been replaced with a square of wood, a Cupid has lost its head. The picture radiates a good dinner, perspiring heat, lechery and gentle decay. After these gentlemen have belched, farted and had their laced coffee, they presumably gather in Mathilde von Merkens' huge salon, with its smell of mould, and there they make music. They are, like the angels, perfect.

I was desperately ashamed of my superficial and artificial comedy (*Now About These Women*). This shame was instructive but disagreeable. I had had too much else to think about as I had just become director of Dramaten, facing my first season without the prospect of pulling out. So I grasped at the simplest solutions. I would have preferred to resign, but had committed myself. All the contracts were drawn up and everything prepared down to the last detail. The script was fun and everyone was pleased.

Sometimes considerably more courage is required to put on the brakes than to fire the rocket. I lacked the courage and realized, too late, what sort of film I ought to have made.

Punishment was not unforthcoming. The whole affair was a dismal failure, with the audience as well as financially.

The war came. Though several theatres and concert halls were closed, and many other musical groups disbanded, the Vogler Quartet had special permission to go on touring.

One autumn day, Andrea and the other musicians found themselves in East Prussia, near Königsberg. They were living in a small seaside hotel on the coast and playing in the vicinity.

One evening, Andrea was walking along the shore by herself, the sun setting in glowing mist, the sea absolutely calm. Artillery fire could be heard in the distance. Andrea suddenly stopped, aware of two powerful, simultaneous experiences: one that she was pregnant, the other that a guardian angel protected her.

A few days later, the towns round Königsberg were captured by Russian troops. Andrea, her daughter, her husband and the other musicians were taken to an assembly point. Their travel permit was regarded with suspicion, and they were all locked into a cellar. Through windows high up in the wall, they could see an asphalted school playground. Their instruments were confiscated. Jonathan Vogler was ordered to undress and was taken with other prisoners to the school yard to be shot. Through some administrative hitch, they were left standing up against the wall for several hours, then they were ordered back to the cellar. The next day the same procedure was repeated.

The guards raped the women prisoners. So as not to terrify her daughter, Andrea allowed the men to make use of her. She reckoned she had been raped twenty-three or twenty-four times.

A few days later, Russian élite units arrived in town, an administration was set up and some Russian soldiers were shot as a deterrent: the Red Army does not plunder the destitute or rape the defenceless.

The cellar room was transformed from a prison into a dwelling. Vogler was given back his clothes and had a breakdown, lay in a corner shaking all over, but he kept quiet. Andrea and the other musicians set off on a hunt for food.

During one of their expeditions, she met the town's theatre director and some actors. They decided to visit the Commandant to get some kind of theatre and musical activities going. Andrea spoke Russian, so told a lieutenant-colonel about the project and he was interested. Through some unfathomable organizational caprice the musicians got back their instruments, undamaged.

A few days later, Andrea and the theatre director announced a soirée in the town hall. The top floor had gone, but the main hall was fairly intact. At eight o'clock, the premises were full to overflowing with townspeople, refugees and the Russian occupiers. They played Bach, Schubert and Brahms. The theatre director and the remains of his company performed scenes from *Faust*. They continued for several hours, until heavy rain coming through the unprotected flooring above put an end to the festivities.

The performance was repeated, a great success. The entrance fee was a piece of coal, an egg, a dab of butter or some other necessity. Andrea administered and organized and also saw that her husband and the other musicians practiced regularly.

After the war, Jonathan Vogler abandoned his wife and became professor at some German academy. He was by then quite white-haired, his complexion as if painted with chalk, his black eyes burning like coals, his stomach now grotesque and his heart trouble chronic. He lived with three permanent mistresses.

Andrea settled down in Stuttgart and established herself as a music teacher. Käbi Laretei, her devoted pupil, was treated with unsentimental kindness and flint-hard resolve.

Käbi's problem was serious. She had made a career out of

talented musical generosity, warmth and temperament com-
bined with beauty and radiance. But this exquisite building
stood on very shaky ground. She lacked sound technique. The
result was a dangerous uncertainty beneath the glamorous
self-confidence. Her concerts could be brilliant or appalling,
depending on circumstances.

Käbi Laretei went to Andrea Vogler-Corelli to construct a
firm foundation beneath that lovely building. It turned out to
be a tough task extending over many years. Meanwhile an
intimate friendship grew between the two women.

I was occasionally allowed to be present at her lessons, at
which the same rigorous standards applied as with Torsten
Hammarén. A phrase plucked apart into its constituent parts,
practised with pedantic fingering for hours, then reassembled
when the time was ripe.

Andrea liked Käbi's big pianist's hands, her temperament
and her musical talent, but complained about her indolence.
She was merciless; Käbi was restless, but submitted. The
whole became far-reaching, like an analysis, the solutions
nearly always of a technical kind, but turning on spiritual
considerations in the course of the work. 'Finger joints, hand,
lower arm, upper arm, shoulder, spine, posture, fingering.
Don't cheat, don't hurry when in two minds, stop and think.
From that bar you have the answer to the whole phrase. Carry
on, you must breathe there. Why do you hold your breath all
the time, dear child? There's only half an hour left now, have a
little patience and you'll get your tea. If the second finger joint
is troubling you, then the trouble is here.' (A ringed forefinger
between the pupil's shoulder-blades). 'Now play F-sharp
twenty times, no, thirty times, but *think what you're doing*!
First with your forefinger, then middle finger. Where does it all
come from? *That's it*. The force comes from the stomach,
don't cheat with your posture. There's no instrument, never
will be, that can render the dynamism Beethoven imagined in
his silent world. See, now it sounds lovely. You who have so
much beauty in you, you must learn to bring it out. Let's go on
then. Here you have a premonition of what will happen to us

twenty-nine bars later; you hardly notice it, but it's important. No padding in Beethoven, he speaks persuasively, furiously, sorrowfully, cheerfully, painfully, never mumbling. You mustn't mumble, never produce common stuff! You must know what you want even if it's wrong. Meaning and context. Go ahead now. That doesn't mean everything has to be emphasized; there's a difference between emphasis and significance. Now let's go on, be patient, practise patience. When you want to stop, you have to connect up to a special battery that doubles your effort. There's nothing so awful as a guilty conscience in art. Stop there. A C. My friend Horowitz went to the piano every morning after breakfast and played a number of C-major chords. He said he was washing his ears.'

I listened to Andrea and thought about theatre, about myself and actors, our sloppiness, our ignorance, the damned common stuff we produce in exchange for payment.

In our remote cultural landscape, we certainly have had a number of outstanding actors who lack basic technique. Relying on undoubted charisma, they go on stage and set up a kind of sexual relationship with the audience. When that relationship is not there, they grow confused, forget their lines (which they haven't learnt properly), become diffuse and slurred, a nightmare for their fellow players and the prompter. They have been brilliant amateurs with moments, perhaps whole evenings, of dazzling inspiration, but with uneven greyness, stimulants, drugs and alcohol in between.

The great Gösta Ekman is a good example. His experience, his magical charisma and his brilliance were of no use to him. His misery can be seen in his films. The camera reveals his humbug, his emptiness and uncertainty, his lack of sexual identity.

His premières were probably magnificent. But the fifth performance? Or the fiftieth? I saw his Hamlet on a perfectly ordinary Thursday. It was a private display of arrogance and unmotivated affectation performed in diligent dialogue with his increasingly agitated prompter.

*　　*　　*

For a few summers, Käbi and I rented a house in the archipelago on north Ornö, a patrician villa in stone, on a headland with a view out towards Jungfrufjärden and the inlet to Dalarö. The headland was separated from the rest of the island by thick ancient forest which was marching towards the house and had already invaded the strawberry bed and potato patch. A moist dimness reigned within it, orchids gone wild glimmering in the twilight and the mosquitoes angry and poisonous.

In this exotic environment, we celebrated summer – Käbi, her mother, our German maid, Rosie, and I. Käbi was pregnant and suffering from a harmless but extremely annoying complaint called restless legs. She had continuous itching in knees and toes, so had to move about all the time. Nights were the worst, as she couldn't sleep.

Käbi often used to complain over little things, but she endured this suffering with patience and fat Russian novels. She went on endless wanderings through the dark hours, sometimes falling asleep as she walked, and when she woke she found she had done things she had been quite unaware of.

One night I was woken by a bang and a cry of horror. Käbi was lying at the bottom of the stairs. She had fallen asleep while walking and tumbled headlong. She escaped with a fright and a few grazes.

My sleeping mechanism fell apart and my insomnia, or poor sleep, became chronic.

I am still all right as long as I sleep for four or five hours. I am often drawn up in a spiral out of deep slumber, an irresistible force which makes me wonder where it hides itself. Is it diffuse feelings of guilt or an inextinguishable need to control reality? I don't know. The only key thing is to make the night endurable with books, music, biscuits and mineral water. Worst are the 'hours of the wolf' in the small hours between three and five. That is when the demons come: mortification, loathing, fear, and rage. There is no point in trying to suppress them, for that makes it worse. When my eyes tire of reading, there is music. I close my eyes and listen with concentration and give the demons free rein: come on then, I know you, I know how you function, you just carry on until you tire of it. After a while the bottom falls out of them and they become foolish, then disappear, and I sleep for a few hours.

Daniel Sebastian was born by caesarian on 7 September 1962, Käbi and Andrea Vogler labouring ceaselessly at the keyboard until the last hour. The evening after the delivery, when Käbi had fallen asleep after seven months of torment, Andrea took the score of The Magic Flute down from the shelf. I told her about my dream of a production and Andrea looked up the chorus sung by the Guards and the Fiery Helmets. She pointed out how remarkable it was that Mozart, a Catholic, had chosen a Bach-inspired chorus for his and Schikaneder's message. She showed me in the score and said: 'This must be the keel of the boat. The Magic Flute is difficult to steer. Without a keel, it doesn't work at all. The Bach chorus is the keel.'

We leafed back and came to Papageno's and Pamino's cheerful flight from Monostatos followed by the duet 'Bei Männern, welche Liebe fühlen'. 'Look here,' she said, pointing. 'Almost like a parenthesis, here's another message. Love as the best thing in life. Love as the innermost meaning in life.'

A production stretches its tentacle roots a long way down through time and dreams. I like to imagine the roots as dwelling in the special room of the soul, where they lie maturing comfortably like mighty cheeses. Some, reluctantly or quite enthusiastically and quite often, come into view; others do not emerge at all. They see no necessity to take part in this perpetual production.

This store of slow ideas and swift flashes of inspiration begins to ebb away now, but I feel no sense of sadness or loss.

19

By the early 1970s, I had made some dubious films, but earned quite a lot of money. Personally I was in poor shape after my grandiosely thought-out but unsuccessful production with myself and Liv Ullmann in the main parts and the steles of Fårö as the setting. One protagonist had moved on and I was left on the set. I did quite a good production of *A Dream Play*, fell in love with the love of a young actress, was appalled at the mechanism of repetition, retreated to my island and, during a long attack of melancholy, wrote a film called *Cries and Whispers*.

I collected up my savings, persuaded the four main characters to invest their fees as shareholders and borrowed half a million kronor from the Film Institute. This caused immediate resentment among many film makers who complained that Bergman was taking the bread from the mouths of his poor Swedish colleagues although he could finance his films abroad. That was not the case. After a row of semi-failures, there were no backers, either at home or abroad. Fine. I have always appreciated the honest brutality of the international film world. One need never doubt one's worth in the market. Mine was zero. For the second time in my life, the critics had started talking about my career coming to an end. Strangely enough, I remained unaffected.

We made the film in an atmosphere of cheerful confidence. The setting was a decayed old manor house outside Mariefred, the park sufficiently overgrown and the lovely rooms in such bad condition that we could do what we liked with them. We lived and worked there for eight weeks.

Sometimes I probably do mourn the fact that I no longer make films. This is natural and it passes. Most of all I miss working with Sven Nykvist, perhaps because we are both utterly captivated by the problems of light, the gentle, dangerous, dreamlike, living, dead, clear, misty, hot, violent, bare, sudden, dark, springlike, falling, straight, slanting, sensual, subdued, limited, poisonous, calming, pale light. Light.

It took time to complete *Cries and Whispers*. The sound work and laboratory trials became lengthy and expensive. Without waiting for the result, we started on *Scenes from a Marriage*, mostly for fun. In the midst of shooting, my lawyer phoned to tell me that the money would run out within a month. I sold the Scandinavian rights to television and saved our six-hour film by a whisker.

It turned out to be difficult to find an American distributor for *Cries and Whispers*. Paul Kohner, my agent, a wily old trader, took a lot of trouble with no result. A well-known distributor turned to Kohner after a screening and yelled, 'I'll charge you for this damned screening.' In the end, a small firm specializing in horror films and soft porn took pity on us. There was a gap in one of New York's quality theatres – a Visconti film had not been completed on time. Two days before Christmas, *Cries and Whispers* had its world première.

Ingrid and I had married in November and moved into an apartment house in Karlaplan, about as beautiful as a slab of toffee, on the site of the Red House where Strindberg lived with Harriet Bosse. On the first night, I was woken by faint piano music coming through the floor. It was Schumann's *Aufschwung*, one of Strindberg's favourite pieces. A friendly greeting, perhaps?

We prepared for Christmas with a certain sense of unease about the future. Käbi used to say she didn't care about money, but that money was good for the nerves. I was rather sorry that Cinematograph's activities would probably have to cease.

The day before Christmas Eve, Paul Kohner telephoned. His voice sounded strange and he was mumbling. 'It's a rave, Ingmar. It's a rave!' I didn't know what a rave was and it took some time to absorb this triumph. Ten days later *Cries and Whispers* had been sold to most countries where movie theatres still existed.

Cinematograph moved into spacious premises. We fixed up a lovely screening room with perfect equipment, our office became a pleasant meeting place and a centre of quietly expanding activities. I established myself as a film producer and worked on projects with other directors.

I don't think I was a particularly good film producer, because I made great efforts not to be domineering, and thus became dishonest, far too encouraging and undemanding. I had various opportunities to reflect on Lorens Marmstedt's brilliance as a producer, his firmness, ruthlessness, honesty and guts, but also his tact, understanding and sensitivity. If we had had a single producer of Marmstedt's capacity, our most gifted film makers would not be so wasted: Jan Troell, Vilgot Sjöman, Kay Pollak, Roy Andersson, Mai Zetterling, Marianne Ahrne, Kjell Grede, Bo Widerberg. Long fruitless periods of uncertainty and insecurity, overcompensating self-esteem and rejected projects. Suddenly some financial support, then silence, indifference and chicken-livered promotion. Misfortune, failure, the little grey smile we give when our worst fears are realized. What did we tell you?

A good marriage, good friends, a well-situated and smoothly functioning firm. Gentle winds were blowing round my somewhat protruding ears and life tasted better than ever. *Scenes from a Marriage* was one success, *The Magic Flute* another.

Just to rub shoulders with fame for once, Ingrid and I went to Hollywood. I was officially invited to hold a seminar at the Film School in Los Angeles, which fitted in excellently, on the surface an irreproachable excuse, but secretly an unfamiliar and almost forbidden indulgence.

It was all beyond our expectations: the poisonous yellow sky above Los Angeles, the official luncheon with directors and actors, the indescribable dinner at Dino De Laurentiis' palace with its vista over the city and the Pacific, his wife Silvana Mangano, the perfect beauty of the 1950s, now a wandering skeleton with a well made-up cranium and restless wounded eyes, their beautiful fifteen year-old daughter inseparable from her father, the bad food, the smooth nonchalant friendliness.

Another event on another evening – my agent Paul Kohner, a veteran of Hollywood, had invited some elderly directors to dinner, William Wyler, Billy Wilder, William Wellman. The atmosphere was light-hearted, almost jolly. We talked about the direct and superb dramatic verve of American films; William Wellman told us how at the beginning of the 1920s he had learnt the profession by directing two-acters. These entailed establishing the situation quickly. A scene showing the dusty street outside a saloon, a small dog sitting on the steps. The hero comes out of the door, pats the dog and rides off. The villain comes out of the door, kicks the dog and rides away. The drama can start. Within a minute, the audience has decided on its antipathies and sympathies.

Earlier that year, I had read Arthur Janov's *Primal Scream*, a powerful and controversial book I admired. It propounded a psychiatric therapy with participating patients and relatively passive therapists. His theories were fresh and bold, lucidly and fascinatingly laid out. I was extremely stimulated and started developing a television film in four parts along Janov lines. As his clinic was in Los Angeles, I asked Paul Kohner to arrange a meeting. Arthur Janov came to Kohner's office, with his lovely woman friend. He was a slender, almost fragile man, with curly grey hair and an attractive Jewish face. We were immediately on the same wavelength. We were curious and unembarrassed, ignoring the conventions, and swiftly tried to get down to essentials.

Many years ago out at Film Town I was visited by Jerome Robbins and his exquisitely beautiful oriental companion. That experience was similar, the immediate contact, the easy but scorching touch, the sense of loss on parting and the urgent assurances of a speedy reunion.

But that did not happen this time, and nor does it ever happen *quite* like that. It is sabotaged by the peasantlike Bergman embarrassment, timidity in face of unpredictable emotions. Best to withdraw, say nothing, evade the issue, life is risky enough as it is, thank you. Carefully, I retreat, my curiosity turned into anxiety. Thank God for the great everyday. That can be supervised and directed.

Face to Face was intended to be a film about dreams and reality. The dreams were to become tangible reality. Reality would dissolve and become dream. I have occasionally managed to move unhindered between dream and reality, in *Persona, Sawdust and Tinsel* and *Cries and Whispers*. This time it was more difficult. My intentions required an inspiration which failed me. The dream sequences became synthetic, the reality blurred. There are a few solid scenes here and there, and Liv Ullmann struggled like a lion, but not even she could save the culmination, the primal scream which amounted to enthusiastic but ill-digested fruit of my reading. Artistic licence sneered through the thin fabric.

It was growing dark without my seeing the darkness.

Italian television wanted to do a film about the life of Jesus. There were powerful backers behind the project and a five-man delegation arrived in Sweden to commission the work. I responded with a detailed synopsis on the last forty-eight hours of the Saviour's life. Each episode was about one of the main characters in the drama: Pontius Pilate and his wife; Peter who denied Him; Mary, mother of Jesus; Mary Magdalene; the soldier who plaited the crown of thorns; Simon of Cyrene who carried the cross; Judas the betrayer. Each of these characters had an episode in which their confrontation with the drama of the Passion irretrievably destroyed their reality and changed their lives. I told the television people that I wanted to film it on Fårö. The town hall round Visby would be the wall round Jerusalem. The sea below the steles was to be Lake Gennesaret and I wanted to raise the cross on Langhammar's stony hill.

The Italians read it, pondered and backed away bleakly. They paid up with good grace and passed the assignment to Franco Zeffirelli; it became the life and death of Jesus in a pretty picture book, a real *biblia pauperum*.

It was growing darker but I did not see the darkness.

My life was pleasant and at last free of exhausting conflicts. I had learnt to deal with my demons and was also able to realize one of the dreams of my childhood. A hundred year-old semi-derelict barn belonged to the restored house at Dämba on Fårö. We rebuilt it and used it as a primitive film studio for *Scenes from a Marriage*. When the filming was over, we turned the studio into a screening room with an ingenious editing area in the hayloft.

When *The Magic Flute* editing was completed, we invited some of those who had been involved, together with some inhabitants of Fårö and a number of children, to our world première. It was August and a full moon, the mist sweeping in over Dämba Marsh, the old house and mill glowing in the low cold light. The house's own ghost, the Righteous Judge, sighed in the lilac bushes.

In the interval, we lit Bengal lights and drank champagne and apple juice, toasting the Dragon, the Speaker's ragged glove, Papagena, who had had a daughter, and the successful conclusion of my lifelong journey with *The Magic Flute* in my luggage.

As one gets on in years, the need for distraction declines. I am grateful for kindly, uneventful days and not too sleepless nights. My Fårö screening-room gives me untold pleasure. Through the friendly accommodation of the Film Institute's Cinematheque, I can borrow from their inexhaustible store of old films. My chair is comfortable, the room cosy, it grows dark and the first trembling picture is outlined on the white wall. It is quiet, the projector humming faintly in the well-insulated projection room. The shadows move, turning their faces towards me, urging me to pay attention to their destinies.

Sixty years have gone by but the excitement is still the same.

20

In 1970, Laurence Olivier had persuaded me to stage *Hedda Gabler* at the National Theatre in London, with Maggie Smith in the title rôle. I packed my suitcase and left, with considerable inner resistance and full of forebodings.

My hotel room was dark and dirty, the traffic noisy outside, shaking the building and rattling the windowpanes. There was a smell of damp and mould and the radiator to the right of the door made rumbling noises. Some small shiny insects, beautiful but out of place, lived in the bath. The supper with the new Lord Olivier and the actors to welcome me turned out badly, the food Javanese and inedible. One of the actors was already drunk. He told me that Strindberg and Ibsen were unplayable dinosaurs, which simply went to prove that bourgeois theatre was on its way out. I asked why the hell he was taking part in *Hedda Gabler*, and he said that there were 5000 unemployed actors and actresses in London. Lord Olivier smiled a little wryly and told me that our friend was an excellent actor, and the fact that he became revolutionary when drunk was nothing to worry about. We broke up early.

The National Theatre was provisionally playing in rented premises while the new theatre was being built on the south bank. The rehearsal room was a concrete and corrugated iron shed in a spacious yard containing stinking garbage bins. When the sun blazed down on the metal roof, the heat was almost unbearable. There were no windows. Iron pillars every five metres held up the roof, so the scenery had to be placed behind and in front of these stanchions. There were two lavatories between the rehearsal room and the temporary administration hut. They were forever overflowing and stank of urine and rotten fish.

The actors were excellent, some of them outstanding. Their professionalism and speed frightened me a little and I at once realized their working methods were different from ours. They had learnt their lines by the first rehearsal. As soon as they had the scenery, they started acting at a fast tempo. I asked them to slow down a little and they loyally tried to, but it bewildered them.

Lord Olivier had cancer, but appeared in his administration hut every morning at nine o'clock, worked all day and played Shylock several nights a week, two performances on some days. One Saturday I went to see him in his cramped and uncomfortable dressing room after the first performance. He was sitting in his underclothes and a ragged make-up overall, deathly pale and sweating profusely. Some unappetizing sandwiches were floating about on a dish. He was drinking champagne, one glass, two glasses, then a third. Then the make-up person came and touched him up, the dresser helped him on with Shylock's worn frock coat, he inserted the rôle's special false teeth and reached for his bowler hat.

I could not help thinking about our young Swedish actors complaining about having to rehearse in the daytime and perform at night. Or even worse, having to perform at a matinée and then again at an evening performance. What hard work! How bad for their artistry! How difficult the next day! How disastrous for their family life!

I high-handedly moved to the Savoy Hotel and swore I was prepared to pay whatever it cost. Lord Olivier offered me his pied-à-terre at the top of a high-rise in one of the more genteel areas of the city. He assured me I would not be disturbed. He and his wife, Joan Plowright, lived in Brighton, and he might spend the odd night in London occasionally, but we would not embarrass one another. I thanked him for his thoughtfulness and moved in, to be welcomed by a Dickensian character who was his housekeeper. She was Irish, four feet tall and moved crabwise. In the evenings she read her prayers so loudly, I first thought it was a service being broadcast through a loud-speaker in her room.

At first sight, the apartment was elegant, but turned out to be dirty, the expensive sofas grubby, the wallpaper torn, and there were interesting damp formations on the ceilings. Everything was dusty or stained. The breakfast cups were not properly washed up, the glasses had lip-marks on them, the wall-to-wall carpets were worn out, the picture windows streaky.

Practically every morning, I met Lord Olivier at breakfast. For me, it was instructive. Laurence Olivier held seminars over our cups of coffee and lectured me on the subject of Shakespeare. My enthusiasm knew no bounds. I asked questions, he answered, taking his time, occasionally 'phoning to say he could not attend some morning meeting, then sitting down and having yet another cup of coffee.

That singularly modulated voice spoke from a lifetime with Shakespeare, about discoveries, adversities, insights and ex-periences. Slowly but with joy I began to understand English actors' profound intimacy with and straightforward practical handling of a force of nature which could have crushed them or bound them to slavery. They lived fairly freely within a tradition – tender-hearted, arrogant, aggressive, but free. Their theatre, the short rehearsal times, the severe pressure, the compulsion to reach their audience, was direct and unmerciful. Their contact with their tradition was multi-dimensional and anarchic. Laurence Olivier carried on the tradition but also rebelled. Thanks to constant collaboration with younger and older colleagues, who lived under the same severe but creative circumstances, his relationships within his overwhelming professional life were constantly changing. His rapport with his art became fathomable, managable, and yet always dangerous, exhausting and surprising.

We met several times, but then that all came to an end. Lord Olivier had just filmed his production of *Three Sisters*. I thought the film sloppily made, badly edited and wretchedly photographed. It also lacked close-ups. I tried to say all this as politely as possible, praising the quality of the performances and the actors, especially Joan Plowright, a matchless Masha. It was no use. Laurence Olivier suddenly turned very formal. Our earlier cordiality and common professional interest changed into mutual squabbling over minor details.

He came to the *Hedda Gabler* dress rehearsal half an hour late, made no apology, but aired some sarcastic (if true) opinions on weaknesses in the production.

On the day of the première, I left London, which I had hated with every fibre in my body. It was a light May evening in Stockholm. I stood down by the North Bridge looking at the fishermen in the boats and their green scoop nets. A brass band was playing in Kungsträdgården. I had never seen such beautiful women. The air was clear and easy to breathe, the cherry blossom fragrant and an astringent chill rose from the rushing water.

*   *   *

During the 1960s, Charlie Chaplin was on a visit to Stockholm to publicize his recent autobiography. Lasse Bergström, his publisher, asked me if I would like to meet the great man at the Grand Hotel, and indeed I would. One morning at ten o'clock, we knocked on the door, and it was immediately opened by Chaplin himself, impeccably dressed in a dark well-tailored suit, the Legion of Honour's little button in his lapel. That hoarse multi-toned voice politely welcomed us, and his wife, Oona, and two young daughters, as lovely as gazelles, came out of an inner room.

We at once started talking about his book. I asked him when he had found out for the first time that he caused laughter, that people laughed at him in particular. He nodded eagerly and willingly told me.

He had been employed by Keystone in a group of artists who went under the name of the Keystone Kops. They did hazardous numbers before a static camera, like a variety show on a stage. One day they were told to chase a huge bearded villain who was made-up white. It was, you might say, a routine assignment. After a great deal of running and falling about, by the afternoon they had managed to catch the villain and he was seated on the ground surrounded by policemen hitting him on the head with their truncheons. Chaplin had the idea of not banging repeatedly with his truncheon as he had been told. Instead he made sure he was in a visible place in the circle. There he spent a long time carefully aiming his truncheon. He started on the penultimate blow several times, but always stopped at the last moment. When, gradually and after careful preparation, he let the blow fall, he missed and fell over. The film was shown at a Nickelodeon. He went to see the result.

The movie audience, seeing the blow miss its target, laughed for the first time at Charlie Chaplin.

*   *   *

Greta Garbo came on a quick visit to Sweden to consult a Swedish doctor. A friend telephoned me to say the star had asked to visit Film Town late one afternoon. She had declined a reception committee and asked whether I would meet her and show her around her old stamping ground.

Just after six, one cold early spring day, a shiny black limousine drew up in the studio yard. My assistant and I welcomed her and, after some confusion and rather forced conversation, Greta Garbo and I were left alone in my modest work room. My assistant looked after her friend, offering her brandy and the latest gossip.

The room was cramped, a desk, a chair and a sagging sofa. I sat at my desk, the desk lamp switched on. Greta Garbo sat on the sofa. 'This was Stiller's room,' she declared at once, looking round. I didn't know what to say, so replied that Gustaf Molander had had this room before me. 'Yes, this is Stiller's room, I know for sure.' We talked rather vaguely about Stiller and Sjöström, and she told me Stiller had directed her in a Hollywood film, even though he had already been fired. 'Fired and ill. I knew nothing. He never complained and I had problems of my own.'

Silence fell.

Suddenly she took off her concealing sunglasses and said, 'This is what I look like, Mr Bergman.' Her smile was swift and dazzling, teasing.

It is hard to say whether great myths are unremittingly magical because they are myths or whether the magic is an illusion, created by us consumers; but at that particular instant there was no doubt. In the half-light in that cramped room, her beauty was imperishable. If she had been an angel from one of the gospels, I would have said her beauty floated about her. It existed like a vitality around the big pure features of her face, her forehead, the intersection of her eyes, the nobly-shaped chin, the sensitivity of her nostrils. She immediately registered my reaction, was exhilarated and started talking about her work on Selma Lagerlöf's *Gösta Berling's Saga*.

We went up to the Little Studio and looked into the west corner, where there was still a dent in the floor after the fire in Ekeby. She mentioned names of assistants and electricians, all but one now dead. For some inexplicable reason, Mauritz Stiller had driven the remaining one out of the studio. He had stood to attention when being reprimanded, then had turned on his heel and marched out. After that, he never again set foot indoors and became Film Town's odd-job man and gardener. If he liked a director, he stood to attention, shouldering his rake, sometimes singing a few bars of the king's anthem. Any director he did not like often found a heap of leaves or snow in front of his car.

Greta Garbo laughed her dry, pure laugh. She remembered that he had fed her with home-made ginger biscuits. She had never dared refuse them.

We made a hasty tour round the area. She was wearing an elegant trouser-suit, moving energetically, her body vital and attractive. As there were slippery patches on the steep road, she took my arm. When we returned to my room, she was cheerful and relaxed. My assistant and his guest were romping in the next room.

'Alf Sjöberg wanted us to make a film together. We sat talking in a car out in Djurgården all one summer night. He was so persuasive, he was irresistible. I accepted, but changed my mind the next morning and refused. That was awfully stupid of me. Do you also think that was stupid, Mr Bergman?'

She leant over the desk so that the lower half of her face was lit by the desk lamp.

Then I saw what I had not seen! Her mouth was ugly, a pale slit surrounded by transverse wrinkles. It was strange and disturbing. All that beauty and in the middle of the beauty a shrill discord. No plastic surgeon or make-up man could conjure away that mouth and what it told me. She at once read my thoughts and grew silent, bored. A few minutes later we said goodbye.

I have studied her in her last film, when she was thirty-six. Her face is beautiful but tense, her mouth without softness, her gaze largely unconcentrated and sorrowful despite the comedy. Her audience perhaps had an inkling of what her make-up mirror had already told her.

*   *   *

In the summer of 1983, I produced Molière's *Don Juan* for the Salzburg Festival. The planning had gone on for about three years, beginning during the honeymoon period between me and the Residenz Theatre director, the Austrian Kurt Meisel, who was to do Sganarelle. Later he kicked me out of the theatre, but the contract with Salzburg remained valid. I chose another Sganarelle, Hilmar Thate, who had been frozen out of East Germany. There was also a brilliant company at my disposal, with Michael Degen as the ageing Don Juan.

Rehearsals began in Munich. The polishing was completed over fourteen days in the ugly and cramped Hof Theatre in Salzburg, which had one advantage only: the air-conditioning functioned excellently. That summer was hot, the hottest on record.

I do not believe in national characteristics, but Austrians do seem to be a special tribe, certainly the kind who thrive on the festival in the town of Salzburg. Their kindness knew no bounds; the lack of efficiency, the over-organization, the mendacity, the bureaucracy and the smooth indolence were marked.

The administration soon discovered that with my production of *Don Juan* they had acquired a bull in a china shop. The smiles grew colder, but failed to provide any relief from the raging heat.

I was invited to visit Herbert von Karajan, who was preparing a repeat production of *Rosenkavalier*, his proudest creation, in the Great Festival Hall.

His car fetched me and took me to the private office deep inside the huge building. He arrived a few minutes late, a small slender man with a large head. As he had undergone a serious operation on his back six months previously and dragged one leg, an assistant was supporting him. We sat down in a comfortable inner room in exquisite grey tones, agreeably impersonal, cool and elegant. Assistants, secretaries and helpers withdrew. The rehearsal of *Rosenkavalier* with orchestra and soloists was due to start in half an hour.

The Maestro came straight to the point. He wanted to do *Turandot* as an opera film for television with me as director. He stared at me with his pale cold eyes. (I usually think *Turandot* an unpleasant, cumbersome, perverted mess, a child of its time.) I was totally absorbed by this little man's hypnotically pale gaze and heard myself saying this was a great honour, that I had always been fascinated by *Turandot*, that the music was puzzling but overpowering and I could think of nothing more stimulating than to be allowed to collaborate with Herbert von Karajan.

The production was fixed for the spring of 1989. Karajan named a number of stars in the world of opera and suggested a designer and studio. The film would be based on a recording he was aiming to make in the autumn of 1987.

Everything suddenly became unreal, the production of *Turandot* the only real thing. I knew the man in front of me was seventy-five, I ten years younger. In 1989 an eighty-one year-old conductor and a seventy-one year-old director would together breathe life into this mummified oddity! The grotesqueness of the project never occurred to me. I was helplessly fascinated.

With the preliminary planning over, the Maestro started talking about Strauss and *Rosenkavalier*. He had conducted it for the first time as a twenty year-old. He had lived with it all his life and found it constantly new and challenging. He suddenly stopped. 'I saw your production of *A Dream Play*. You direct as if you were a musician. You've a feeling for rhythm, the musicality, pitch. That was in your *Magic Flute* too. In parts it was charming, but I didn't like it. You'd switched some scenes at the end. You can't do that with Mozart. Everything is organic.'

An assistant had already peered round the door to say it was time for the rehearsal. Karajan waved him away. They can wait.

After a while he got up with some difficulty and reached for his stick. An assistant materialized and guided us along stone corridors to the Festival Theatre, a terrifying place with seating for thousands. As we slowly moved forward, we were transformed into an imperial procession of assistants, helpers, opera singers of all sexes, obsequious critics, bowing journalists and a shattered daughter.

The soloists were ready on the stage, surrounded by a ghastly set from the 1950s. 'I have had the original designs copied in detail. The stage designers of the day are either insane or idiots, or both.' The Vienna Philharmonic was waiting in the orchestra pit and in the auditorium were hundreds of officials and indefinable citizens of this empire.

When the slender figure with his dragging leg appeared, everyone stood up and remained standing until the Maestro was lifted over the orchestra rail and in place on the rostrum.

The work started immediately. We were drowned in a wave of devastating, repellent beauty.

21

My self-imposed exile started in Paris in 1976. By chance, after some roving around, I ended up in Munich. By chance again, I went to the Residenz Theatre, which in Bavaria is the equivalent of Stockholm's Royal Dramatic Theatre, with its three stages, about the same number of staff, the same state grant, the same number of productions. I put on eleven productions there, gained a number of experiences and committed a rather larger number of follies.

The actual theatre building is squeezed between the Opera House and the Residenz, facing on to Max-Joseph Platz, and resembles what the Bavarians call a 'Schnaps-Idee', which it is too. The building was put together fairly soon after the war and in contrast to the handsome Opera House is the ugliest imaginable both inside and out.

The auditorium seats over a thousand and resembles a cinema from the days of the Nazis. The floor of the auditorium is level and visibility wretched, the seats narrow, close together and hellishly uncomfortable. If you are small, the seating is slightly better, but then your view is obscured. If you are as tall as the average Swede, you see better, but sit in a vise. The relationship between stage and auditorium is nonexistent. The stage never begins and the auditorium never comes to an end, or vice-versa. The colours are rat-grey and dirty brick-red, with grandiloquent gold ornamentation on the barriers between sections. A horrible neon chandelier winks in the ceiling and the neon wall-lamps give out a loud buzzing sound. The theatre machinery is worn out and switched off because the authorities have declared it highly dangerous. Administration offices and dressing rooms are cramped and inhuman, and the odour of German cleansing material associated with delousing or a barracklike brothel hovers over everything.

West Germany has a great many municipal theatres, some of which attract the best, partly because they pay well and partly because there is no risk of sinking into oblivion. Theatre directors and critics are mobile and come from all corners to find out what you are up to. Compared with other countries, the arts pages in the major papers are extremely interested and clearly consider theatre should not be included in sections for video and pop. Hardly a day goes by without a full report on some theatrical event or a contribution to the perpetually raging debate on theatre.

There are hardly any permanent producers or stage designers, which has great advantages. The actors have annual contracts and can be arbitrarily dismissed. Only those who have been employed for more than fifteen years cannot be given the sack. So insecurity is total, which has advantages as well as disadvantages. The advantages are obvious and need no comment. The disadvantages are intrigues, the abuse of power, aggression, obsequiousness, fear and rootlessness. A theatre director moves and takes with him twenty or thirty actors from his previous theatre and puts twenty or thirty out on to the street. This system is accepted even by the unions and is never questioned.

The pace of work is intense. At least eight plays are produced on the Big Stage, four on the Annexe Stage and a variable number on the Experimental Stage. Performances are given every day, no week off, rehearsals six days a week and also in the evenings. The repertoire is adhered to, programmes changing from day to day, thirty or so productions kept going for several years. A highly praised production may be over ten years old.

Professionalism is valued highly, as are knowledge, skill and the ability to tolerate adversities, persecution and insecurity without complaint.

So the work is hard, rehearsal times rarely more than eight to ten weeks. The private therapy for producers and actors practised in countries with a gentler theatrical climate and a more enthusiastic attitude to amateurism has no financial basis. So all activity is fiercely directed at results, while at the same time no theatre is so anarchic and questioning as German theatre, except possibly that of Poland.

When I went to Munich, I thought I was quite good at the German language. I was to discover otherwise.

The first time I was confronted with the problem was at the first joint reading of Strindberg's *A Dream Play*. Forty-four splendid actors and actresses sat looking at me expectantly, not to say benevolently. I was a fiasco, stammering, unable to find the right words, muddling articles and syntax, flushing, sweating and thinking that if I survived this I could survive anything. 'It isn't easy to be a human being' in German is '*Es ist Schade um die Menschen*'. That is nowhere near Strindberg's mildly conciliatory cry.

The first years were hard. I felt like an invalid robbed of arms and legs, and I realized that the right word at that fleeting exact moment had been my surest instrument as an instructor of actors, the word that does not break the rhythm of the work, nor disturb the actor's concentration or my own listening, the swift, effective word that is born intuitively and is exactly right. With anger, sorrow and impatience, I was made to realize that this word was not to be born out of my sloppy conversational German.

After a few years, I learnt to make contact with actors who understood intuitively what I had to say. We gradually succeeded in setting up a signalling system which was eventually fairly satisfactory. The fact that despite this handicap of mine I did some of my best productions in Munich is due more to the sensitivity of the German actors, their quick grasp and their patience, than to the gibberish I myself accomplished. At my age learning another language properly was out of the question. I got by with what little I remembered and with random success.

There is something splendid about the theatre audiences of Munich. They are faithfully initiated and cut through all social layers. They can be extremely critical and like giving vent to their dissatisfaction by whistling and booing. What is interesting about these audiences is that they go to the theatre regardless of whether a performance has been slated or praised sky-high. I do not mean to say they do not believe the critics in the daily papers – they certainly read them – but they retain the right to decide for themselves whether they like a performance or not.

Average attendance is about 90 per cent and applause great if audiences consider they have had a good evening. Slowly, almost reluctantly, they leave the theatre, standing about in groups discussing their impressions of the evening. Gradually the beer halls in Maximilianstrasse fill up, as do the little cafés down the side streets. The evening is humid and warm, thunder threatening somewhere over the mountains, the traffic roaring. I stand there, uneasy and excited, breathing in cooking smells, car fumes and the heavy scents from the dim parks, listening to thousands of footsteps and the alien language and thinking: I am undoubtedly abroad.

I suddenly feel homesick for my own audience which applauds so kindly for four curtain calls, then leaves the theatre as if fire has broken out. When I go down to Nybroplan, the snow is swirling round the silent sooty marble palace. The wind comes from the tundras beyond the sea and some ragged punks are bawling out their loneliness in the white desolation.

My early reception in Munich was magnificent. I was

received with open arms. Bergman flees from that socialist hell in the north and finds refuge in Bavaria's democratic society, lovingly hugged in the huge bearlike embrace of Franz-Josef Strauss.

At a private party in my honour, I was photographed with the Great One. He used it in his subsequent election campaign. Welcoming parties succeeded one another. *The Magic Flute* kept attracting enthusiastic audiences in the largest movie theatre in the city. *Scenes from a Marriage* was shown on television with follow-ups and discussions. Both the hospitality and the curiosity were devastating. I tried to meet all this goodwill halfway and made efforts to be courteous to everyone, realizing too late that Bavaria is a politicized community through and through, with insurmountable barriers between parties and factions.

In a very short time I managed to make a fool of myself.

I blundered into the Residenz Theatre, bringing with me principles and ideas evolved over a long professional life in a fairly sheltered corner on the outskirts of the world. I made the stupid error of trying out Swedish models in German circumstances. Thus I spent a great deal of time and energy on trying to make the decision-making processes in the theatre more democratic.

That was stupid of me.

I forced through meetings of the company and managed to get going a representative body of actors, consisting of five members who were given an advisory function. This plan quite literally fell apart. In this context, it should be said that Bavaria's National Theatre has no board, but is administered directly from the Ministry of Arts and is the responsibility of some pompous organ player who is more inaccessible than the Emperor of China.

When, after much agonizing by the company, my advisory council had at last been formed and started working, I realized what a monster I had helped to create. Hatred that had accumulated and festered for years now came to light, and obsequiousness and fear reached hitherto unimagined heights. Hostilities between different factions flared up. Intrigues and cat-and-mouse games on a scale no one in Sweden would have believed possible – not even in church circles – became the daily fare.

Our theatre director was in his seventies and came from Vienna. He was a brilliant actor, who was unfortunately married to a beautiful but considerably less brilliant actress. To compensate for this, she was megalomaniac, acting-mad and an intriguer. Our director and his Clytemnestra ruled supreme, having together fought their way through the humiliation and grandeur of German theatre.

This director lived under the illusion that he ran the theatre with paternal wisdom, but the newly formed actors' council abruptly disillusioned him. For obvious reasons, he regarded me as the destroyer of a loving relationship between father and child. I was his bitterest enemy. In this he was energetically supported by his wife, who was playing Olga in my production of *Three Sisters*. I had been irritated by her way of speaking down in her throat, which she presumably thought sexy. I solemnly advised her to take elocution lessons and she never forgave me.

Thus began the struggle between my superior and myself. Our mode of conflict was crude, our weapons blunt. The conflict was made all the more tragic by the fact that we had previously liked and admired each other.

The result of all this was that the theatre was put under a meaningless and great strain. In my eagerness to do everything for the best, I had forgotten one fundamental thing – these actors had no security whatsoever. Their cowardice was understandable. Their courage was incredible.

In June 1981, I was sacked on the spot.

My productions were taken out of the repertoire and I was banned from the theatre. All this to the accompaniment of accusations and insults that were passed on to the press and the Arts Ministry. I am not saying I was treated unfairly. If I had been the director, I would probably have done the same, but sooner.

Six months later I was back. The old director had left and a new one had appeared after a press and political campaign of the filthiest kind, inconceivable in a society more open than Bavaria. It was instructive and rather exciting for anyone on the outside, but terrible and humiliating for the victims.

Other follies: I declined to have anything to do with the press in Munich. I was well and truly made to eat my words. I refused to communicate with either major or minor critics. That was rather stupid of me, because a certain interplay between victims and executioners is an important factor in this strictly ritualistic Bavarian game of exaltation and degradation.

My friend Erland Josephson had once said that one should be careful of getting to know people because then one started liking them. That's exactly what happened to me. I became fond of many of my colleagues and it was painful to break the ties. These ties delayed my departure by at least two years.

I have never in my life had such a bad press as I had during my nine years in Munich. Productions, films, interviews and other appearances were treated with scorn and a bored contempt that was almost fascinating. But there were exceptions.

A few explanations: my first productions were certainly not particularly good, uncertain and conventional in a tedious way, which of course created some fundamental confusion. I also refused on principle to explain the thought processes behind my productions, which gave rise to even more irritation.

By the time I'd improved and was occasionally on really good form, the damage had been done. People were fed up with this insufferable Scandinavian who thought such a lot of himself. Then the invective began to fly; I was booed at the première of *Miss Julie*, a remarkably stimulating experience.

A producer has to take a bow alongside the actors, at least at a première. If he is not there, a schism arises. At first the actors received their applause and bravos. I came on stage and a deafening booing broke out. What do you do? Nothing. You stay there and bow with a sheepish smile. At the same time I thought: Now, Bergman, this is something new to you. After all, it's good that people can be so furious. About nothing. 'What's Hecuba to him as he to Hecuba. . . ?'

The stage floor is smeared with monster snot. Ibsen's poor Ghost drags his feet through the sticky mess, for this monster snot, as each and everyone at once realizes, represents bourgeois decadence. Hamlet's father pushes the Ghost under a hospital bed, naked, of course. A planned *Merchant of Venice* ends on the parade ground of the nearby Dachau concentration camp. The audience is taken there in buses. After the spectacle, Shylock stands there alone, in camp uniform, lit by powerful spots. Wagner's *Flying Dutchman* starts in a spacious Biedermeier salon, and the ship crashes in through the walls. Enzenberger's *Sinking of the Titanic* is played with a huge aquarium in the middle of the stage, a terrifying carp swimming inside it. As the disaster continues, the actors descend to the carp. At the same theatre, *Miss Julie* is played as a three-hour silent-film farce, the actors in white make-up, shrieking incessantly and gesticulating insanely. And so on. And so on. All this was at first somewhat surprising to me. Then I understood that it was a fine German theatrical tradition, tough and vigorous. Total freedom, total questioning, sharpened with professional desperation.

For a barbarian from Sweden, who had absorbed faithfulness to the letter with his mother's milk, all this was terrible but fun.

The audience raged and applauded, the critics raged and applauded, I myself felt my head going hot, the ground rocking beneath my feet. What is this I see, what is this I hear, is it me – or?

Gradually, I decided I really had to take a stand. Everyone does, and that's good for you, even if the next day you take it all back and maintain the opposite. So most of what tumbled over me on the German stage was not total freedom, but total neurosis.

What do the poor devils have to think up to get audiences? How do they get the critics even to raise their eyebrows? A young producer is given the considerable task of putting on *The Broken Jug*. He has seen it himself seven times in different settings. He knows his audience has seen twenty-one versions since childhood and the critics have yawned their way through it fifty-eight times. So he has to be audacious if he is to make an impression at all.

That is not freedom.

In the middle of all this chaos bloomed great theatrical experiences, brilliant interpretations, decisive even explosive break-throughs.

People went to the theatre, and moaned about it or loved it. Or moaned *and* loved it. The press followed suit. Crises in local theatres were constantly exploding. There were scandals. Critics gave performers hell or were given hell themselves. To put it briefly, it was a devilish uproar. A great many crises, but hardly a crisis.

*   *   *

A hot wind rises in the deserts of Africa, blows through Italy, climbs over the Alps and gives off its moisture there, then floats like molten metal down over the plateau and strikes Munich. In the morning it can be sleeting and two degrees below zero, and at midday when you come out of the darkness of the theatre it can be twenty degrees in the shade and the air trembling with corrosive transparent heat. The distant Alps seem so close you can almost touch them with your hand. People and animals go a little mad, but unfortunately not in a very pleasant way. Traffic accidents are more frequent, more important operations are cancelled and the suicide rate rises, nice dogs bite and cats flash like lightning. The rehearsals at the theatre grow more emotionally charged than usual. The city becomes electric and I sleepless and furious.

This wind is called *Föhn* and is feared with some justification. The evening papers give it banner headlines and the inhabitants of Munich drink beer brewed from wheat with a juicy slice of lemon at the bottom of the glass.

In an air raid in 1944, the inner city, with all its churches, ancient buildings and handsome opera house, was razed to the ground. Immediately after the war, it was decided to rebuild it all so that it would look exactly the same as before the raid. The opera house was lovingly recreated down to the last detail. There are still 200 seats from which one can see nothing, only hear.

In this remarkable building, one trembling white *Föhn* day, Karl Böhm was conducting a dress rehearsal of *Fidelio*. I was sitting in the front row, diagonally behind the conductor's rostrum, and was able to follow the old maestro's every movement and mood. I faintly remember that the production was horrible and the sets hideously trendy, but that is irrelevant. Karl Böhm conducted his pampered but virtuosi Bavarians with tiny hand movements – how chorus and soloists could see his signals was a mystery. He sat slightly hunched, never raised his arms, never got up, never turned a page of the score.

This plodding fiasco of an operatic monster was suddenly transformed into a clear springlike experience. I realized that I had just heard *Fidelio* for the first time, to put it simply that I had never grasped it before. A decisive fundamental experience, an internal tremor, euphoria, gratitude, a whole stream of unexpected reactions.

Everything looked simple, the notes in place, no remarkable tricks, nothing astonishing, the tempi never heard. The interpretation was what the Germans with light irony call *werktreu* [faithful to the work]. The miracle was nevertheless a fact.

* * *

Many years ago I saw a Walt Disney cartoon about a penguin who longed for the South Seas. He eventually realized his dream and ended up in the warm blue waters around an island with rustling palms. But there he pinned pictures of the

Antarctic on to a palm tree. He was homesick, and busy building a new boat that would take him back.

I am like that penguin. While I was working at the Residenz Theatre, I often thought about the Dramatic Theatre and longed to be back with my own language, friends and fellowship. Now I am home and long for the challenges, the rows, the bloody battles and death-defying actors.

At my age, the impossible is a spur. I understand Ibsen's Master-Builder Solness, who starts climbing the church tower even though he suffers from vertigo. The analysts say (so considerately) that the urge towards the impossible has something to do with receding potency. What else could an analyst say?

I think I am driven by other motives. Failure can have a fresh and astringent taste, adversity stirs up aggression and shakes life into creativity which might otherwise remain dormant. It's fun to cling to the north-west wall of Mount Everest. Before I am silenced for biological reasons, I very much want to be contradicted and questioned. Not just by myself. That happens every day. I want to be a pest, a trouble-maker, and hard to pigeon-hole.

The impossible is all too tempting, for I have nothing to lose. Neither have I anything to gain apart from benevolent approval in a few newspapers, approval which the readers will have forgotten in ten minutes, I myself in ten days.

The truth in our interpretations is bound by time. Our theatre productions do indeed disappear into merciful obscurity. But individual moments of greatness or misery are still illuminated by a mild light. And the films still exist and bear witness to the cruel fickleness of artistic truth. A few steles rise above the crushed pebbles.

In a moment of angry clear-sightedness, I realize that my theatre belongs to the 1950s and my teachers to the 1920s. That insight makes me watchful and impatient. I must separate ingrained concepts and important experiences, rout out old solutions without necessarily replacing them with new ones.

Euripides, the play builder, sits exiled in Macedonia in his old age, writing the *Bacchae*. He builds his wall block by block in a fury, contradictions colliding with contradictions, worship with blasphemy, workaday with ritual. He has grown tired of moralizing and sees that the game with the gods has been conclusively toppled. Commentators have spoken of the ageing poet's weariness. It is the other way round. Euripides' weighty sculpture represents mankind, the gods and the world in merciless and meaningless movement beneath an empty sky.

The *Bacchae* bears witness to the courage to break the moulds.

22

On Tuesday 27 December 1983, the lights of Stockholm went out just as dusk was falling. We were rehearsing *King Lear* in a large lovely room up under Dramaten's roof. An assembly of sixty souls, actors, dancers and assistants.

The mad king stood in the middle of the stage, surrounded by all kinds of rabble, maintaining life was a stage for fools. The lights went out, everyone laughed, the blinds were drawn up. The wind was driving wet snow at the windowpanes, the leaden daylight trickling hesitantly into the rehearsal room. Someone said on the internal telephone that the theatre, the whole area, possibly the whole city was in darkness.

I suggested that we wait for a while. Electricity cuts in a city last only a few minutes at most. We sat down on the floor and on chairs, chatting quietly. A few inveterate smokers went out into the waiting room, but returned at once, driven back by the Stygian darkness.

Minutes went by, the shadowless daylight turning grey, the king standing slightly to one side, still wearing his wide black coat and crowned with a dishevelled wreath of flowers which might have belonged to Ophelia or Anna or Sganarelle. His lips were moving, his hand beating time, his eyes closed.

Gloucester, his bloodstained bandage over his ripped-out eyes, peered out and said with a slight stutter that he was a dab hand at fried herrings. Some of the lovely dancers had sat down in a corner and were listening to satirical Albany, who was wearing a sword, boots and a jogging-suit. They occasionally laughed, grateful but restrained, because the atmosphere in the big room was slightly subdued, though not at all unpleasant.

Edgar, our safety-at-work man, said that the platform really must have a railing. He had taken off his glasses and was talking eagerly to the stage manager, who was taking notes. Honest Kent was lying flat on his back, the beginning of lumbago or some other damned problem. Fair Cordelia had hunted out a candle and was gliding through the darkness of the waiting room on her way for a pee and a cigarette, two insistent needs.

Half an hour went by. The snowstorm was increasing and it was now quite dark in the furthest corners. The conductor and our musical performers, boys and girls with good voices, were sitting in the middle of the floor in a circle round five lighted candles, singing a madrigal.

We all fell silent and listened. The voices were gently coiling round us, the storm howling, no street lighting dispersing the uncertain dying daylight, which was disappearing ever more rapidly. The song wandered through our senses and our faces became blurred. Time had ceased and there we were, deep in a world that was always there, always close. We needed only a madrigal, a snowstorm and a blacked-out city. We played with time every day in our profession, extending, shortening, suspending it. Now it occurred naturally without our devoting a thought to the phenomenon. Time was fragile, a surface construction and now it had totally vanished.

King Lear was a continent. We equipped expeditions which with varying skill and success mapped a few heaths, a river, a few shores, a mountain, forests. All the countries of the world equipped expeditions; sometimes we came across one another on our wanderings and established in despair that what was an inland lake yesterday had turned into a mountain today. We drew our maps, commented and described, but nothing fitted. An experienced interpreter clarified the fourth act. It had to be like that. The king was cheerful, his madness indulgent. The same interpreter grew grey and feeble in his volcanic outburst in the second act. The piece opened on an absurd note: best make it all into a game, full of laughter and party mood. The king had had a seductive but dangerous idea. He himself laughed. But the wandering drama? The transformation? Who had the power and physical endurance to create the broken-heartedness at the most distant frontier? At first all was order and within a second the world hurtled into chaos, a universal disaster.

I knew what it was about and had experienced the drama in the skin of my soul. The scars had not healed. How could I translate my experience so that the king managed to tear down his laboriously fortified barrier against disorder and degradation?

But our performers should not be weighed down by profundity. They have to be swift, extrovert, comprehensible. We Swedes had no experience, no Shakespearean tradition, only bad schooling. Could desire replace technique? Or would we die in the morass of so many words? We who had practised only Strindberg's straight dialogue which stands on its own feet. Could ordinary working actors and actresses give expression to Gloucester's double agony? Kent's phoney anger? Edgar's pretended madness? Regan's demonic evil?

Our expedition made its way across the heath, the heat scorching, and we sweated. Suddenly the sun plunged like a glowing stone, the darkness grew impenetrable, and we realized we were in a quagmire with bottomless depths. Days and days: *this* was the moment of truth, a fixed point, *at last*, now we would be calmly methodical. From here to there was two metres and seventeen centimetres. We noted it down. Better measure it again. Now it was 14,000 metres!

Audience, producer, actor, critic, each and everyone saw his *King Lear* differently – sometimes vaguely, sometimes an illusion, each according to individual intuition and feeling.

Every attempt at description was fruitless but captivating.

Come on. Let's play the concept game together.

Some turned their noses to the north-west and prophesied towards the sun, others closed their eyes and, chin on chest, mumbled to the south. Who could come up with the very best description of Beethoven's String Quartet in B-minor Opus 130, third movement, Andante con moto, ma non troppo? Let's read, let's listen! I thought *that* was good. Though a little tedious. But good! Macrocosmos, inversion, counterpoint; structured, dialectic, mimetic? Faster or slower? Faster *and* slower? Though really a little more structured? I was so moved I cried, remembering that Beethoven, the amazing old devil, had been deaf. Putting music into words was rhapsodic, fabulous, for the oscillation of the notes affected emotion. Putting theatre into words was considered possible because words were said to be subject to reason. Good Lord!

Ibsen and his liars, Strindberg's earthquakes, Molière's rage, gliding on treacherous alexandrines, Shakespeare's continents. Bloody difficult! What about the absurdists, the trendy, the inventive? Aren't *they* predictable, easily repeated, tempting and fun, handy little kicks, fast food for the impatient?

Now I take you by the arm, my dearly beloved friend, and shake you cautiously. Are you listening to me? You've now said those words every day several times a day. You should know that those words in particular entail an appeal to your experience. They have been shaped, laboriously or voluptuously, at prodigious speed or at snail's pace. Now I shake your arm: you see, I see, I understand, the moment is triumphant, the day has not been in vain, our irresolute life has at last been given meaning and colour. The flabby whoring has been transformed into love. Amazing! Bloody marvellous!

23

Someone says I should write about my friends. That is unrealistic, unless one is very old and one's friends have already left this earth. Otherwise one ends up in an informal balancing act between indiscretion and keeping secrets. Relax, you will be allowed to read what I write.

Someone wrote a detailed confession and his ex-mistress was naturally allowed to read the manuscript. She went to the toilet and threw up, then demanded that her name should be eliminated. The author agreed to her request, but at the same time took out all his positive judgements and reinforced the negative ones.

Friendship, like love, is extremely clear-sighted. The essence of friendship includes openness, a passion for the truth. It is a relief to see your friend's face or hear his voice on the telephone, to talk about just what is most painful and urgent, to hear the friend himself confess what he has hardly dared to think. Friendship often has a touch of sensuality. The friend's shape, his face, eyes, lips, voice, movements and tone of voice are inscribed on your mind, a secret code which gives you the confidence to reveal yourself in true fellowship.

A love relationship explodes into conflicts; that is unavoidable. Friendship is tasted more sparingly, without the same need for commotion and purgings. Occasionally sand sticks between the vulnerable surfaces of contact, and then sorrow and difficulties arise. I think: I can manage perfectly well without that idiot! Then a little time goes by and the unpleasant sensation of missing him makes itself felt on various levels, sometimes obviously, often discreetly.

Now I am making contact, things mustn't be like this. It is a matter of keeping track of our capital. We weed out, clean and replace.

The result is uncertain: better, worse, or as before. We cannot know. Friendship never depends on promises or protestation, nor on time and space. Friendship is absolutely undemanding, except on one point. Friendship demands honesty, the only demand, but difficult.

A close friend emigrated after a life of extrovert activity. He settled on the Riviera, rented a three-room apartment, sat on the balcony and made rya rugs. His considerably younger woman friend continued working back at home, but she went to visit the comfortable balcony for several months a year. The friend fell silent, our conversations forging their way through a tough undergrowth of reserve, and it took time and trouble to keep communications open. His messages became more and more cryptic. Why the hell have you gone off to a balcony on the Mediterranean! You're dying slowly and politely without the corpse-spots showing! We conversed according to ritual. I knew he had some worry on his mind which he was not confiding to me. Yes, thanks, everything's fine. It's snowing on the palm trees but the magnolia is in flower.

I couldn't tell him I knew about his anxiety. I didn't want to hurt him by reproaching him for his lack of candour.

For that matter, we are practically contemporaries – perhaps this is what the beginning of true ageing is like. More and more, we lose our way in obscure halls and winding unswept corridors. We talk to each other through faulty local telephones and stumble headlong over a reserve hard to detect.

An actor friend of mine wrote a captivating piece of radio drama, which I asked if I could produce. A few months later, I asked him if he would like to play the Ghost and the First Player in my production of *Hamlet*. After some agonizing, he turned me down. I was furious and said that in that case I wouldn't do his radio play. Shocked with good reason, he retorted that he did not see the connection, which to me was obvious. After a good deal of to-ing and fro-ing, we sorted out our differences without upsetting our positions. However, our friendship was affected.

A socially and politically successful friend of mine suffers from a neurotic fear of every form of direct aggressiveness. He jokingly refers to himself as a *besserwisser*, a know-all, which he also is. I rather like being lectured at, as he teaches me various things. Many years ago he lectured me rather a lot on my vacillating position in the international film market, something which I knew more about than anyone else. He lectured seven times and on the eighth I got furious and advised him in no uncertain terms to shut up and go to hell. It took several years for our friendship to recover.

On the whole I have no illusions about my own talent for friendship. I am indeed faithful, but extremely suspicious. If I think I am being betrayed, I am quick to betray. If I feel cut off, I cut off, a dubious and very Bergmanlike talent.

I find women friends easier. Openness is obvious (I like to think), undemandingness is total (I hope), loyalty invulnerable (I imagine). Intuition moves without prejudice, emotion is undisguised, there is no prestige involved. Conflicts which arise are trusting and not infectious. Together we have danced every imaginable turn: suffering, tenderness, passion, foolishness, betrayal, anger, comedy, tedium, love, lies, joy, jealousies, adultery, overstepping boundaries, good faith. And here are even more: tears, eroticism, mere eroticism, disasters, triumphs, troubles, abuse, fights, anxiety, pining, eggs, sperm, bleeding, departure, panties. Here are even more – best to finish before the rails run out – impotence, lechery, terror, the proximity of death, death itself, black nights, sleepless nights, white nights, music, breakfasts, breasts, lips, pictures. Turn towards the camera and behold another jumble of images: skin, dog, rituals, roast duck, whale steak, bad oysters, cheating and fiddling, rapes, fine clothes, jewellery, touches, kisses, shoulders, hips, strange lights, streets, towns, rivals, seducers, hairs in the comb, long letters, explanations, all that laughter, ageing, aches, spectacles, hands, hands, hands. Now the aria comes to a close: shadows, gentleness, I will help you, the shoreline, the sea. Now all is quiet. My father's old gold watch with its cracked glass ticks away on its stand on my desk. It says seven minutes to twelve.

No, I won't write about my friends. It's impossible. Nor will I write about my wife, Ingrid.

Some years ago I produced a not very successful film script called *Love with no Lovers*. It turned into a panorama of West German life and I think it was coloured by the powerless rage of the prisoner, certainly not a fair picture.

Out of this giant, which died a natural death, I carved a steak that became a film for television called *From the Life of the Marionettes*. It was not liked, but belongs among my best films, an opinion shared by a few.

In the wrecked screenplay (with a playing time of about six hours), as a counterweight to the confusion of the basic structure, there was a paraphrase of Ovid's tale of Philemon and Baucis. The god wanders disguised on earth with the intention of learning about his creation. One cool spring evening by the sea, he comes to a decaying farm on the edge of the village community, occupied by an elderly farmer and his wife. They invite him to supper and a night's lodging. The next morning the god continues his journey after the old people have been allowed to make one wish: they do not want death to separate them. The god responds to their wish and turns them into a huge tree to shade the farm.

My wife and I live near each other. One of us thinks and the other answers, or the other way round. I have no means of describing our affinity.

One problem is insoluble. One day the blow will fall and separate us. No friendly god will turn us into a tree to shade the farm. I have a talent for imagining most of life's situations. I plug in my intuition and my imagination and appropriate emotions pour in, colouring and deepening.

Nevertheless I lack the means of imagining the moment of separation. As I am neither able nor willing to imagine another life, some kind of life beyond the frontier, the perspective is appalling. From a somebody I will become a nobody. That nobody will not even have the memory of an affinity.

24

When Father was on holiday in Våroms in the middle of July, he was restless and uneasy, taking long walks through the forests on his own and sleeping in outfield buildings and barns.

One Sunday, he was to preach in Amsberg chapel. The morning was thundery and oppressive, the sun and horseflies stinging, a dark-blue bank of clouds above the hills.

It had been decided long before that I should accompany him. Father put me on the front carrier of the bicycle and the food pack and a case containing his cassock on the back. I was bare-footed and wearing blue striped shorts and a blouse of the same material with a turned down collar. I had a bandage round my wrist because I had scratched a mosquito bite and it had become infected. Father was wearing black trousers, bicycle clips, black laced boots, white shirt, white hat and a thin summer jacket.

I can confirm all this, because I have recently seen a photograph. Gertrud, a young friend of the family, can just be seen in the background. She is looking at Father with love in her eyes and smiling spitefully. Gertrud was my favourite and it would have been good if she had come too, for she often laughed and put Father in a good mood. They used to sing together. Grandmother can be seen in the background on her way to the privy. My brother is presumably leaning over some hateful homework and my sister still asleep. I am nearly eight. Mother is holding the camera. She enjoyed taking photographs.

So we set off in the smell of resin and hot moss down the forest slope, which was steep with pines and ant-hills on both sides, the bilberry plants already laden with unripe berries. We passed the gardener's washing hanging on the line. A few weeks earlier, my brother and his friends from the Mission House had stolen strawberries, squashed them and drawn obscene figures on Mrs Tornqvist's sheets. We were all heavily suspected, but let off for lack of evidence. It was then the turn of the gardener's sons, although they were innocent.

I did not know whether or not I should tell, despite everything, as I had good reason to take revenge on my brother. One day he had dangled a fat angling worm in front of my nose and said: 'I'll give you five öre if you eat this worm.' I managed to get the worm down and, when I had swallowed the last bit, my brother had said: 'If you're so damned stupid as to eat a worm, I'm not going to give you five öre.'

I was too easily deceived. I also had adenoids, so often breathed through my mouth, which made me look stupid.

'Take Grandmother's umbrella,' my brother had said. 'Put it up. I'll help you. Now, if you jump from the upstairs balcony, you'll fly.' I was stopped at the last minute and wept with rage, not because I had been deceived, but because one couldn't fly with Grandmother's umbrella.

'You're a Sunday's child, Ingmar, so you can see fairies,' Old Lalla had said. 'But you mustn't forget to hold two crossed twigs in front of you.'

I don't know how much Lalla believed of what she said, but I crept away. I didn't see any fairies, but I did see a little grey man with a bright spiteful face. He was holding a girl by the hand, and she was no bigger than my middle finger. I wanted to capture her, but the gnome and his daughter got away.

When we lived in Villagatan, wandering musicians used to come and play, and one day a whole family arrived. Father came into the dining room and said: 'We've sold Ingmar to the gypsies. We got quite a good price.' I wailed with terror, then suddenly everyone started laughing and Mother took me on her knee, held my head and rocked me gently. They were all surprised I was so credulous. 'He's gullible and has no sense of humour.'

We had now reached the hill by the post office and I had to get off the bicycle and walk. As I was bare-foot, I walked along the verge where the grass was soft and trampled. We said good morning to the postmaster, who was on his way to the railway station to load the mail on to the morning train to Krylbo, his mailbag on a small cart. Lasse was sitting on the steps. He was too tall and his arms dangled. When we passed he wobbled his head and bellowed. I guardedly said hello back to him. Lasse had just taught me a song. The prick and the cunt were to see who'd be first. The prick drove so hard that the cunt went and burst. I understood neither content nor spirit, but I did realize it was no verse of a hymn.

After the hill, I could mount again and Father told me to stick my feet out. A year before I had caught my foot in Uncle Ernst's spokes and had broken some small bones. We got up speed and were soon past Berglund's big farm where we fetched our milk and pinched apples. Dolly barked hoarsely and ran along on the lead fastened to a wire between two pines. After the farm came a ghost house and then the Mission House, where the numerous Frykholm children lived while their parents were working for God in the African field. A cheerful and loving Christianity reigned in the Mission House, with no rules or coercion. The children went barefoot all day and didn't have to wash. Meals were taken standing up at the table whenever they were hungry, and Bengt Frykholm owned a magic theatre which he had made from instructions in *Allers Family Journal*. The children's signature tune, however, was never sung inside the Mission House.

I was born in Africa
My papa there was king
Giraffe, ape and crocodile
were toys when I was young.
Choohaddi-eyaloo!
Fat missionary makes good stew.

We were now scudding along at a good speed down the long
slope to Solbacka, the road close to the river, the sun burning,
the wheels whistling and crunching and the surface of the water
glinting. The bank of clouds beyond the hills was still there and
swelling. Father was singing quietly to himself, the morning
train whistling far away. I thought of my own train with a sense
of loss. I could have been at home at Våroms at that moment,
laying out my railway on the little path to the turfed cellar. A
trip with my father was always a ticklish undertaking. You
never knew how it would end. Sometimes he remained in a
good mood all day, sometimes the demons caught up with him
and he turned taciturn, evasive and irritable.

Some traps taking people to church were already waiting at
the ferry place, as well as a very old man with a dirty cow and a
few boys on their way to Djuptärn to go swimming and fishing
for perch.

Steel wires were stretched across the river and the ferry was
fastened to the cables with iron loops and rusty wheels. The
whole thing was operated by hand. The men grasped the cables
with heavy gripping instruments of tarred wood, so that the
flat-bottomed craft was hauled back and forth across the dark
flowing channel of the river, where drifting logs thumped
against its sides.

Father at once fell into conversation with the women in one
of the traps. I sat down on the boards up at the front and
lowered my feet into the water, icy cold even in high summer
and flowing brown and fiercely round my legs and feet.

Ever since my childhood, the river has existed in my dreams.
Always dark and swirling like the Gråda river by the railway
bridge, the logs smelling of bark and resin as they slowly swing

round in the strong current, and sharp stones protruding menacingly below the swirling surface of the water. The river channel cuts deeply between the banks where thin alders and birches find root; the water is lit by the sun for a few moments, then dies and becomes blacker than ever. The ceaseless movement towards the curve of the river, the subdued murmur.

We sometimes went swimming by the river bank, taking a path that ran steeply down the slope by Våroms, across the railway embankment and the road, then across Berglund's meadow and down the river bank, which was fairly low on our side. A timber raft we could dive from was tied up there. I once came up underneath the raft and couldn't get back to the surface. I was not in the least frightened, but opened my eyes and saw the swaying water plants, my own bubbles of air, the sunlight lighting up the brown water, and the small fish lurking among the stones sunk into the mud. Later I remember lying on the raft spewing up water and mucus and everyone talking at once.

Now I was sitting on the edge of the ferry, cooling the burning soles of my feet and the mosquito bites round my ankles. Suddenly someone took me by the shoulders, threw me backwards, and I received a slashing blow on the head. Father was furious. 'You know that's forbidden. Don't you see you could be pulled under?' He hit me again. I didn't cry, but I was full of hatred. Bloody hoodlum. Always hitting. I'll kill him. I won't forgive him. When we get back home, I'll think up a painful death for him. He can beg for mercy. I'll hear him scream with terror.

The logs thumped, the water murmured and I stood to one side, but kept in sight. Father was helping pull the ferry, struggling with the heavy chunk of wood. I could see he was angry too.

We landed, the water washing up over the planks, the traps driving ashore, the jetty swaying and lurching. Father said goodbye. He always found it easy to talk to people. The boys going fishing smiled scornfully and picked up their rods. The old man with the dirty cow trotted up the slope.

'Come on now, you fathead,' Father said in a friendly voice. I didn't move, and turned my head away, tempted to start crying, now that Father sounded friendly. He came over to me and shoved me in the back. 'You must have seen I was frightened. You might have drowned and no one would have noticed.' He shoved me again. Then he took his bicycle and wheeled it over the wet planks. The ferryman was letting new people on board.

Father held out his large hand and felt for mine, and my rage ran out of me in a second. He had been frightened. That was understandable. If you're frightened, you get angry, I understood that. Now he was being nice. He had hit me too hard and was regretting it.

The slope up from the ferry stage was steep and I helped push the bicycle. At the top, the heat rose like a wall and the fine sand swirled up in little whirlwinds with no coolness. Father's black trousers and boots were already dusty.

We arrived just as they were ringing for ten o'clock. The churchyard was shady; some women in black were watering the flowers on the graves and there was a smell of new-mown grass and tar. It was gently cool under the stone porchway. The churchwarden who had been ringing the bell followed Father into the sacristy, where there was a basin and a can of water in the cupboard. Father took off his shirt and washed, then donned a clean shirt, his dog collar and cassock. Next he sat down at the desk and wrote down the hymn numbers on a piece of paper. I went with the churchwarden to help put up the right numbers in the church. We didn't speak while we were carrying out our important task; a wrong number would be catastrophic.

I knew that Father had to be left alone now, so I went out into the churchyard and read the inscriptions on the gravestones, especially in the children's section, the dome of the sky white above the dark foliage of the ash trees. The heat lay motionless. A few bumble bees. A mosquito. A cow lowing. Drowsy. Doze for a while. Asleep.

*   *   *

While I was making preparations for *Winter Light*, I went around looking at churches in Uppland in the early spring. I usually borrowed the key from the organist and sat for a few hours in the church, watching the light wander and thinking how I would work out the end of my film. Everything had been written down and planned, all except the actual ending.

One Sunday, I phoned Father early in the morning and asked him if he would like to come with me on an outing. Mother was in hospital after her first heart attack and Father had isolated himself. His hands and feet had grown worse and he now walked with a stick and wore orthopaedic boots. With self-discipline and strength of will, he continued his duties in the parish of the royal palace. He was seventy-five.

It was a misty early spring day with strong light above the snow. We arrived in good time at the little church north of Upsala to find four churchgoers ahead of us waiting in the narrow pews. The churchwarden and verger were whispering in the porch and the woman organist was rummaging in the organ loft. When the summoning bell faded away over the plain, the pastor had still not appeared. A long silence ensued in heaven and on earth. Father shifted uneasily and kept muttering. A few minutes later came the sound of a rushing car on the slippery ground outside, a door slammed and the pastor came puffing down the aisle.

When he got to the altar rail, he turned round and looked over his congregation with red-rimmed eyes, a thin, long-haired man, his trim beard scarcely hiding his receding chin. He swung his arms like a skier and coughed, his hair curly on the crown of his head, his forehead turning red. 'I am sick,' said the pastor. 'I've got a high temperature and have a chill.' He sought for sympathy in our eyes. 'I have permission to give you a short service; there will be no communion. I'll preach as best I can, then we'll sing a hymn and that will have to do. I'll just go into the sacristy and put on my cassock.' He bowed and for a few moments stood irresolutely as if waiting for applause or at least some sign of understanding, but when no one reacted, he disappeared through a heavy door.

Father started rising from the pew. He was upset. 'I must speak to that creature. Let me pass.' He got out of the pew and limped into the sacristy, leaning heavily on his stick. A short and agitated conversation ensued.

A few minutes later, the churchwarden appeared. He smiled in embarrassment and explained that there would be a communion service. An older colleague would assist the pastor.

The introductory hymn was sung by the organist and the few churchgoers. At the end of the second verse, Father came in, in white vestments and with his stick. When the hymn was over, he turned to us and spoke in his calm free voice: 'Holy, holy, holy Lord God of Hosts, heaven and earth are full of thy glory. Glory be to thee, O Lord most High.'

Thus I was given the end of *Winter Light* and the codification of a rule I have always followed and was to follow from then on: *irrespective of everything, you will hold your communion*. It is important to the churchgoer, but even more important to you. We shall have to see if it is important to God. If there is no other god than your hope as such, it is important to that god too.

*   *   *

I had slept well on a bench in the shade and now the summoning bell was ringing and I pattered into church in my bare feet. The pastor's wife took my hand and pressed me down at her side in the front pew below the pulpit. I would rather have sat in the organ loft, but the pastor's wife was in the advanced stages of pregnancy and I couldn't possibly squeeze past her. I immediately felt the need to pee and realized my distress would last a long time. (Church services and bad theatre last longer than anything else in the world. If you ever feel life is rushing along too fast, go to church or the theatre. Then time stops and you think there's something wrong with your watch and as Strindberg says in *Storm*: 'Life is short but it can be long while it lasts.')

Like all churchgoers at all times, I have often become lost in altar pieces, triptyches, crucifixes, stained glass windows and murals, where I could find Jesus and the robbers in blood and torment; Mary leaning on St John, woman behold thy son, behold thy mother. Mary Magdalene, the sinner. Who'd been the latest to fuck her? The Knight playing chess with Death. Death sawing down the Tree of Life, a terrified wretch wringing his hands at the top. Death leading the dance to the Dark Lands, wielding his scythe like a flag, the congregation capering in a long line and the jester bringing up the rear. The devils keeping the pot boiling, the sinners hurtling headlong into the depths and Adam and Eve discovering their nakedness. Some churches are like aquaria, not a bare patch. People everywhere, saints, prophets, angels, devils and demons all alive and flourishing. The here-and-beyond billowing over walls and arches. Reality and imagination merged into robust myth-making. Sinner, behold thy labours, behold what awaits thee round the corner, behold the shadow behind thy back!

I was a teacher for a few years at the drama school in Malmö. We were to put on a performance but did not know what to play, and then I thought about my childhood's church murals with all their pictures. In a few afternoons, I wrote a little play called *Wood Painting* with a part for every student. The school's most handsome youth was unfortunately the least gifted (he was to go into operetta). He played the Knight. The Saracens had cut out his tongue, so he was dumb.

Wood Painting gradually became *The Seventh Seal*, an uneven film which lies close to my heart, because it was made under difficult circumstances in a surge of vitality and delight. In the witch's night forest, where she is executed, you can just catch a glimpse between the trees of the high-rise windows of Råsunda, the suburb next to the studio. The procession of flagellants marches across a derelict site on which the new studio laboratory would be erected.

The image of the Dance of Death beneath the dark cloud was achieved at hectic speed because most of the actors had finished for the day. Assistants, electricians, a make-up man and two summer visitors, who never knew what it was all about, had to dress up in the costumes of those condemned

to death. A camera with no sound was set up and the picture
shot before the cloud dissolved.

*   *   *

I never dared go to sleep when Father was preaching. He saw
everything. A friend of the family's had once fallen asleep
during the early morning Christmas service in the Sophiahemmet Hospital chapel. Father interrupted his sermon and said
perfectly calmly: 'Wake up, Einar. What is to come concerns
you.' Then he spoke on the theme of the last shall be first.
Uncle Einar was the deputy archivist at the Foreign Department and dreamt of becoming the senior archivist. He was a
bachelor and played the violin.

After the service, coffee was served at the parsonage, where
there was a fat yellow-haired son of my age. We were given
juice and buns. Oscar was disgusting. He had eczema on his
scalp and wore a cap of dirty, pink-spotted bandages and kept
scratching himself. He smelt of disinfectant. We were sent to
the nursery, which Oscar had turned into a church with an
altar, candlesticks, crucifix and coloured tissue paper stuck to
the windows, a chamber organ in the corner. The smell of
disinfectant and dead flies was strong. Oscar asked me if I
wanted to hear a sermon or whether I'd like to play funerals.
He had a little child's coffin in the wardrobe. I said I didn't
believe in God. Oscar scratched his head and assured me that
the existence of God had been scientifically proved, and that
the world's greatest scientist was a Russian called Einstein –
he had caught a glimpse of the face of God deep down in his
mathematical formulae. I replied that I had no intention of
swallowing that bit of deceit. We almost quarrelled. Oscar
was stronger than I and twisted my arm, demanding that I
admit to the existence of God. It hurt and frightened me, but
I refrained from calling for help. Oscar was presumably
mad. Idiots have to have their own way, otherwise you never
know what might happen. I hastily admitted my belief in the
existence of God.

After I had made my confession, we sulked in separate corners. In time, we said our farewells and parted. Father had packed his cassock and collar, pushed his hat on the back of his head and had me climb up on the front carrier. The pastor and his wife wanted us to wait until the storm had passed – the sun was already on the edge of a thick cloud but shining brightly, the heat suffocating with approaching rain. Father thanked them and smiled. We would no doubt escape it. Anyhow, a little cooling rain would be pleasant. The pastor's wife pressed me to her big bosom, her belly full to bursting; she smelt of sweat. I almost fell off the carrier. The pastor shook hands. He had thick lips and sprayed saliva as he spoke. Oscar was nowhere to be seen.

At last we got away. Nothing was said, but I sensed Father was relieved. He was humming the tune of some summer hymn and pedalling away. We whizzed along at speed.

As we passed the turning to Djuptärn, Father suggested we should take a quick dip. I thought that a good idea, so we turned off on to the little path down through a pastureland heavy with the acrid fragrance of bracken and old reeds.

The lake was circular and considered bottomless, the path ending in a narrow strip of sand bordering on the water and running steeply down into the darkness. We undressed. Father threw himself backwards into the water, puffing and blowing. I was more cautious, took a few strokes and let myself sink below the surface, where there was no bottom, no plants, nothing.

Then we sat on the bank and dried off in the oppressive heat, surrounded by flying insects. Father had straight shoulders, a high chest, long strong legs and a big penis with scarcely any hair. His arms were muscular with a lot of brown spots on his white skin. I sat between his knees like Jesus hanging on his cross in that old triptych. Father had found a deep purple flower on the shore and was wondering what it was called. He pulled it apart and guessed. He knew almost everything about flowers and birds.

Although we were full after the abundance of food at the

parsonage, we finished up our sandwiches and shared a lemonade.

It grew darker, a few wasps made swift attacks on our sandwiches, and suddenly there were innumerable circles on the shiny surface of the water, then they vanished almost at once.

We decided we had to be off.

* * *

When Father became a widower, I often went to see him and we talked to each other on friendly terms. One day I was with his housekeeper, dealing with a few practical problems. We heard him slowly shuffling down the corridor, then he knocked on the door and came into the room, peering in the strong light. He had clearly been asleep. He looked at us in surprise and said: 'Has Karin come home yet?' At the same moment he realized his painful confusion and smiled in embarrassment. Mother had been dead for four years and he had made a fool of himself by asking after her. Before either of us had time to say anything, he waved his stick dismissively and went back to his room.

A note in my work journal, 22 April 1970: Father is dying. I went to see him on Sunday at Sophiahemmet Hospital. He was asleep and snoring. Edit, who stays with him day and night, woke him and left the room. His face is the face of a dying man, but his eyes are clear and strangely expressive. He whispered something, but it was impossible to understand what he wanted to say. I suppose he was slightly confused. It was captivating to see the way his eyes changed expression several times: challenging, questioning, impatient, frightened, seeking contact. When I rose to leave, he suddenly took my hand and his voice blurred. He was reading something and I realized it was the Blessing. A dying father calling down God's blessing on his son. Everything happened very swiftly and unexpectedly.

25 April 1970: Father still alive. That is, he is profoundly unconscious, his strong heart the only thing functioning. Edit

thinks she is communing with him by holding his hand. She speaks to him and he responds through the hand. It is unfathomable but poignant. They are childhood friends.

29 April 1970: Father is dead. He passed away on Sunday at twenty past four in the afternoon. His death was peaceful. I find it difficult to explain what I felt about seeing him. He was totally unrecognizable, his face most of all reminding me of pictures of the dead in the concentration camps. It was a face of death. I think of him from a despairing distance, but with tenderness. Things are bad for Bergman this day, despite the friendly light over the sea. The yearning for something at last to touch me, to give me grace. Things are bad this day. Not that I feel ill – on the contrary – but my soul. . . .

*   *   *

When we emerged from the birch woods out on to the plain of wide fields we saw the summer lightning over the hills. Heavy drops fell into the dust on the road and made streaks and patterns. 'We should go round the world like this, you and me, Father,' I said. Father laughed and gave me his hat to hold. We were both in a good mood. The hailstorm came as we were going uphill towards the deserted village. In the course of a minute or so, the storm descended, lightning flashing through all the black, the thunderclaps becoming a ceaseless roar. The heavy rain turned into thick lumps of ice. Father and I ran to the nearest deserted farm, where there was a wagon shed and a few abandoned carts. The roof had gone but we sheltered under what had once been a hayloft.

We sat on a huge beam and looked out through the open doorway. A tall birch on the slope outside was twice struck by lightning, smoke pouring out of its trunk and the foliage swinging about as if in torment, the roar shaking the ground. I sat huddled close to Father's knee. His trousers smelt wet, his face was soaked and he wiped it with his sleeve. 'Are you scared?' Father asked. I said I wasn't scared, but I thought: Perhaps this is the Last Judgement, when the angels blow on their trumpets and the star called Wormwood falls into the sea. I had indeed denied the existence of God, but I did not think I would be punished, because God the Father, with Jesus on his right hand, would see to it that I was hidden.

The gusts of wind suddenly grew fierce and chilly. It turned cold and my teeth started chattering. Father took off his jacket and wrapped it round me. It was wet but warm from Father's warmth. Sometimes the landscape disappeared behind a curtain of rain. The storm had stopped, but hailstones were still lying on the ground. Outside the shed, a pool of water had formed and started running under the stones on which the shed stood. The light was grey and unsteady, like dusk with no sunset. The thunder retreated and dulled, the rain turning from a stormy flood into a steady stream.

We set off. We had already been away from home far too long and it was past dinner time. Part of the road was a rushing stream, making cycling hard work, and the bicycle suddenly skidded. I pulled up my legs and rolled down a grassy slope. Father fell on the road. When I got up, he was lying there quite motionless, one leg under the bicycle and his head down. *Now Father's dead.*

A moment later he turned his head and asked if I had hurt myself, then he began to laugh his ordinary cheerful laugh. He got up and picked up the bike. He had a little graze on his cheek which was bleeding. We were dirty, wet and muddy, and it was still raining. We walked beside each other, Father laughing now and again, as if relieved.

There was a large farm just before we got to the ferry. Father knocked on the door and asked if he could use the telephone, but the old man said the storm had cut it off. The old woman offered us coffee. She decided I had to undress and then she rubbed me with a hard towel all over my body. Then she produced a pair of coarse linen underpants, a nightshirt, a cardigan and a pair of thick woollen socks. At first I refused to put on women's clothing, but Father turned stern and I had to obey. Father borrowed a pair of trousers from the old man and put on his cassock, slipping an old leather waistcoat on top of the cassock. The old man harnessed a trap with a hood and we got back to Våroms at dusk.

Everyone laughed at our outfits.

That same evening my brother and two friends of the same age flew from the Mission House on a magic carpet out of the window and away over the forest. The conspirators were sleeping on mattresses they had pulled together in a cramped room next to the nursery. I was told sternly to stay in my bed and not to move.

I could not possibly take part in the flying trip, for I was too small. And it was uncertain whether the magic carpet would hold more than three fliers. Through the half-open door I heard whispered conversations and suppressed laughter, the thunder rolling in the distance and the rain hissing on the roof. Now and again soundless flashes of lightning lit up the room.

Then I quite clearly heard the window being opened. The magic carpet was thrown out on to the porch roof and the fliers climbed out after it. A gust of wind struck the house, making the walls creak, and the rain increased. I couldn't control myself and rushed into the next room, but it was empty, the rug gone, the window open to the night and the curtain fluttering in the draught. The lightning revealed my brother floating away over the edge of the forest on the red-checked rug, together with Bengt and Sten Frykholm.

They were tired and silent the next morning. At family breakfast, when I tried to bring up the subject of their flight, I was silenced by my brother's threatening looks.

25

One Sunday in December, I was listening to Bach's Christmas Oratorio in Hedvig Eleonora Church. It was afternoon. Snow had been falling, silently, with no wind. Then the sun came out.

I was sitting on the left, high up under the vaulted roof. The gold-shimmering moving sunlight was reflected strongly in the row of windows in the parsonage opposite the church, forming figures and patterns on the inner abutment of the arch, the direct light slanting through the dome in brilliant shafts. The mosaic window by the altar flared for a few moments, then was extinguished, a soundless explosion of dull red, blue and golden brown. The chorale moved confidentially through the darkening church: Bach's piety heals the torment of our faithlessness. The trembling uneasy light patterns on the wall moved upwards, narrowed, lost their strength and were extinguished. The D-minor trumpets raised their jubilant cries to the Saviour. A gentle greyish-blue light filled the church with sudden stillness, timeless stillness.

It had grown cold, the street lights not yet on, the snow already crunching underfoot, my breath steaming, severe cold for Advent. What will the winter be like? It will be hard to bear now. Bach's chorale was still moving like colourful floating veils in my consciousness, flitting back and forth across thresholds and through opened doors. Joy.

In my mind, in a rash moment, I cross the Sunday-quiet Storgatan and go into the parsonage. It smells of scouring powder and holiness, just as it did fifty years before.

The big apartment is silent and deserted, the light from the snow moving over the salon ceiling, a desk lamp shining in Mother's room, the dining room in darkness. Someone hurries past, leaning slightly forward, through the pantry passage. Low voices can be heard in the distance, women's voices, a peaceful buzz of chat, spoons delicately clinking against porcelain. It is Sunday afternoon coffee time at the kitchen table.

I take off my overcoat and shoes and pad across the creaking and newly polished parquet flooring of the dining room. Mother is sitting at her desk, her glasses on her nose, her not yet white hair in slight disorder as she leans over her diary, writing with a slim fountain pen. The picture is smooth and compelling, but microscopic. Her left hand is resting on the desk overlay, the fingers short and strong, the back of her hand criss-crossed with blue veins, the heavy wedding rings and the diamond ring gleaming between them. Her nails are cut short, the cuticles neglected.

She quickly turns her head and catches sight of me. (How I have yearned for this moment. Ever since Mother died, I have yearned for this moment.) She smiles a little formally, at once closes her book and takes off her glasses. I kiss her filially, on the forehead and the brown mole by her left eye.

'I know I'm disturbing you. This is Mother's own special moment, I know. Father's resting before dinner and Mother's reading, or writing in her diary. I've just been in church listening to Bach's Christmas Oratorio. It was beautiful, the light was beautiful and all the time I thought: Now I'll make an attempt, this time it will be successful.'

Mother smiles. Ironically, I think. I know what she's thinking! You passed Storgatan quite often on your way to your theatre, every day. You rarely or never thought of coming to see us then. No, I suppose I didn't. I am a Bergman. Don't disturb, don't intrude. Anyhow there's always talk about my children. I can't talk about my children, as I never see them. And all that emotional blackmail. You could, just for my sake. Don't be angry, now, Mother! We won't put all our cards on the table. There's no point. Let me just sit for a few minutes in this old chair. We needn't even speak to each other. If Mother would just go on writing in her diary. The washing machine. I was going to buy a washing machine, wasn't I, for Christ's sake. Mother should have a washing machine, I thought now and again, but of course nothing came of it.

Mother gets up and walks swiftly (always quick steps) out into the dining room, disappearing into the darkness. Then I can hear rummaging in the salon. She lights the lamp on the round table, comes back, lies down on the bed with the dark-red counterpane and pulls her grey-blue shawl over her.

'I'm still tired,' she says apologetically.

'I want to ask Mother about something urgent. Several years ago, I think it was in the summer of 1980, I was sitting in my workroom in Fårö and it was raining, that soft quiet summer rain, as if it were going to rain all day, the kind that doesn't exist any more. I was reading and listening to the rain. Then I felt that Mother was very near me, beside me. I could have held out my hand and taken hers. It wasn't that I had fallen asleep. I'm sure of that, and it wasn't even a supernatural event. I knew Mother was with me in the room, or did I imagine it? I can't make it out. Now I'm asking, Mother.'

'It probably wasn't me,' she says calmly. 'I'm still far too tired. Are you sure it wasn't someone else?'

I shake my head; despondency, the feeling of trespassing.

'We became friends, we became friends, didn't we? The old apportioning of rôles of mother and son were dissolved, and we became friends? We spoke openly and intimately. Didn't we? Did life become comprehensible? Did I get anywhere near to understanding? No, don't think I'm sitting here getting confused, crushed by self-reproaches. That's not so at all. But friendship? Weren't the rôles unchanged, only what was said rewritten? The game took place on my conditions. But love? I know, we don't use such terms in our family. Father talks about God's love in church. But here at home? What was it like for us? How did we cope with that divided heart, that compressed hatred?'

'You must talk to someone else about that. I'm too tired.'

'With whom? I can't even talk to myself. Mother's tired now. Fair enough. I can also feel a dull weariness through my nerves and guts. Mother said: "Now you must amuse yourself, go and play with your new toys. No, I don't like being caressed. You're too caressing. You behave like a girl."

'Mother sometimes said she was never accepted by Grandmother. Grandmother gave all her love to her youngest child, the one who died. Who got Mother's love?'

She turns her face to the light from the desk lamp and now I see the dark gaze that can be neither returned nor endured.

'I know,' I say swiftly, with a shudder I find hard to control. 'The flowers thrived. The creepers climbed, the new shoots were green. The flowers thrived, but *us*? Why did everything become so miserable? Was it the Bergman paralysis, or was it something else?

'I remember some sorrow my brother had caused. Mother came out of this room and went through the salon. We were in there and Mother staggered to the left. I thought – she's acting, but she's overacting, that wasn't at all convincing.

'Were we given masks instead of faces? Were we given hysteria instead of feelings? Were we given shame and guilt instead of love and forgiveness?'

Mother gestures towards her hair, her gaze sombre and still. I don't think she even blinks.

'Why did my brother become an invalid? Why was my sister crushed into a scream? Why did I live with a never-healing infected sore that went right through my body? I have no wish to hand out blame. I'm no debt collector. I just want to know why our misery became so terrible behind that brittle social prestige. Why were my brother and sister affected so terribly, despite all the care, support and trust? Why was I incapable of normal human relationships for so long?'

Mother sits up, looks away and draws a deep breath. I see that she has a little band-aid on her left forefinger. A little gold watch is ticking busily on the bedside table. She swallows several times.

'I have a huge arsenal of explanations, for every feeling, every movement or bodily indisposition, for why I use just these words. One nods so understandingly. That's how it must be! And yet I hurtle headlong through the abyss of life. That sounds magnificent, hurtling through the abyss of life. But the abyss is a fact, and it is also bottomless. One doesn't even kill oneself in a stony ravine or on the surface of the water. I am calling for Mother as I always have. When it was night and I had a fever. When I came back from school. When I ran through the hospital grounds in the dark, chased by some ghost. When I stretched out my hand to reach Mother that rainy afternoon on Fårö. I don't know. I know nothing. What is it we are going through together? We won't be able to cope with this. Yes, it's true. I have high blood pressure. That happened during a time of humiliation and degradation. My cheeks burn and I hear someone howling, myself, I suppose.

'I must control myself and calm down. This meeting hasn't turned out at all as I had imagined. We were to be a little melancholy and talk quietly about these mysteries. You were to listen and explain. Everything was to mould itself as cleanly and perfectly as a Bach chorale. Why have we never used the intimate *du* to Mother or Father? Why did we have to speak to our parents in a distancing grammatical absurdity?

'We found Mother's diaries in the safe-deposit. After Mother's death, Father sat every day with a strong magnifying glass, trying to make out the microscopic, partly coded writings. Slowly he realized that he had never known the woman he had been married to for fifty years. Why didn't Mother burn the diaries? Planned retribution, I suppose? Now I am speaking and you don't understand me. I'm telling you what is innermost in me and please don't respond by saying nothing. Please don't say nothing in the way you always did when I pleaded, wept and raged.'

I now see that Mother is dissolving. Her legs have disappeared under the shawl, her pale face has separated from her neck and is floating in front of the oriental draperies, her eyes half closed. The dark gaze is turned inwards, the forefinger with the band-aid on it lies motionless against the edge of the gold watch. Her slim body sinks into the pattern of the counterpane.

I make an effort, but not too great a one.

'We quarrelled. Mother slapped my face. I hit back. Why did we quarrel? Terrible showdowns, slamming doors, furious tears. Why did we quarrel? I don't remember what about, except that last one about Father in hospital. Was it jealousy, seeking contact or just our upbringing? I remember our reconciliations, the gentle relief. But the lies?'

The faint smell of frying herrings emerges from the kitchen. Father coughs far away in his study. He is getting up from his midday rest and sitting down at his desk with a cigarillo and his Hebrew grammar.

*　　*　　*

A few years ago I made a little film of Mother's face. I made it with an 8 mm camera and a special lens. As I had stolen all the family photograph albums when Father died, I had access to considerable material. So the film was about Mother's face, Karin's face, from the first photograph, when she was three, to the last, a passport photograph taken a few months before her final heart attack.

Day after day, I studied hundreds of photographs through the enlarging and restricted lens. Her ageing father's proud favourite, amiably arrogant. The schoolgirl with her friends at Aunt Rosa's dame school. The year is 1890. The girl is wriggling in distress. She is wearing a large embroidered pinafore. Her friends don't have pinafores. Confirmation in an expensively patterned white blouse cut in Russian style, a

Chekhov girl, yearning and mysterious. The young nurse in uniform, a qualified professional woman, determined and confident. The engagement photograph, taken in Orsa in 1912. A masterly shot of intuitive understanding, the fiancé sitting at a table in his first pastor's uniform, reading a book. The fiancée sitting at the same table with her handwork put down in front of her. She is embroidering a cloth. She is leaning slightly forward and looking into the camera, the light coming from above, shading her eyes, which are dark and wide open. Two solitaries with no common boundary. The next photograph is touching. Mother is in a tall armchair, a large dog sitting in front of her. She is laughing cheerfully (one of the few photographs in which Mother is laughing). She is free, newly married.

A little parsonage in the Hälsinge woods, far away from the hatred between 'Ma' and 'her nice pastor', as she called him. The first pregnancy, Mother leaning with abandon on Father's shoulder, he smiling, proudly protective, not very, but enough. Her lips are swollen as if from many kisses, her eyes are veiled, her face soft and open.

Then come the Stockholm photographs. The handsome couple with their pretty well-cared for children in a sunny apartment on a quiet street in quiet Östermalm. Well-coiffed, well-dressed, eyes masked, smile formal, lovely jewellery, lively, adorable. They have adopted their rôles and are acting them out with enthusiasm.

Another photograph of Mother laughing. She is sitting on the veranda steps at Våroms and I am on her lap, at most four years old, my brother propped against the railing, eight years old. She is wearing a light simple cotton frock and despite the heat she has high sturdy boots on her feet. She is holding me in a firm grip with both hands over my stomach. Mother's hands, short, strong, the nails cut short, the cuticles bitten. What I remember best, after all, is her hand with its deep life line, that dry soft hand, the network of veins. Flowers, children, animals. Responsibility, care, strength. Occasional tenderness. Forever duty.

I browse on. Mother disappears more and more from the seething collective of family photographs. She has now had an operation, her womb and ovaries have been removed, and she is peering slightly, in a light elegant dress, her smile no longer reaching her eyes. More photographs. Now she has straightened up after having planted some cuttings in a pot. Her hands are earthy and hang slightly in perplexity. Fatigue, possibly anguish, she and Father have been abandoned. Children and grandchildren have gone. They are Bergman children. Don't disturb, don't disturb.

Then comes the final one, the passport photograph. Mother loved travel, theatre, books, films and people. Father loathed travel, unplanned visits and strangers. His illness grew worse and he was embarrassed by his fumbling, the head-shaking, his difficulties in walking. Mother became more and more tied. She occasionally got away and went to Italy. Her passport had run out and a new one was needed. Her daughter had married and moved to England. The passport photograph was taken. Mother had had two heart attacks. It looks as if an icy wind had blown across her face, shifting her features a fraction. Her eyes are veiled. She, who had always read, now cannot read. Her heart is miserly with the supply of blood. The hair above the broad low forehead is brushed back and iron grey, her mouth smiling hesitantly. You have to smile at photographers. The soft skin of her cheeks is baggy and crisscrossed with creases and furrows, the lips dried up.

*　　*　　*

So I have now been to Hedvig Eleonora church one Sunday afternoon at the beginning of Advent. I have seen reflections of light in the vaulting and I have managed to get into the apartment three floors up. I have found Mother leaning over her diary and she has given me permission to talk to her.

I immediately become incoherent and ask about things I thought buried.

I call her to account – accusing her. Mother talks about her tiredness. She has often done that recently. Now she has thinned down and is scarcely visible. I must think about what I have, not what I have lost or have never had. I will collect my treasures, a few luminous things with a special lustre.

In one short moment, I fathom her pain when faced with the fiasco of life. She was no liver-of-a-lie like Father. She was no believer. She had the strength to take the blame even when her share of the blame was doubtful. Her moment of impassioned theatre did not obscure her insight and her insight revealed the catastrophe of her life.

So I am now sitting in her chair accusing her of crimes she has never committed. I am asking questions to which there are no answers. I am turning my searchlight on to details of details.

I stubbornly ask how and why. In a sudden brilliant but probably pointless flash of insight, I think I catch a glimpse of Grandmother's cold strength behind the drama of my parents. As a young woman, Grandmother had married an ageing man with three sons not much younger than she was. Her husband died after a short marriage, leaving his wife with five children. What had *she* been forced to suppress and destroy?

The solution is probably simple, but the mystery remains unsolved. What I can certainly see is that our family were people of good will but with a disastrous heritage of guilty conscience and too great demands made on them.

I searched in Mother's diary for July 1918, in which it said:

Have been too ill to write in recent weeks. Erik has had Spanish 'flu for the second time. Our son was born on Sunday morning on 14 July. He immediately contracted a high temperature and severe diarrhoea. He looks like a tiny skeleton with a big fiery red nose. He stubbornly refuses to open his eyes. I had no milk after a few days because of my illness. Then he was baptized in an emergency here at the hospital. He is called Ernst Ingmar. Ma has taken him to Våroms, where she found a wet nurse. Ma is bitter about Erik's inability to solve our practical problems. Erik resents

Ma's interference in our private life. I lie here helpless and miserable. Sometimes when I am alone, I cry. If the boy dies, Ma says she will look after Dag, and I am to take up my profession again. She wants Erik and me to separate as soon as possible 'before in his mad hatred he thinks up some other new insanity'. I don't think I have the right to leave Erik. He is overwrought and his nerves have been bad all spring. Ma says he feigns it, but I don't believe that. I pray to God with no confidence. One will probably have to manage alone as best one can.

Fårö 25.9.86.

Ingmar Bergman:
A Chronology
by Peter Cowie

Ingmar Bergman:
A Chronology
by Peter Cowie

Film titles appear in *italics*, stage plays in CAPITAL LETTERS.

1918   Ernst Ingmar Bergman born 14 July in Uppsala, Sweden. Parents Erik (curate at Hedvig Eleonora Church, Stockholm) and Karin (née Åkerblom).

1920   Family moves to Villagatan 22, Östermalm (Stockholm).

1922   Margareta (sister to Ingmar) born.

1924   Father appointed Chaplain to the Royal Hospital, Sophiahemmet.

1934   Father appointed parish priest at Hedvig Eleonora Church, and family moves to Storgatan 7, Stockholm.
        IB attends Palmgren's School, Östermalm (basis for *Frenzy/Torment*).
        Spends one month during summer in Thuringia (Germany), and visits Berlin on way home to Sweden.

1937   Takes his Student Examination (matriculation).

1938   Brief spell of compulsory military service in Strangnäs.
        Enters Stockholm University.
        (May) Stages first plays at Mäster-Olofsgården: OUTWARD BOUND (Vane), LUCKY PETER'S JOURNEY (Strindberg), THE BLUE BIRD (Maeterlinck), MASTER OLOF (Strindberg).

1939   Applies, unsuccessfully, for job at Royal Dramatic Theatre, Stockholm. Obtains post as production assistant at Stockholm Opera.

1940   Leaves Stockholm University.
MACBETH (Shakespeare), Mäster-Olofsgården, Stockholm.
THE PELICAN (Strindberg), Student Theatre, Stockholm.

1941   A MIDSUMMER NIGHT'S DREAM (Shakespeare), Stockholm Civic Centre:
THE GHOST SONATA (Strindberg), Stockholm Civic Centre.

1942   Carl Anders Dymling appointed head of Svensk Filmindustri.
(May) BEPPO THE CLOWN (Else Fisher), People's Park, Stockholm.
(September) THE DEATH OF PUNCH (own play), Student Theatre, Stockholm.
Invited to join Svensk Filmindustri by Stina Bergman.

1943   (January) Starts work at script department of Svensk Filmindustri.
(March) Marries Else Fisher.
TIVOLI (Hjalmar Bergman, no kin), Student Theatre, Stockholm.
JUST BEFORE ONE WAKES (Bengt Olof Vos), Student Theatre, Stockholm.
WHO AM I? (Carl Erik Soya), Student Theatre, Stockholm.
U-BOAT 39 (Rudolf Värnlund), Playwrights' Studio, Stockholm.
NIELS EBBESEN (Kaj Munk), Playwrights' Studio, Stockholm.
(December) Daughter, Lena, born.

1944   (February–May) IB's first screenplay to be accepted, *Frenzy/ Torment*, is filmed by Alf Sjöberg.
THE PLAYHOUSE (Hjalmar Bergman), Playwrights' Studio, Stockholm.
MR. SLEEMAN'S COMING (Hjalmar Bergman), Playwrights' Studio, Stockholm.
(April) Appointed head of Helsingborg City Theatre.
(September) LADY ASCHEBERG OF WIDTSKÖVLE (Brita von Horn/Elsa Collin), Helsingborg City Theatre.
(October) WHO AM I? (Carl Erik Soya), Helsingborg City Theatre.
(October) *Frenzy/Torment* opens.
(November) MACBETH (Shakespeare), Helsingborg City Theatre.

1945   (February) SCAPIN, PIMPEL, AND KASPER (own play), Helsingborg City Theatre.
(February) THE SAGA (Hjalmar Bergman), Helsingborg City Theatre.

(April) MORALITY REDUCED (Sune Bergström), Helsing-borg City Theatre.

(July) Starts filming *Crisis*.

(September) JACOBOWSKY AND THE COLONEL (Franz Werfel), Helsingborg City Theatre.

(November) RABIES (Olle Hedberg), Helsingborg City Theatre.

(November) THE PELICAN (Strindberg), Malmö City Theatre.

Divorced from Else Fisher.

Marries Ellen Lundström.

Daughter, Eva, born.

1946   (February) *Crisis* opens.

(March) REQUIEM (Björn-Erik Höijer), Helsingborg City Theatre.

Joins Lorens Marmstedt at Terrafilm.

(summer) Films *It Rains on Our Love/The Man with an Umbrella*.

(September) RAKEL AND THE MOVIE THEATER DOOR-MAN (own play), Malmö City Theatre.

(autumn) Joins Gothenburg City Theatre as a director.

(November) CALIGULA (Albert Camus), Gothenburg City Theatre.

(November) *It Rains on Our Love/The Man with an Umbrella* opens.

Son, Jan, born.

1947   Writes screenplay for *Woman without a Face* (dir. Gustaf Molander).

Writes JACK AMONG THE ACTORS.

(January) THE DAY ENDS EARLY (own play), Gothenburg City Theatre.

(March) MAGIC (G. K. Chesterton), Gothenburg City Theatre.

Directs radio versions of two Strindberg plays, PLAYING WITH FIRE and DUTCHMAN.

(spring) films *A Ship Bound for India/The Land of Desire*.

(September) *A Ship Bound for India/The Land of Desire* opens.

(October) TO MY TERROR (own play), Gothenburg City Theatre.

(autumn) Films *Music in Darkness/Night is My Future* (dir. only).

1948   Twins, Anna and Mats, born.

(January) *Music in Darkness/Night is My Future* opens.

(February) DANCING ON THE WHARF (Björn-Erik Höijer), Gothenburg City Theatre.

(March) MACBETH (Shakespeare), Gothenburg City Theatre.

(spring) Films *Port of Call*.
(September) THIEVES' CARNIVAL (Jean Anouilh), Gothenburg City Theatre.
Collaborates on screenplay of *Eva* (dir. Gustaf Molander).
(October) *Port of Call* opens.
(November) Films *Prison/ The Devil's Wanton*.
(November) Radio production of MOTHER LOVE (Strindberg).
(December) DRAW BLANK (own play), Helsingborg City Theatre.

1949 (January–February) Films *Thirst/ Three Strange Loves* (dir. only).
(February) A WILD BIRD (Jean Anouilh), Gothenburg City Theatre.
(March) A STREETCAR NAMED DESIRE (Tennessee Williams), Gothenburg City Theatre.
(March) *Prison/ The Devil's Wanton* opens.
Radio production of DRAW BLANK (own play).
(July–August) Films *To Joy*.
Goes to Paris for three months with Gun Hagberg.
(October) *Thirst/ Three Strange Loves* opens.
Contract with Gothenburg City Theatre expires.

1950 Supplies synopsis for *While the City Sleeps* (dir. Lars-Eric Kjellgren).
(February) *To Joy* opens.
(February) DIVINE WORDS (Don Ramón de Valle-Inclán), Gothenburg City Theatre.
(April–June) Films *Summer Interlude/ Illicit Interlude*.
(July–August) Films *This Can't Happen Here/ High Tension* (dir. only).
(October) THE THREEPENNY OPERA (Brecht), Intima Theatre, Stockholm.
(October) *This Can't Happen Here/ High Tension* opens.
(December) A SHADOW (Hjalmar Bergman) and MEDEA (Jean Anouilh), double bill at Intima Theatre, Stockholm.
Divorced from Ellen Lundström.

1951 Writes screenplay for *Divorced* (dir. Gustaf Molander).
Marries Gun Hagberg.
(April) LIGHT IN THE HOVEL (Björn-Erik Höijer), Royal Dramatic Theatre, Stockholm.
(May) Son, Ingmar, born.
(May) THE CITY (own play), radio production dir. by Olof Molander.

(October) *Summer Interlude/ Illicit Interlude* opens.
(November) THE ROSE TATTOO (Tennessee Williams), Norrköping City Theatre.
During studio shutdown in Sweden, IB directs various cinema commercials for 'Bris' soap.

1952   (February) THE MURDER IN BARJÄRNA (own play), Malmö City Theatre.
Appointed a director at Malmö City Theatre.
(June–July) Films *Waiting Women/ Secrets of Women*.
(August) Films *Summer with Monika/ Monika*.
Relationship with Harriet Andersson begins.
(November) THE VIRGIN BRIDE (Strindberg), Malmö City Theatre.
(November) *Waiting Women/ Secrets of Women* opens.
Produces three plays for radio: THERE ARE CRIMES AND CRIMES (Strindberg), EASTER (Strindberg), and BLOOD WEDDING (Lorca).

1953   (February) *Summer with Monika/ Monika* opens.
(February–June) Films *Sawdust and Tinsel/ The Naked Night*.
(July–September) Films *A Lesson in Love*.
(September) *Sawdust and Tinsel/ The Naked Night* opens.
(October) THE DUTCHMAN (Strindberg), radio production.
(November) SIX CHARACTERS IN SEARCH OF AN AUTHOR (Pirandello), Malmö City Theatre.
(December) THE CASTLE (Franz Kafka/ Max Brod), Malmö City Theatre.

1954   (March) THE GHOST SONATA (Strindberg), Malmö City Theatre.
(June–August) Films *Journey into Autumn/ Dreams*.
(October) *A Lesson in Love* opens.
(October) THE MERRY WIDOW (Lehar), Malmö City Theatre.

1955   (January) DON JUAN (Molière), Malmö City Theatre.
(February) THE TEAHOUSE OF THE AUGUST MOON (John Patrick), Malmö City Theatre.
(March) PAINTING ON WOOD (own play), Malmö City Theatre.
(June–August) Films *Smiles of a Summer Night*.
Relationship with Bibi Andersson begins.
(August) *Journey into Autumn/ Dreams* opens.
(October) LEA AND RAKEL (Vilhelm Moberg), Malmö City Theatre.

(autumn) PAINTING ON WOOD (own play), Royal Dramatic Theatre, Stockholm (dir. Bengt Ekerot).

(December) *Smiles of a Summer Night* opens.

1956   (January) THE POOR BRIDE (Alexander Ostrovsky), Malmö City Theatre.

Writes screenplay for LAST COUPLE OUT (dir. Alf Sjöberg).

(May) *Smiles of a Summer Night* wins Special Jury Prize at Cannes Festival.

THE OLD PLAY OF EVERYMAN (Hugo von Hoffmansthal), radio production.

(July–August) Films *The Seventh Seal*.

(October) CAT ON A HOT TIN ROOF (Tennessee Williams), Malmö City Theatre.

(December) ERIK XIV (Strindberg), Malmö City Theatre.

1957   (February) *The Seventh Seal* opens.

(March) PEER GYNT (Ibsen), Malmö City Theatre.

(April) MR. SLEEMAN'S COMING (Hjalmar Bergman), IB's first TV production.

(May) *The Seventh Seal* wins Special Jury Prize at Cannes Festival.

(July–August) Films *Wild Strawberries*.

(November–December) Films *So Close to Life/ Brink of Life*.

(December) THE MISANTHROPE (Molière), Malmö City Theatre.

(December) *Wild Strawberries* opens.

1958   (February) THE VENETIAN (anon.), TV production.

(February–August) Films *The Face/ The Magician* at intervals.

(March) *So Close to Life/ Brink of Life* opens, and wins three prizes at the Cannes Festival in May.

(April) THE SAGA (Hjalmar Bergman), Malmö City Theatre.

(June) *Wild Strawberries* carries off Golden Bear at Berlin Festival.

(October) URFAUST (Goethe), Malmö City Theatre.

(December) THE PEOPLE OF VÄRMLAND (F. A. Dahlgren), Malmö City Theatre.

(December) *The Face/ The Magician* opens.

1959   Joins Royal Dramatic Theatre, Stockholm, as a director.

(May–July) Films *The Virgin Spring* (dir. only).

(September) Marries Käbi Laretei.

(October–January 1960) Films *The Devil's Eye*.

1960   (January) STORM WEATHER (Strindberg), TV production.

(February) *The Virgin Spring* opens.

(July–September) Films *Through a Glass Darkly*.
(August) FIRST WARNING (Strindberg), TV production.
(October) *The Devil's Eye* opens.

1961 (January) THE SEA GULL (Chekhov), Royal Dramatic Theatre, Stockholm.
(January) PLAYING WITH FIRE (Strindberg), radio production.
Carl Anders Dymling dies; IB appointed Artistic Adviser at Svensk Filmindustri.
Writes screenplay for THE PLEASURE GARDEN (dir. Alf Kjellin), with Erland Josephson, under joint pseudonym, 'Buntel Eriksson'.
(April) *The Virgin Spring* wins Academy Award as 'Best Foreign Film'.
(April) THE RAKE'S PROGRESS (Stravinsky), Stockholm Opera.
(October) *Through a Glass Darkly* opens.
October–January 1962) Films *Winter Light*.

1962 (April) *Through a Glass Darkly* wins Academy Award as 'Best Foreign Film'.
(July–September) Films *The Silence*.
(September) Son, Daniel Sebastian, born.

1963 (January) Appointed Head of Royal Dramatic Theatre, Stockholm.
(February) *Winter Light* opens.
A DREAM PLAY (Strindberg), TV production.
(July) Takes up his duties at Royal Dramatic Theatre.
(May–July) Films *Now About These Women/ All These Women*.
(September) *The Silence* opens.
(October) WHO'S AFRAID OF VIRGINIA WOOLF? (Edward Albee), Royal Dramatic Theatre, Stockholm.
(October) THE SAGA (Hjalmar Bergman), Royal Dramatic Theatre, Stockholm.

1964 (June) THREE KNIVES FROM WEI (Harry Martinson), Royal Dramatic Theatre, Stockholm.
(June) *Now About These Women/ All These Women* opens.
(October) HEDDA GABLER (Ibsen), Royal Dramatic Theatre, Stockholm.

1965 IB ill with viral infection during early months of year (cancels plans to stage THE MAGIC FLUTE in Hamburg).

(July–September) Films *Persona*.
Relationship with Liv Ullmann begins.
Wins Erasmus Prize (*ex-aequo* with Charles Chaplin).
(December) TINY ALICE (Edward Albee), Royal Dramatic Theatre, Stockholm.

1966 (February) THE INVESTIGATION (Peter Weiss), Royal Dramatic Theatre, Stockholm.
(March) IB's mother dies.
United Artists pays $1 million for rights to *Persona* and IB's next film.
Daughter, Linn, born by Liv Ullmann.
(May–September) Films *Hour of the Wolf*.
(October) *Persona* opens.
(November) THE SCHOOL FOR WIVES (Molière), Royal Dramatic Theatre, Stockholm.
Resigns as Head of Royal Dramatic Theatre.
Builds house on island of Fårö (completed 1967).

1967 (March) episode, 'Daniel', in portmanteau film *Stimulantia* opens.
(April) SIX CHARACTERS IN SEARCH OF AN AUTHOR (Pirandello), National Theatre, Oslo.
(September–November) Films *The Shame/Shame*.
Persona AG (Swiss company) established.

1968 (February) *Hour of the Wolf* opens.
Cinematograph AB (Swedish production company) established.
(May–June) Films *The Rite/The Ritual*.
(September) *The Shame/Shame* opens.
(September–October) Films *A Passion/The Passion of Anna*.

1969 (February) *The Shame/Shame* receives an Academy Award nomination as 'Best Foreign Film'.
(March) *The Rite/The Ritual* aired on TV.
(March) WOYZECK (Georg Büchner), Royal Dramatic Theatre, Stockholm.
(March–May) Films *The Fårö Document*.
Writes teleplay, THE LIE (aired following year in various countries, under different directors).
(November) *A Passion/The Passion of Anna* opens.

1970 (January) *The Fårö Document* aired on TV.
(March) A DREAM PLAY (Strindberg), Royal Dramatic Theatre, Stockholm.
(April) IB's father dies.
(June) HEDDA GABLER (Ibsen), National Theatre, London.

(September–November) Films *The Touch* (first English-language film).

1971   Gun Hagberg (then known as Gun Grut) killed in car crash in Yugoslavia.
(March) SHOW (Lars Forssell), Royal Dramatic Theatre, Stockholm.
(April) Liv Ullmann accepts Irving Thalberg Memorial Award on IB's behalf on Oscars' night in Hollywood.
(August) *The Touch* opens.
(autumn) Films *Cries and Whispers*.
(November) Marries Ingrid von Rosen.
Moves into apartment in Karlaplan, Stockholm.

1972   (March) THE WILD DUCK (Ibsen), Royal Dramatic Theatre, Stockholm.
(summer and autumn) Films *Scenes from a Marriage*.
(December) Svensk Filmindustri announces that IB will make lavish screen version of *The Merry Widow*, starring Barbra Streisand.
Project founders.
(December) *Cries and Whispers* opens (in United States).

1973   (January) THE GHOST SONATA (Strindberg), Royal Dramatic Theatre, Stockholm.
(March) *Cries and Whispers* opens (in Sweden).
(April–May) *Scenes from a Marriage* screened in six weekly episodes on Swedish TV.
(April) THE MISANTHROPE (Molière), Danish Royal Theatre, Copenhagen.
(May) IB attends Cannes Festival, with *Cries and Whispers*.
A LITTLE NIGHT MUSIC, based on *Smiles of a Summer Night*, opens on Broadway.

1974   (February) TO DAMASCUS (Strindberg), Royal Dramatic Theatre, Stockholm.
(April) Sven Nykvist wins Academy Award for Cinematography on *Cries and Whispers*.
(spring) Films *The Magic Flute*.

1975   (January) *The Magic Flute* aired on TV.
(March) TWELFTH NIGHT (Shakespeare), Royal Dramatic Theatre, Stockholm.
IB flies to United States to meet Dino De Laurentiis, who agrees to finance *Face to Face*.
(April–July) Films *Face to Face*.

Writes screenplay (not filmed to date) entitled *The Petrified Prince*.

IB given Honorary PhD at Stockholm University.

1976   (January) IB arrested during rehearsals for THE DANCE OF DEATH.

(April) IB leaves Sweden in voluntary exile.

(April–May) *Face to Face* screened in four weekly episodes on Swedish TV.

IB given contract at Residenztheater, Munich.

(August) IB wins Goethe Prize.

(September) Moves into apartment in Munich.

(autumn) Films *The Serpent's Egg* in Bavaria Studios, Munich.

1977   (February) *Paradise Place* opens (prod. IB, dir. Gunnel Lindblom).

(May) A DREAM PLAY (Strindberg), Residenztheater, Munich.

(October) *The Serpent's Egg* opens.

(September–October) Films *Autumn Sonata* in Oslo.

1978   (June) THREE SISTERS (Chekhov), Residenztheater, Munich.

(July) IB celebrates 60th birthday on Fårö with all his children in attendance.

(August) THE DANCE OF DEATH (Strindberg) resumes rehearsals, but is again halted due to mortal illness of Anders Ek.

(October) *Autumn Sonata* opens.

1979   (January) TARTUFFE (Molière), Residenztheater, Munich.

(April) HEDDA GABLER (Ibsen), Residenztheater, Munich.

(summer) Writes screenplay for *Fanny and Alexander*.

(August) TWELFTH NIGHT (Shakespeare), Royal Dramatic Theatre, Stockholm.

(October) Films *From the Life of the Marionettes*.

(November) IB officially exonerated in tax affair.

(December) *The Fårö Document 1979* aired on TV.

1980   Alf Sjöberg dies.

(May) YVONNE, PRINCESS OF BURGUNDY (Witold Gombrowicz), Residenztheater, Munich.

(July) *From the Life of the Marionettes* opens (in Oxford).

(November) Production of *Fanny and Alexander* announced at press conference.

1981   (April) Double bill of A DOLL'S HOUSE (Ibsen) and MISS JULIE (Strindberg) at Residenztheater, Munich, plus SCENES FROM A MARRIAGE (own play) at theatre across street on same night.

(June) IB fired from Residenztheater, Munich.
(November–early summer 1982) Films *Fanny and Alexander*.
(December) Reinstated at Residenztheater (under new management).

1982   IB announces retirement from the cinema.
(December) *Fanny and Alexander* opens.
(September) IB appears at National Film Theatre, London.

1983   Films *After the Rehearsal* (for TV).
DON JUAN (Molière), Hof Theater, Salzburg.
Films *Karin's Face*, a short tribute to his mother.
(September) IB attends Venice Festival, with complete version of *Fanny and Alexander*.

1984   KING LEAR (Shakespeare), Royal Dramatic Theatre, Stockholm.
(April) *Fanny and Alexander* wins four Academy Awards.
(May) *After the Rehearsal* screened at Cannes Festival.

1985   (June) JOHN GABRIEL BORKMAN (Ibsen), Bavarian State Theatre, Munich.
Films *The Blessed Ones* for TV (dir. only).
Dag Bergman dies.

1986   (February) Olof Palme assassinated in Stockholm.
(April) A DREAM PLAY (Strindberg), Royal Dramatic Theatre, Stockholm.
(September) IB completes autobiography, 'Laterna Magica'.
(December) MISS JULIE (Strindberg), Royal Dramatic Theatre, Stockholm.
(December) HAMLET (Shakespeare), Royal Dramatic Theatre, Stockholm.

1987   Autobiography published in Sweden.
IB told by doctors to rest from his usual theatre schedule.

1988   (April) LONG DAY'S JOURNEY INTO NIGHT (O'Neill), Royal Drmatic Theatre, Stockholm.

Index

Index

TEIKYO WESTMAR UNIV. LIBRARY

PN 1998.3 .B47 A3 1988
Bergman, Ingmar, 1918-
The magic lantern
      (94-284)

DEMCO